A BILLION TO ONE

The Story of Herzog, Heine, Geduld, Inc.

A BILLION TO ONE

The Story of Herzog, Heine, Geduld, Inc.

John E. Herzog

A Billion to One: The Story of Herzog, Heine, Geduld, Inc.

Copyright © 2017 John E. Herzog. All rights reserved.
Printed in the United States of America. No part of this book may be used, reproduced, translated, electronically stored, or transmitted in any manner whatsoever without prior written permission from the publisher, except by reviewers, who may quote brief passages in their reviews.

Published by:
Museum of American Finance
48 Wall Street
New York, NY 10005
www.MoAF.org

ISBN: 978-0-9642630-2-4

Design by Alan Barnett

Imperial Impressions, Inc.

Printing and Binding by Imperial Impressions, Inc.
Phone: (201) 960-1804

*This book is respectfully dedicated to
Diana E. Herzog, whose calm and reasonable counsel
and abiding trust over fifty years gave me the confidence
to do things, and then to write about them.
Her love will be always with me.*

Contents

Foreword vii

Preface xiii

Acknowledgements xv

1. Go West Young Man 1

2. Struggle for Survival: 1926–1931 7

3. Developing a Business: 1931–1940 15

4. Business Maturity 21

5. Softly Blowing Reveille 27

6. Beginning the Trek 35

7. Change and New Growth 41

8. R. M. Smythe & Co. Joins the Office 47

9. An Improving Market Environment 51

10. Confidently Moving Ahead	61
11. Difficult Years, Complex Problems	69
12. More Change and Bigger Growth	83
13. Bright New Days Dawning	87
14. Onward and Upward	99
15. Back Home in Town	107
16. A Rapidly Changing Milieu	115
17. More Exposure and Greater Opportunity	119
18. The Year of the Crash of 1987	125
19. In the Aftermath	133
20. The Early Nineties	145
21. New Office and New Challenge: 1995	163
22. The Home Stretch	171
23. A New Century	191
Appendix: Herzog, Heine, Geduld, Inc. Income and Expense History	199
Index	217

Foreword

John Herzog's history of Herzog, Heine, Geduld, the Nasdaq market-making firm he led for nearly four decades, is called "A Billion to One." It could as well have been titled, "One to a Billion," with the One being John's father, Robert (Bob) Herzog, who in 1926 co-founded Herzog & Co., a small stock and bond trading firm and then led it for four decades, and the Billion being almost the dollar value of the firm when Merrill Lynch purchased the vastly larger Herzog, Heine, Geduld in 2000.

John's story illustrates two great themes of U.S. economic history. One is entrepreneurial achievement. Bob Herzog kept the firm small from 1926 to 1959, when young John, age 23, joined it as its fifth employee. Although Herzog & Co. was barely larger in terms of employees and business done in 1959 than it had been in 1926, it had managed to survive the Great Crash of 1929, the Great Depression of the 1930s, World War II, and the early years of the Cold War. It was a survivor, unlike many financial firms, small and large, that disappeared over that troubled third of a century. John makes a good case that it was his father's principles that made Herzog & Co. a survivor. He passed those principles on to his son, who along with the Geduld brothers and Max Heine would take Herzog, Heine, Geduld to great heights as a major Nasdaq market maker from the 1970s to 2000.

The other great American theme is immigrant success. John's grandfather, Armin, arrived in the United States as an immigrant from Hungary just before the outbreak of World War I, and then in 1915 arranged for his wife, teenage son Bob, and Bob's two sisters to join him in America. Immigrants to America needed to convert their European currencies to dollars, and often to convert dollars to European currencies to make remittances to Europe. Grandfather Armin and father Bob understood currency trading and made it their business. After the war, which resulted in New York replacing London as the leading world financial center, Bob Herzog moved from currency trading into trading, at the NYSE bond brokers G. & A. Seligman, the dollar-denominated bond issues that financed European postwar reconstruction. And then, as an experienced currency and bond trader, Bob Herzog, age 25 and barely a decade in America, started his own firm in 1926.

Most of John's story, however, is about his years at the firm, initially Herzog & Co., and eventually Herzog, Heine, Geduld, from 1959 to 2000. Unlike his exceedingly cautious father, John saw opportunities for growing the firm and was willing to take the risks to make that happen. He sometimes made mistakes, and he learned from them. This is a very honest tale. He also made some great decisions, including notably bringing Irwin and Buzzy Geduld, and later Max Heine, into the firm. Like a great surfboarder, Herzog, Heine, Geduld caught the great wave of Nasdaq's growth and the expansion of securities trading generally in the last three decades of the twentieth century. The firm rode that wave a long way, mostly by being in the forefront of technological innovation in the markets, and by hiring excellent employees and treating them well. When John writes about the number of securities in which HHG made markets, its daily trading volumes, and it daily and monthly profits around the year 2000, and compares them with the tiny figures typical when he started at the firm four decades earlier, one senses that he himself can hardly believe the incredible differences.

There is a subplot to John's story that I for one would wish that he had further developed. I met John in 1990 when I arrived at NYU's Stern School to teach economic and financial history. My colleague Ed Altman quickly sought me out to say that I had to meet John Herzog, who recently founded a museum devoted to American financial history, partly to promote a better public understanding of the capital markets after they had been tarnished by the crash of October 19, 1987. I leapt at the opportunity to meet John. We quickly became friends and I began to work with the museum in its various activities, eventually become a board member (succeeding Ed Altman) and board chairman (succeeding John). I soon learned that John had collected historical financial documents, including securities, since around 1960, and that parts of his great collection became the basis of the museum's collection. And that early on he had purchased R. M. Smythe & Co., a long-established dealer in such documents, which he and his wife, Diana, managed. The related stories of the Museum of American Finance and the Smythe firm appear to be tangential to the main story of Herzog, Heine, Geduld in the pages that follow. But the reader may be assured that they were hardly tangential to John's career and his family.

As a scholar and as John's long-time collaborator at the museum he founded, I welcome this fine addition to the literature of financial history, as well as to the great American themes of immigrant success and entrepreneurial achievement.

> — *Richard Sylla*
> *Professor Emeritus of Economics and, 1990–2015,*
> *Henry Kaufman Professor of the History of Financial*
> *Institutions and Markets, New York University*

Preface

This book is about Herzog, Heine, Geduld, the brokerage firm my father started in 1926, which I joined in 1959. "Herzog" became a New York Stock Exchange member firm in 1976 and was a market maker in Nasdaq stocks. This book is necessarily also autobiographical, as four decades of my own career were at the firm, ending on the day it was sold to Merrill Lynch in 2000. But I also had another career as a lifelong collector of historic financial documents. During my forty years in the trading business my wife Diana headed a numismatic auction house, R. M. Smythe & Co, which we owned together until 2008 when the business was sold to Spink in London. Those two parallel careers led to yet another. In response to the market Crash of 1987, I founded the Museum of American Finance, seeded with some of my own collection of historic documents. As a financial industry executive, I wanted to enhance people's understanding of the capital markets by displaying and celebrating the history of America's financial experience. The museum has grown to become a Smithsonian affiliate and a popular tourist attraction on Wall Street.

Diana and I attended Museum events. At one of these events we met two friends of ours, Lily Wey and her husband Alan Frishman, and we arranged to have dinner with them following the presentation. During dinner Lily was very pleased to let us know that Harvard Business School had agreed to create a case study with her company as the subject. This was a great compliment for Lily and her young company. Hearing this, I shared with Lily that years back, I responded to Harvard's request for a copy of my master's thesis for their entrepreneurial history collection. Alan asked me for a copy, and Diana and I quickly read it again, realizing that our recollections had become clouded by time. Alan told me he enjoyed reading it, as did others to whom we gave copies. Diana and I pleasantly re-lived memories of forty-five years earlier.

I digitized the original thesis, thinking I might make a few changes. Time passed, and I decided to tell the rest of the story of the firm I helped build, later joined by Irwin and Buzzy Geduld. Gradually, the urgency grew, and soon Bridget, a college intern was sorting through files in an accumulation of corrugated boxes which held the story.

The original thesis research was done during my father's lifetime, and his recollections were mainly intact. With his help, I could confirm facts and events. The thesis was appropriately academic and dispassionate, and four decades later it seemed remarkably incomplete. In it I had attempted to describe the management history of our family firm. From its start in 1926, I traced how world events and changes in the securities industry shaped the four-person firm I joined in 1959 and the 13-person firm it had become in 1968 when I wrote the thesis. Now I will tell how those same factors led us to become the 750-employee firm we were when we closed the sale to Merrill. My former partners and several employees have helped me tell this story, and they have added perspective, color and roundness.

Looking back from 2016, I realize that the principles my father lived by deeply influenced the firm long after I assumed leadership with my new partners. In his simple letter to a trader, recovered years later, he would reveal the principles which led to many years of successful and satisfying growth. They are meaningful to all who trade, and a cautionary tale about managing risk and constant change with discipline. My objective now is to tell the story of the firm and the dramatic changes in the securities industry which occurred in the twentieth century and how his principles guided and endured.

This is a story of a small firm which grew to great importance nationally and was then absorbed into the fabric of a far larger and more prominent brokerage organization. I hope this story will make interesting reading and that the experiences described will help educate a new generation of managers and risk takers. Of this need I have no doubt.

—John E. Herzog
October 2016

Acknowledgements

It would have been impossible to undertake a book of this sort without the unwavering help and support of my family — my father and mother, my wife Diana, my daughters Mary and Sarah, and my brother Bill, all of whom have contributed meaningfully to the finished product. Their encouragement in weak moments and reassurance during numerous bouts of self-doubt have been essential to the work.

More very reliable memory was provided during several office lunches with Buzzy Geduld. His perspective and help was extremely valuable. My editor, Samantha Brand, was instructive in every way and her experience remains essential. Others from the old firm include Harvey Wacht and Joe Frazzitta. Mark Anderson organized all the old financial information we could find into understandable form, a great help. Gail Langan performed miracles with a number of the old photos in the book, and many others not included. There has been help for the project itself from Tulis McCall, Jim Grosso, and Robin Majlak and from Bridget Fraher, who sorted a dozen boxes of files into a chronological sequence for reference in writing. And the initial impetus and inspiration for telling the story came from Lily Wey and Alan Frishman, whose case study of their business for Harvard led me on this road. Helen Hockney has been helpful at many times, remembering things I had forgotten. Important design and proofreading help came from Abby Suckle and Mariana Oller, earning great appreciation. Professor Richard Sylla and David Cowen helped me to understand some larger issues which was a great benefit. The veteran of twenty-five years of often conflicting design instructions from many of us, Alan Barnett, accepted this book, making me very happy, and then introduced me to Michelle Gluckow, the printer, who true to her promise created a lovely product.

—*John E. Herzog*
March 2017

CHAPTER 1

Go West Young Man

Awakened from a sound sleep by his anxious mother Rose, Robert must dress and get ready for the passage to America. He appeared, just in time to board the ship, and Robert Imre Herzeg knew he was on the way to America. He and his mother and his sisters, Lily and Elizabeth, boarded the Rotterdam on September 6th, 1915, by family legend the last passenger ship to leave Holland before the Great War, and they were all relieved that their voyage had begun. The days were long, and hours passed with very few ships, if any, to be seen. Night brought a murky blackness which tricked the imagination, collapsing perspective and awareness of space.

Fearing the imminent outbreak of the war following the assassination of Archduke Ferdinand, Armin Herzeg sent for his wife and their three children. A year earlier, Armin had come to America joining many of his Hungarian countrymen in New York seeking safety and opportunity. Political events accelerated the schedule. Robert looked forward to seeing his father, and soon he would learn about the opportunities his father saw in their new country across the Atlantic.

Armin's family joined a tide of Eastern European immigration which had been going on for years. Among other surprises, their new home was nothing like their spacious apartment in Budapest, situated only a few blocks from Parliament, with a fine balcony where Elizabeth dried her long hair in the sun. In this new country Rose had to make her own tomato puree for her delicious dinners, unlike Budapest where she could buy as much as she wished. School in New York would be nothing like the Jesuit school Robert had attended where young boys' heads were shaved in the summer. As they passed through immigration, the family name was changed to the more anglicized spelling, Herzog. In young Robert's pocket, his fingers clung to some currency and coins from home, but that would soon change.

Armin had been learning about life in New York. He realized he could develop some income with his knowledge of European money, as newly arrived Europeans discovered that the banknotes they brought sewn into their clothes were of little use on the teeming avenues of New York's Lower East Side. Those who wished to send some of their earnings back home had a similar need for exchange. Armin found opportunity as a currency trader. Seeking trade, he made the rounds of the Lower East Side up and down the avenues.

With newfound familiarity and confidence, Robert joined his father when school was out, and on weekends, excitedly walking First and Second Avenues. Father and "Budzy," as his sisters called him, were at the ready, prepared to buy or sell notes and extract a fair profit. They would be mindful of factors local and distant which might impact scarcity and demand and Armin would adjust accordingly. He soon learned that events could not be anticipated or controlled, but his mark-up could. He would build a reputation based on fairness, integrity and reliability.

After a year at school, Robert's part time currency trading was interrupted by a period of more conventional work, first at Keuffel and Esser on Fulton Street, where he helped an agent for a steel mill compile mailing lists, and later at the Chatham and Phenix Bank, which eventually became part of Manufacturers Hanover. His facility with math helped his work there as a teller and ledger clerk. At 17, a lateral move to the Central Mercantile Bank was fortuitous in that he worked under Michael Kletz who would later become a successful underwriter of small over-the-counter issues. While he learned from Kletz, he was equally attracted by the monthly wage of $50, and the 50 cents supper money provided when he worked past 8 p.m. Advancing the commerce of others held attraction, signaling work which would come along later.

Global commercial relationships resumed following the end of the war and Robert knew there would be many new opportunities for him. Now there was a great deal of potential business between the United States and Europe as people began catching up with the backlog. Armistice Day ushered in a new era of peace, a great economic stimulus, as my father always reminded me.

By 1919, Robert was helping his father make travel arrangements and manage the currency needs of people returning to post-war Europe. Confident and optimistic, he moved up to $18 a week at Knauthe, Nachod & Kuhne, one of the leading foreign exchange and trading names of the day, often referred to as "KN&K." After the end of the war when there was big volume in foreign remittances, Robert was well situated. New friends and changing times led him to Josephthal & Co. where for $75 per week he traded currencies and handled remittances. In August 1921, he moved on to Simmons & Co., trading currencies. In that office there was a long desk which accommodated four traders, and when the market closed, currency trading gave way to craps. Now known as Bob in business circles, his parents worried about his late hours, and Armin would come down to Wall Street to pick Bob up late at night and take him home.

Reconstruction in Europe was financed in part by high yielding foreign dollar bonds. With his trading and language skills, Robert found a position at G. & A. Seligman, New York Stock Exchange bond brokers. At Seligman, his suggestion to trade these new bond issues, and previously outstanding foreign internal issues was accepted. This worked out well and was an important step to a brighter future. His working day was long, and relaxation coveted.

After a business and pleasure trip to Europe, Herzog returned home in 1926 and met Nat Chadwick, an old friend who had decided to go into the brokerage business. Nat knew Bob from his days on the trading desk at Cowen & Co., and they had become good friends. Chadwick was five years older than Bob and had that extra experience which was so important. Happy to see his old friend, and knowing him to be trustworthy, Chadwick suggested they go into business together, and here the story begins. Parmer, Herzog & Chadwick began doing business on July 20, 1926. Well, almost. The person these two young men had chosen as their third partner, Devore Parmer, turned out to be a problem rather than a help.

Parmer was a fellow whose prior firm had been in Kansas City. He specialized in speculative oil and mining securities, and in the Seligman days he had traded with Herzog in some of the riskiest German and Austrian bonds with very low recovery value. Parmer's younger partners were not aware that his unsavory reputation prevented them from installing private wires with the firms they were close to. These direct telephone connections from one office to another for special relationship clients were very important, and have remained so. Wires required prior approval from the New York Stock Exchange, and the Exchange withheld permission because Parmer was a partner. Solving their first business problem required diplomacy, and Herzog and Chadwick convinced Parmer that they needed to be on their own. Parmer, the old soldier by ten years, soon left, realizing that his reputation as a promoter of speculative investments saddled him with a reputation that was not acceptable in New York.

A new partnership was formed. Herzog & Chadwick did foreign bond trading and general brokerage. Chadwick's reputation was built at the reputable Cowen & Co., and the two partners were optimistic about their future together. They had learned a valuable lesson. They would be more careful in choosing partners and employees and would always safeguard their reputations and the public perception of their firm. While both men solicited customers and looked for new business, Bob was the inside operations man, and took charge of the administrative needs of the young firm. Chadwick was well connected and adept at the social scene after business hours.

Most over-the-counter trading activity in the early days was in bank and insurance stocks. Commercial banks were a good source of business, as were stock brokers and underwriters. As the business expanded, the partners needed additional money for trading and working capital. They made a deal with Orrin Zoline who lent the partners $10,000 at 6% and got a weekly salary of $75, and 50% of firm profits for the first three months. Capital was costly, but Herzog thought it was a good deal and they would not have survived without the loan. Zoline also contributed the use of his New York Curb Market membership. The Curb Market, which became the American Stock Exchange, was where numerous lower priced and more speculative stocks traded. Zoline's contribution was vital, but the direction he wished to go in was not shared by Herzog or Chadwick.

Assets and contacts are important, but personality is the hidden element which must mesh in a firm destined for success. Zoline wanted to do more business with individuals in Curb stocks, but Herzog and Chadwick were wary of expanding their retail customer business. He also wanted to become a specialist on the Curb, a member responsible for making an orderly market in specific stocks. More strong disagreement followed, and the partnership with Zoline was dissolved in early 1928. It was also the year that Chadwick decided to leave the firm to go to California, writing in an emotional letter to Herzog, "It is not without a feeling of much regret that I do this." Living in San Francisco, their friendship was still going strong in 1977, when he wrote my father, congratulating him on an article about the firm he saw in the newspaper.

Effective February 6, 1928, the firm was to be known as Herzog & Co., and the partners were limited to Herzog and his sisters Lily and Elizabeth. Now just 27, Herzog was alone and nearly out of capital. Problems securing capital would remain a constant challenge, but Herzog persevered, doing a small amount of business and thinking optimistically.

Years later, during another worrisome, profitless period, my father reiterated this experience, and the lesson that simply being in business nurtured hope for better days ahead. He recalled a story about a former clerk who worked in his building. While others denigrated this man, my father always respected him, and a casual friendship developed. Then one day the clerk was absent, having moved on without telling anyone. A year later, he called unexpectedly from California where he had become quite successful. He remembered my father's kindness and sent many orders to Herzog & Co. helping the firm stay in business. My father's respect for all people was an important lesson for me, and my tolerance for people considered difficult by others often made me "the only person he will listen to." I learned early that in business patience often led to a good result, while a hot temper was rarely profitable.

During this period, foreign bonds which then yielded 6%-8% were in great demand, as these returns were more generous than those in the home market. Investors were not thinking that a day might come when the interest on these bonds would not be paid. Popular demand led to higher and higher prices. Europe was delighted to sell these issues since capital was scarce after the war, and the industrial redevelopment then going on required large sums of money. Business for the firm picked up as investors sought these issues.

CHAPTER 2

Struggle for Survival
1926–1931

Robert Herzog kept his business going. There were problems, but he handled them, always looking ahead. He was self-supporting. I recall him telling me in the earliest days of my career that a year might consist of one good month and eleven poor ones, when the challenge was to break even. He warned that the ups and downs came quickly and without warning. His wariness served him well, and his modest success allowed him to pursue leisure activities. A fine horseback rider, he joined Westchester Country Club, where he kept a horse. There he met John W. Campbell, the credit-rating leader, and his wife Princess. The Campbell Apartment in Grand Central Terminal was his office.

Bob's bachelor apartment at 10 Park Avenue was conveniently located and comfortable. Views from his apartment were the source of some great photographs of Park Avenue. Bob studied photography at The New School, taking a course at which Edward Steichen, who later created "The Family of Man" was a guest lecturer. With new friends from Budapest Laci and Geza Rona, he began taking day trips, exploring their new country. An outing to Branford and Guilford, Connecticut by street car was a favorite, as were other trips up the Hudson Valley, to the resort area where lots of New Yorkers enjoyed a breath of country air. On one of these visits to Fleischmanns, Bob met and talked with Norma Englander, there with her parents Jacob and Mary. Bob never forgot the image of Norma sitting on a rock by a stream, wearing a purple dress.

Capital was difficult to locate and the cost to get it was high, but Herzog did what he needed to do to keep his company afloat. Management problems were daunting, and for a small firm the difference between blue skies and a crisis is often measured in days, not weeks or months. It was a constant challenge to seek new and useful relationships, and encourage social or business friends to become customers of the firm. When my father found someone willing to invest in his business, philosophical differences often proved more onerous than the deal terms.

My father shared these experiences and they were of tremendous value to me and my future partners. We were fortunate, and recent research has confirmed the value of "intergenerational mentoring." Firms having this benefit are more likely to succeed than those lacking an experienced founder or leader willing to share his institutional memory with the next generation of managers.

Herzog had been building a group of friends, and began to attend industry events, and about this time in 1928 Benjamin Grody began working with the firm. He was tall and well-dressed, dark, with a mustache and pleasant smile and an ever-present pocket handkerchief in his single-breasted suits. His influence and contacts were useful. He was well trained in financial research, and worked on ferreting out special situations which he then described and added to the list of stocks and bonds the firm traded. A market maker finds stocks he likes, and advertises his willingness to buy or sell shares of that stock to any other dealer who calls. Grody's research was distributed to out of town dealers, most of whom felt very detached from Wall Street. Bob Herzog helped change that by taking short trips to visit dealers in different cities. One of these trips was to Richmond, Virginia, where he visited Scott and Stringfellow, a well-established local firm. Many years later, in New Orleans, I met one of their senior executives. We were introduced, and he embraced me saying how much he had enjoyed the relationship between the firms during his years in the business. Bob's early trips resulted in more order flow for Herzog & Co. and business increased. Grody had a fine telephone personality, an extremely important skill in a business of this sort, and he developed business from many new sources.

There were several other additions at about this time. My father, now in his late twenties and more confident, created a Public Utility Bond Department and a Trading Department, and these new areas were listed in the Security Dealers of North America, the important industry directory of the day. Along with each specialty, the name of the firm's trader was listed. These designations in the directory gave some status to his new employees and were designed to impress the out-of-town brokers. Bob was optimistic. Expansion seemed perfectly logical; there was business to be gained as the market spiraled ahead.

Herzog was eager to cash in on the higher volume of trading activity. This optimism meant personnel needs. Harold Neulander was added as the first non-producing employee of the firm in 1927. He had been with the firm for about two years when he began to trade a little bit. On February 11, 1929, John J. Meyers, Jr., a trader, joined the firm after leaving Moore, Leonard & Lynch, a Pittsburgh firm. Meyers had met Herzog at a traders' dinner, and he felt there would be good opportunity at a New York firm.

On April 15, 1929, George L. Busch, an old social and golfing friend of Herzog's was admitted to the firm without a change in the firm name. Busch had worked in the commercial loan business, but he wanted to work on Wall Street. His personality was well suited to this job, as he was gregarious and extroverted. He drove a bright yellow 1929 Nash, known more familiarly as a "Rumble Seat Cabriolet." The stock market was rising and though he had no previous experience, Busch felt that he could develop commission orders from customers. As a gesture of good faith, he put up $2,500, but his partnership was based on friendship.

Trading activity at the firm was mostly in bank and insurance stocks, and the most common price range for these issues was between $300 and $1,000 per share. These stocks traded over-the-counter because of the issuers' reluctance to release detailed operating information which would then be available to competitors. Stock Exchange rules required far more public disclosure than the over-the-counter market.

Markets were not as "close" as they became in later years and markups and trading profits were far greater. Each quotation consists of a "bid" price at which the trader would buy, and an "offering" price or "ask" price, at which the trader would sell. The quotation "24 bid, offered at 25" meant the trader, or market-maker, would buy 100 shares at $24 per share, or sell 100 shares at $25 per share. If 100 shares were traded, a profit of $100 would be made. These small profits were the life blood of trading, and the reason why adding volume was crucial. This was the business of the firm.

Only a few people saw anything wrong with the market in early 1929 and business went ahead as usual. There was scant economic forecasting as we know it today, nor were there statistical analyses available. There were no margin requirements, so no meaningful action could be taken to cut speculative excess.

In August 1929 the firm started clearing at the Trust Company of North America ("TCNA"). This was the first such account taken by that bank.

Making trades on the telephone is the easiest part of the business. Confirming that the securities have found their way from the seller to the new owner, and have been paid for, with all the correct bookkeeping entries is much more complex and demanding. TCNA would verify the terms of the trade — the "comparison" process, which required a printed record of every trade with its dollar value. This record was delivered to the contra broker and rubber-stamped in agreement as "compared." Physical delivery of the securities days later was time consuming and detail ridden and required security as well. The process was costly and labor intensive, too expensive for Herzog to undertake. It was Bob Herzog's suggestion that TCNA enter the clearing business, and it worked, as they became a leader in this area. This clearing relationship would last for 33 years in essentially the same form, except for a brief period when the firm cleared at Cohen, Simonson & Co.

Phil Chasin managed the Broker's Clearance Department at TCNA. As clearing agents for several other brokers, Chasin's staff toiled, pairing up the trades between the brokers for whom they cleared. Heavy volume in the second half of 1929 meant that some trades offset others, making the physical delivery of securities unnecessary. The decision to outsource this function speaks well of Herzog's vision in a business that stubbornly resisted innovation.

Optimism was rampant and the market moved ever higher. Volume increased to unprecedented levels and speculation was unrestrained. Without regulations retail investors could take positions with 10% to 20% margin, and there were no minimum capital requirements for brokers. Securities were supposed to be delivered and paid for by 2:15 P.M. the next day. But firms couldn't keep up, and they "failed to deliver" with greater frequency. One has difficulty imagining the immense management problems associated solely with the orderly delivery and receipt of securities for payment. For the month preceding the crash, daily volume on the New York Stock Exchange had often been 4 million shares and occasionally 5 million. For the week of the crash, 29 million shares were traded in four days. Everything was written by hand, and delivered by foot. The Computing and Tabulating Company, later IBM, was busy helping firms deal with the paper, but volume outstripped resources. Firms became insolvent and vanished, casualties of the decline and the accompanying back office crisis.

News stories from the day of the Crash give some idea of what happened. *The New York Daily Investment News* said, "The utter helplessness of the situation defies description. With the Stock Exchange ticker tape two hours behind trading on the floor, and member firms unable to obtain quotations from the Exchange, a large part of yesterday's record trading was done in the dark. The bond ticker, over which a few quotations were sent at intervals of 10 minutes, fell behind the bond market for the first time in the history of the Exchange." And "so furious was the trading pace maintained all through the day that tickers kept churning until seven minutes past seven last night, over four hours after the close." At Herzog & Co., even a little extra volume meant a lot more work, and taking the Lexington Avenue subway from Wall Street to the St. George Hotel in Brooklyn for a shower during an all-nighter was one way to keep up.

British Type Investors, a favorite stock of the day, emerged from the day of the Crash unscathed and proud, with a boast that proved regrettable. It was quoted 23 bid, offered at 24½ on October 24, 1929. The next day the famous advertisement appeared in several newspapers, noting that despite four serious breaks in the market, the stock had not budged. Apparently, the public had just overlooked the stock. Immediately after seeing the advertisement, traders were swamped with sell orders. On October 30, 1929, the stock was offered at 20, without a bid.

Herzog & Co. was trading American Founders, another of the favorite financial stocks of the day. Harold Neulander recalled a trade in which he was selling stock on one wire about 60 points above the price at which Herzog was buying it on another wire. A trade of only 100 shares would generate a profit of $6000! While there were mainly losses during the day of the Crash and those immediately before and after, there were profitable trades, usually because of delays in getting accurate prices.

Herzog & Co. was lucky in a way, as the lower volume handled by the firm could be processed without great difficulty, and operations could be kept under tight control. The firm was insulated from much of the Street chaos since it was newer, smaller, and had fewer people on the payroll, and most importantly was subject to the conscientious oversight of the owner.

Investment banking was very different, and corporate finance was also at the beginning of a long period of dramatic change. Investors were often uninformed about specific attributes of the securities themselves, not just the market prices, and the issuing companies realized that the capital markets called for much more attention to the proper design of investment grade securities. To further complicate things, many bank stocks at that time were "double indemnity" stocks, which meant that the registered owner was liable for double the par value of the stock in case of bankruptcy. The par value of a stock is seldom important, so little attention was paid to it until unexpected developments made that necessary. Many mining stocks were also "assessable," so when the company needed more funds it could send a letter to the stockholder, and if he did not send the assessment, his shares became worth much less. Vast changes were going to be needed in banking and finance and these would result in new legislation creating the Securities & Exchange Commission, as well as new rules for the nation's self-regulating stock exchanges.

The problems associated with the Crash touched Herzog & Co. in a very painful way. "Dictum meum pactum" — my word is my bond — is the motto of the Security Traders Association of New York, and this was the basis upon which millions of dollars of transactions were consummated. Four days before Black Friday, October 25, the firm entered into some contracts in Bank of Manhattan "When Issued" stock with a retail client. A "When Issued" contract is one for shares of stock that do not yet exist, but are expected to be issued soon. The purchase price before the Crash was high, and the firm had these contracts on its books four days later when the Crash occurred. When it came time for Herzog's customer to pay at the stipulated pre-crash price, he chose not to, and reneged. This left the firm with a tremendous loss. There were no rules governing customer trading or extension of credit. No effort was made to secure margin for these contracts as the buyers were social friends, and the firm relied on the honor of the customer. Efforts to collect were in vain. When the contracts were finally closed out a month later, about $25,000 was lost, a large part of the firm's capital. Fortunately, because of Herzog's excellent reputation on the Street, a settlement was reached, with part paid in cash, and notes for the balance. The debt was not fully settled until 1933. This loss was to have a deep psychological effect on Robert Herzog. It colored his attitude toward expansion, and demonstrated the peril of financing his trading positions with borrowed money.

When the Crash occurred, the firm was about three years old. Despite its jarring loss on the "When Issueds," it survived, and remained cautious. There were few regulations and only small industry associations. These associations had the most up to date information about what was going on, and they attempted to exert a good influence and promote responsible conduct within the trading community. As regulation increased, the regulators collaborated with the associations to regain public trust, initiate necessary oversight and to encourage smoothly functioning, compliant businesses.

Because of the lack of capital, and the need for income to live, there was very little money to use for positions. A trader's "position limit" is the amount of firm capital he may commit to buying the stocks he was trading, long or short. A trader's positions were tallied each day, and that sum must not exceed his agreed position limit. This was a blessing, as the market had not yet bottomed, and any long positions, by far most of the position risks, would need to be marked down, for real dollar losses month after month. Bob Herzog was never a short seller, a shame. A trader sells a stock "short" when he feels the price of the stock will go down, providing an opportunity to buy the stock back later when the price has fallen. The difference is profit. If a stock is sold short at 60, and the price declines to 40, the profit would be 20 points, or $2000 for each 100 shares sold short.

On January 15, 1930, only nine months after its commencement, the fourth partnership of the firm was dissolved, and George Busch left the firm. To save as much money as possible, Herzog & Co. moved, and became a sub-tenant of Cohen, Simonson & Co. at 60 Broad Street, paying no rent, but agreeing to place its Stock Exchange commission business with Cohen, Simonson and clear its trades through them. Many firms were feeling the pinch by this time and gloomy predictions about the future became more numerous. Note the difference between the agreement with Orrin Zoline of two years before: a $10,000 loan at 6% plus $75 per week salary and half the profits for three months, and the arrangement that Cohen, Simonson & Co., members of the Stock Exchange, was willing to make now. Rent was free; there were no fixed charges, and no profits to share. A survival mentality had gripped a frightened nation and its businesses. This was only the beginning; the worst was yet to come.

By early 1930, the dreams of investors, and ordinary citizens throughout the country had been shattered. The cataclysm was devastating and a few people jumped out of windows to their deaths. Former executives sold apples on the street, while others built huts in Central Park.

During these troubled years, there were developments on the personal side of Herzog's life. His memory of Norma Englander prevented him from other serious involvements, even when he learned in 1923 that Norma had married another man. He later learned that she had separated from her husband, and was getting a divorce. She now had a son, Bill, who suffered from a mastoid illness. Bob got in touch with Norma, and gave her the name of a doctor he felt certain could cure Bill. The doctor was successful. And so was

Bob, as he began seeing Norma. My brother Bill remembers his "Uncle Bob" in a double-breasted overcoat with velvet lapels, a homburg, and spats, carrying a black walking stick with an ivory handle. Bob drove a yellow Packard convertible with leather seats, and always had a wild cherry Lifesaver in his pocket for Bill.

While banks now have a well-developed practice of maintaining secondary reserves, it was not in use before 1930 and this accounts for some of the illiquidity in the banking system at the time of the Crash. Banks invested funds not needed to meet reserve requirements. They made short term self-liquidating loans to businesses and individuals. This loan portfolio was the source for extra liquidity when the banks needed cash, as portrayed in the movie "It's a Wonderful Life." In the period before the 1930s, there was no market for commercial paper as we know it now, and only a small market for government bonds.

With the advent of a far larger Federal debt and the development of excellent markets for it, banks could employ short term funds profitably with very small risk buying U. S. Treasury bonds. It became unnecessary to disturb the commercial loan portfolio when extra liquidity was needed. This became the secondary reserve area.

As time passed after the Crash, many people left Wall Street, and those remaining inherited the challenges of the Great Depression. Congressional action, regulation and a modification of procedures came slowly. Herzog & Co. was to experience difficult days, but the firm would persevere and succeed.

CHAPTER 3

Developing a Business
1931–1940

The early 1930s were characterized by efforts to stay in business. Herzog tried to use new technology, and on November 21, 1931, the first teletype service became commercially available. Herzog invested in this service. The Security Dealers of North America ("SDNA") directory is an important source of information about the early years of the firm. The company listing in 1931 reads "Brokers in Bonds Specializing in Foreign Industrials and Government Issues." These are the same securities which Herzog had been trading at G & A Seligman & Co. years before. In 1932, the Herzog offices consisted of just one small room and three people: Herzog, Grody and a secretary.

In February 1933, the staff grew with the addition of Louis Weingarten, 40, an association which was to last many profitable years. He had come to New York from Montreal where he had been in several partnerships since 1925. Among these earlier associations were Weingarten & Toolan, and Stone & Co., both over-the-counter firms. Weingarten was energetic and an experienced trader. He travelled to many of the traders' dinners outside New York making valuable contacts for the firm. He was with the firm for approximately six years, when he left to take a position with another firm, then he returned, something which would recur at Herzog. Weingarten would remain an employee for over 30 years. New or returning traders were content not to be partners. As employees, they could avoid many legal responsibilities, and a lot of work. While Herzog closed the books at the end of every month, paid the bills and did payroll, traders simply left when the trading day ended. Being an employee had advantages.

These years were difficult, but those like Bob with a little money to invest in their own businesses saw plenty of opportunity. It was a time of "Scotch weeks" and pay cuts, and it lasted for years. A "Scotch week" was a week without pay, and some people worked years at half pay waiting for better times, happy to keep their jobs. The sad standing joke of the day was that if a firm could not afford to pay a good employee, they would make him a partner, saving his salary.

The large debt resulting from the renege on Bank of Manhattan When Issued contracts had been slowly paid down, and in May 1933 the final settlement of these debts was made. That was a great relief to Herzog, but the experience would influence his future business decision-making. The settlement freed him to pursue his personal life. Norma and Bob had been seeing one another regularly, and they were married at City Hall on May 27th, 1933, with Rose Herzog and Mary Englander in attendance. After the formalities, Bob left to return to the office, as it was Saturday and the market was open half a day then.

Prior to the marriage, Norma lived in Flushing. When Jacob and Mary Englander built their house in Flushing during 1924 and 1925 with profits from Jacob's successful rotogravure business, Norma moved in with her then-husband and young son Bill. The living arrangements did not help her marriage and following her divorce, she remained in Flushing until 1933 when she moved to New York City. Bob and Norma moved back to the Flushing house in 1935 where I grew up. It was a two-story brick home facing 162nd Street. There was a garden in the back and lawns surrounding the house, perfect for touch football. Mature maple trees gave the property character and it was the picture of a lovely residential neighborhood. These were difficult times in the middle of the Great Depression and I remember my mother telling me, above all, that she needed to hold on to this house for her family.

One winter evening after moving back to Flushing, Norma had taken the train home from a day in the city. She walked one long block in the snow from the station, and when she got home, she realized she had lost a $5 bill. She and Bob went back over her steps to try to find it, but they never did, and she was badly shaken by this loss.

As the business climate slowly improved, the firm moved to 30 Broad Street, the office with the wonderful view of the Hudson River. At 500 square feet, with three rooms and a small entrance foyer, the new location was grand. The trading room had a six-position trading table, and a Western Union Teletype. In August 1933, the firm opened an account with the Continental Bank & Trust Company, known at the time as the "Broker's Bank." This was the beginning of an enduring relationship, as this bank became Chemical Bank, with G. Tyler Baldwin, our relationship manager, who was still at his desk when I joined the firm in 1959. Though he was attentive and friendly, he provided little help particularly when we needed capital to add positions at the end of the year. I remember asking for a loan one December when there was lots of stock for sale, the perfect time to be buying. Experience showed us year after year that prices would return to higher levels soon after the New Year. Chemical thought these over-the-counter stocks were too speculative, and they would never help. As expected, once January came along these stocks recovered with big profits.

The firm was doing quite a bit of business with Amro Bank in Amsterdam. Instructions, quotations and confirmations were sent and received by telegram. To ensure secrecy in overseas communications, Herzog used Peterson's International Code. Activity was brisk in what was called the "artificial silk shares." These were German controlled, but Netherlands registered. Companies like American Bemberg, American Enka, Associated Rayon and North American Rayon, were the first synthetic fiber stocks, and along with dollar-denominated foreign loans, these foreign transactions made significant profits.

Mid-1934, Benjamin Grody returned to the firm. Good producers were always in demand, and one firm's stars could be successfully wooed by another firm. This continued as the firm grew and matured. Traders who felt that the firm was not generous enough or that Herzog was too tough would leave to try their luck somewhere else. Usually they returned, realizing that their arrangement at Herzog was fair and equitable. Herzog believed that fairness was the basis for financially rewarding business, and where it was missing, the result was always friction over petty differences and certain parting.

The firm moved again in May 1938, this time to 40 Exchange Place, an office of about 500 square feet without a view but less expensive than 30 Broad Street. This is the office my brother Bill, then 14, remembered visiting with Norma in 1939. There was a stand-up slant top desk at the entrance where stock and bonds and comparisons were received, and inside, Bill remembered a large trading desk.

It's probably impossible for today's investor to imagine the conditions prevailing in the Twenties, Thirties and early Forties. Investing wisely was a challenge. Now it's easy to open an account to buy stocks, and there are endless varieties of securities for general investment. Mutual funds have worked diligently to educate investors over the last 40 or 50 years. Most public companies can be understood without too much difficulty, and research reports are widely available. In the old days, there were no rules requiring disclosure of transactions in securities by insiders. There were so many reorganizations that it was nearly impossible to keep abreast of them. The classic text "Security Analysis" by Benjamin Graham was written in 1934, and but not generally understood until years later.

In addition to the lack of transparency, there were other hazards. There were no industry regulations to protect the customer, and ethical standards were often lower than the ones now firmly backed by legislation and regulatory authority. The needs of the small investor were not a priority. Years ago, many new issues were questionable promotions, while today investors can count on a prospectus and disclosures which must adhere to SEC rules.

The fundamentals of economics were known by few, and not generally relied upon. After all, no one had foreseen the Depression, and no one knew exactly what to do to get things back to "normal." John M. Keynes' seminal work published in 1936 was extremely controversial and remains so. Some of the important thinking of the day can be found in the following quotation from "The Guaranty Survey" of June 24, 1935, headlined "The More Cautiously Government Acts, the More Confidently Business Moves; The time has come not to alter the Constitution but to permit business to solve its own problems...free from political domination that has spread uncertainty, undermined confidence, and brought discouragement."

In 1933, the Securities Act became law. Implementation was unwieldy and the impact of this major legislation could not be determined immediately. Business went on as usual except for a general apprehension especially among the smaller firms. Since the first mention of securities laws, people felt regulation would have a chilling effect on the industry, especially those who prospered before. My father told me that he and his contemporaries thought the new laws were aimed at removing small firms from the securities business. To him, the idea of a watchman was not a pleasant one. He did not pay a lot of attention to various announcements, and when I joined the firm years later, his attitude hadn't changed. He was happy to give me the compliance responsibilities. I viewed the problem differently, and felt the regulations were very helpful. They were there to protect the firm, the customer, the reputation of the industry, and the economic health of the nation. The new rules and oversight were a logical response to continued brokerage failures, and regulation has given popular capitalism a great boost. Without it, we may never have developed our efficient capital markets and the level of individual investor participation we have today. The over-the-counter business was always suspect, and when I joined the firm, I had to work hard to promote these securities and the integrity of the dealers.

The Securities Exchange Act of 1934 had a definite impact; the Federal Reserve could prescribe regulations for credit extended on securities transactions. One section reads in part: "In case a customer purchases a security in the special cash account and does not make full cash payment for the security within seven days, the creditor shall promptly cancel or otherwise liquidate the transaction or the unsettled portion thereof." The dealer was protected from precisely the circumstances which had led to the firm's big loss in 1929. Now the dealer was barred from "overlooking" the fact that a customer's check had not been received on time. Forgetting his own roots, my father would occasionally comment that I should deal with "Americans," as they knew the settlement rules and followed them. He was not sanguine about some of the fast money people he observed in the marketplace, often from more sophisticated European backgrounds.

The New York Security Dealers Association, formed in 1926, was the first self-regulatory body in the industry, the result of a merger of the Bank Stock Dealers Association and the Unlisted Security Dealers Association. This new organization was to represent the interests of Herzog & Co. as well as some 75 other dealers. Membership is for the firm, ordinarily a privilege for the managing partner. Others in the firm may be members, but for voting on any given issue, the firm has only one vote. It promulgated rules for the trading of various securities which for some reason were not standard types.

"STANY," the Security Traders Association of New York, was formed in 1934, thus beginning one of the most enduring industry associations. There was already a national association of traders, known as the National Security Traders Association, "NSTA," known today as the Security Traders Association, of which STANY is the largest affiliate. STANY was the first attempt by the individual New York area traders to associate and its founding provides another indication of the developing maturity of the industry. STANY became a member of the national organization in 1936. It now numbers about 500 members, publishes an annual magazine, and sponsors several panel discussions and social functions throughout the year. STANY is also a sounding board for proposed legislation, and through its officers, expresses opinions to the various regulatory agencies and legislative bodies.

The first form required for the SEC was sent to all dealers in June, 1935, and industry reaction was not enthusiastic. By that time, Herzog, had owned his own firm for nine years and had been in business for 15 years. He had taken serious losses, survived the Crash, and suddenly some men in Washington wanted to know everything about his business. Compliance became a time consuming necessity for every firm. Bob Herzog was doing this work, but he did not spend a lot of time on it, and since regulation was sparse, there was no real problem. Few saw regulation as a key to restoring investor confidence, and increasing public participation in the markets.

July 1939 witnessed the founding of the NASD, the first national self-regulatory association for the brokerage business. Herzog & Co. became a member in February 1940. There was skepticism, particularly among the smaller firms who questioned the organization's usefulness. The NASD has taken on extremely important proportions, and is now the centerpiece of the industry. At first no one foresaw the extent to which self-regulation would progress, or that virtually every detail of the business would be supervised and regulated. The NASD Manual has become the basic reference source for the industry. Rules of Fair Practice are included, as well as procedures for arbitration of disputes. Rulings on unusual contracts are made, and the staff is available to give opinions and recommendations.

People envied the situation of Herzog & Co., but they also knew it was a very risky business, with jeopardy from unexpected places. As the years passed, regulation and innovation reduced the risk in financial services. Capital became more available as investors returned with confidence. The National Association of Securities Dealers Automated Quotation system ("Nasdaq") became well established, and the firm's business improved. We gained respect and the path to profitable growth became clear.

CHAPTER 4

Business Maturity

My father expressed the difficulties of the stock trading business in a letter he wrote to Louis Weingarten. It's very basic, mostly about the trader's position. But within the letter, Herzog reveals all his principles, priorities and attitude towards managing risk. Despite the stunningly paltry sums, here we find the fundamentals that guided me and my partners in all our dealings, the fundamentals which assured our survival and made our success possible. First, some basics about how traders operate. Each trader is allocated a certain amount of firm capital for his trading activities. The trader then decides which stocks he would advertise as a market maker, soliciting inquiries from other firms to buy or sell shares of those companies. The trader would normally develop a position in each of those stocks, and that dollar value exposure is called his position. These positions are the amounts of each stock or bond which he has bought and not sold, in which case it is said that he is "long," or those he has sold but not yet bought, "short" positions. The total value of all these different positions "marked to market" must not be greater than the amount of firm capital he has been allocated. Here we find Herzog on management and the importance of establishing rules, keeping them in plain sight and adhering to them. This letter to Weingarten follows:

> *Roughly, last month we have written the positions down about $350, the month before about $4-450, and so on. It hurts us both, don't tell me it doesn't. I think it is high time we come to some sort of understanding as to positions, so that we don't have the unpleasantness of discussing it every now and then. Here is what I would suggest:*

1. Let's not keep a position beyond a week, if the bid price is below our cost. 2. If there is no trading in a stock for two weeks, we have no right carrying a position in it and out it should go. (Now there is exception to this and it has to be handled intelligently. It does not apply to a stock with which we are familiar and have been in for a long time.) 3. Let's not take a position unless we feel we can make a trading market in the stock. 4. Let's ride our profits and stop our losses. 5. Let's discuss a new position, and take it only if we have made up our minds to abide by the above conditions.

Mind you, we have both been in this business long enough to be able to figure out the angles. At least let's be intelligent about it and recognize the unprofitable aspects, so that we can keep what little we make.

Nothing I have ever read or studied provided better advice. Though written in 1944, nothing has changed, except the numbers have gotten bigger and the consequence of not following my father's advice has become costlier. In the years that followed, when I monitored trading accounts, I realized that there were no new problems. I was gaining confidence following in my father's footsteps, learning that my problems were no different than his and no more complex. This made it much easier for me to talk through these issues with our traders, and to argue convincingly that attention needed to be paid to managing risk all the time. I would be telling a trader that his positions were over his limits, and must be cut. One of the responses was, "Oh, that's easy; I'll just mark to the market!" Another trader was fond of telling me, "My right hand to God, I have a spot for the position!" Even my father, after a lifetime of aggravation with this subject, used to hover around in the trading room. He'd listen to a big trade getting done, and then ask, "Do you have a spot for those, Sonny?"

The Crash of 1929 devalued all in its wake, including emotions and expectations about the future. There were some die-hard optimists still, even as former moguls were reduced to shining shoes, selling apples and taking their places in bread lines. Hope is the fuel of the financial markets. It gets the traders back to try again every day, but "cockeyed optimists" were scarce. My grandfather Jacob Englander captured that feeling completely when he wrote to my father on December 22, 1941. Referring to the slim profits which trading afforded, Englander mentions how sad it is that "the old problem is still there. I can't help feeling that Wall Street is played out, and it is just a loss of time and effort to hang on to it."

Only four days after the invasion of Pearl Harbor, December 11, 1941, bonds and stocks issued by our enemies were suspended from the New York and American Stock Exchanges, and trading in these securities was not permitted by United States brokers. By this time German, Italian and Japanese securities had fallen into disfavor with investors here. As both Herzog and the firm were identified with foreign bonds from years before, some inquiries continued to come in. One day, an individual walked into the office with some bonds issued by the Roman Catholic Welfare Institutions in Germany. He wanted to sell them. A recorded trade was not possible, but a private deal was struck. After the war, these bonds did in fact come back, and they were liquidated. One of these bonds paid for a year's tuition at Cornell.

For less than $100 a month, Herzog moved the firm from Broad Street to 170 Broadway. The office was twice the size with four rooms, a reception area and about 1100 square feet in all. This would be the firm's home for many years. In May 1942, the rent was $83.33 per month. In the summer of '42, Leonard Berlinger was hired from Newburger, Loeb & Co. Berlinger had handled their private wire to Philadelphia, and was thus well acquainted on the Street. He remained with the firm for 23 years, until his retirement. The ability to hire and keep good people increased as the firm grew older and sounder. It enabled us to do a consistently larger quantity of better business. It also added immeasurably to the stability of the firm to have trusted employees over a period of years.

At this point, our family of four included Bob and Norma, Bill, now 17, and myself, six years old. The Englanders had both passed on, and so had Armin Herzog, Bob's father, but his mother, Rose, lived on and Bob supported her for the rest of her life. At home in Flushing during the war years, Bob was an air raid warden, and I remember looking out the window and seeing him at his post on our corner.

The change from wartime to a peace economy was well underway by 1946. This meant opportunities for investment. With great pent-up demand for goods and services, and the money to pay for them, the consumer market once again was in the limelight. Industry set about to supply these goods and Wall Street was ready to do its part. It was in this first post-war year that the NASD instituted registration of each individual person dealing in securities with the public. After this date, not only firm, but also traders and retail salespeople, or customers' men as they were then called, had to register.

During 1944 Herzog became a member of the New York Society of Security Analysts, a fledgling group which invited executives of various companies to visit with them over lunch and address their members, allowing time for discussion. This was one of the first industry bridges between Wall Street and corporate managers. This forum led to countless presentations before a consistently growing number of analysts, and the growth of the organization to one of national importance, primarily responsible for the "Financial Analysts Journal."

To take advantage of the beneficial tax rates accorded corporations and limit the liabilities of the firm's owners, Herzog & Co. incorporated in 1946. This ushered in a period of quiet growth and consolidation with few administrative difficulties. Interestingly, this started an almost 20-year period during which the company did no advertising. Post-war, there was renewed interest in the market and good reason to add another teletype, and the firm's six traders manned the desk and did a fair volume.

Herzog's pride in having achieved 25 years in business prompted a special anniversary dinner at Billy Rose's Diamond Horseshoe in early 1951. He was joined by cashier Murray Gilbert and traders Weinberger, Kennedy, Berlinger, Weingarten and Grody. The surviving photo shows the smartly attired group at the fashionable Paramount Hotel. The last years had been profitable ones, and the firm was highly respected in the trading community. Special stationery as well as specially designed Christmas cards were used. Gilbert would soon exit from the picture to manage a firm which planned to underwrite speculative new issues, something Herzog would find too risky. Herzog responded, coping with the loss of Gilbert by bringing the ledgers home and teaching himself, and me as well, how to complete the monthly reports. Herzog found another task for Berlinger, whose trading activities diminished. Berlinger would write the daily blotters, which were a log of every trade the firm did every day, updated before the start of the next day's trading. The business was profitable, still paying $170 in monthly rent. The experienced cashier grossed $65 per week and the phone bill was $71.19 monthly as the firm approached its 30th year in business. If a trader had a good year, he could anticipate earnings of about $4,000-5,000.

Business continued to prosper, but the firm did not grow. It was logical that I would join the securities business after graduating from Cornell in June 1957, but my career would not start at Herzog. Instead, I joined the back office of Eastman Dillon, Union Securities & Co. as a stock deliver clerk in the New York office at $55 per week. There my job was to prepare physical securities for delivery following a transaction. Stock delivery was just one function within the secure surroundings of what was called "the cage," but after graduating from the New York Institute of Finance, I left operations and New York to become a registered representative at the company's Philadelphia office. Befitting the first hire at the office in many years, I was assigned the firm's dormant accounts. What better way to break into the business as a producer than to face the task of developing revenue from those who hadn't been heard from in years? My exile to Philadelphia did not mean I would lose contact with my father's firm. Herzog & Co. became a source of business for me as they would direct their listed securities business to me since they were not a member firm. My father and I began our first business relationship.

CHAPTER 5

Softly Blowing Reveille

Daybreak came to the downtown corner of Maiden Lane and Broadway at a little before six o'clock, and the outlines of 170 Broadway became clear. The neighborhood is sleepy in May 1959, but a few eateries were making ready for the day. Light entered the corner office of Room 306 through two windows on Maiden Lane and two on Broadway, illuminating the trading table where the Herzog & Co. offices have been since 1942.

Like a sculptor, the light slowly reveals the outlines and then the details of objects all too familiar. The trading table is made in two long halves buckled together underneath. It has been in use since 1926, when Bob Herzog started his business. Over the years, the linoleum top has gotten very dark. There are papers, ash trays, rotary dial telephones, a couple of wire baskets and two time clocks that loudly announce the minutes passing.

At the northwest corner of the table is a heavy secretarial chair with green plastic upholstery, which will soon be in use again. A shelf on the wall opposite the Maiden Lane windows is piled high with National Quotation Bureau "pink sheets" for stocks, "yellow sheets" for bonds, old copies of *The Wall Street Journal*, and a few National Stock Summary books. At the end of the table opposite the Broadway windows is a desk with a disappearing typewriter contraption, and an old Royal typewriter needing repair. Vintage fluorescent lighting fixtures, metal waste baskets, and a few personal trinkets complete the scene.

In the entry area of the office is a stand-up slant top desk. Underneath sits a cube shaped safe about two feet wide, used to store securities and other valuables overnight, and there aren't many of those. The combination lock failed long ago, but the door closes and looks locked. A couple of chairs are there for rare visitors, and a table with an old issue of *Fortune*. There are two other small rooms, and behind them, Bob Herzog's office, with the original 1926 leather couch, red leather chair and round mahogany table, a large walnut desk, chair, pictures on the wall, carpet, and an air conditioner. This scene greeted me on my first day at work at the firm which bore my name. I was to sit at the open position at the trading table, next to my father's place to my left. I sat down in the green chair and wondered what to do next.

There were the people who worked in the office: Louis Weingarten, born in Silesia, the son of a dairy farmer. Louis emigrated from Poland with a terrific recipe for corned beef, and a raspy voice after his years outside on the Curb Exchange. He spoke Polish, German and Yiddish. Louis traded currencies for his own account before working at the Curb Exchange. He was married to Claire, a fiery redheaded radical, who spoke 10 languages, studied under Freud and nurtured a great circle of European friends. She was Austrian, educated in Vienna and lived in Paris in the early 1920s before marrying Louis.

Leonard Berlinger had been with the firm for almost 20 years when I joined, bringing the Newburger private line which rang at his position on the desk. Although he arrived at seven o'clock each morning to hand-write the blotters for the previous day's trading activity, there was time to spare before the start of trading as it was typical at that time to do only four or five trades in a day. Berlinger would give the completed blotter to our secretary, the elderly but lovely, Mary Margaret Lasher who would type out a confirmation for each of the trades before going through the day's mail.

At fifty-eight my father was a handsome and dignified man. He dressed beautifully in double-breasted D'Andrea custom made suits, with shirts from Catanese and Sulka ties. He was gracious, polite and cordial with people, sometimes maddeningly so, and this accounted for his many friends. Though European in background with Hungarian as his first language, he had no trace of an accent. He thoroughly assimilated in his new homeland. A fine athlete, he was a good figure skater, swimmer, tennis player, and rider. He had fallen in love with Norma when they met at Fleischmanns before she was married, and translated Hungarian love poems for her. He found her again after her divorce, and they married in 1933.

Decades removed from the Crash and Depression, that experience remained a profound influence on my father and his approach to risk. His decisions were not hasty. His trading positions were modest. When possible, he would avoid risk and his preference was for a conservative revenue stream, which he would describe as income which would "stick to you." At this time the total capital of the firm was about $40,000, including the family's 1949 Cadillac sedan. Trading positions were thus quite small. Bob had many friends on the Street, and was respected and well liked. Order flow resulted and sometimes there were interesting trading opportunities. There were two private wires, one to Newburger, Loeb & Co., and the other to Bob's close friend, Charlie Banks at Cohen, Simonson & Co., a firm started by former furriers who made the leap to Wall Street. Another source of business was Jim Waters, the head industrials trader at First Boston Corp., who joined us each morning as a passenger when my other job was chauffeur to two smokers in the back seat. These contacts accounted for the four or five trades the firm was doing each day, and on many days, there were also brokerage orders from friends of the family.

My father understood and encouraged my decision to join another firm after my college graduation. I wanted to gain experience. After I left Eastman Dillon, I was talking with my father and wondered aloud about what I was going to do next. He opened his desk drawer to take out a small piece of paper while saying, "Well, son, you could always come to work for the family firm." He handed me an engraved business card with my name on it which he had ordered long before any conversation on this subject. My father had simply waited for the right moment. The time had come, satisfying a long held hope of his. I fell for it, and the deal was $50 a week and half of any trading profits I produced with a position limit of $5000.

While at Eastman Dillon, I went to a training session on personal money management sponsored by the Wellington Fund. There, I learned how to build wealth. The secret was to save 10% of what you earned, and pay yourself first, learning to live on the balance of your take home pay. The stark reality of my meager income began to settle in. I was living at home, paying $10 each week for room and board, so there was little left over. I was stuck in an uncomfortable office with little in the way of gainful work to do, and I lacked the skills that would allow me to earn more.

My arrival at the firm was marked by a letter from my mother, written May 20, 1959:

Dear Herzog and Dear Company,
This is to acknowledge receipt of the card which announces your new association.

> *Be assured that I am deeply gratified by this development. It holds promise of a perfect combination of personalities and attributes and I am firmly convinced that the future will bring deep satisfactions to each of you in this new relationship.*
>
> *Not only do I send you my congratulations and good wishes, but I take this opportunity to assure you of my continued patronage.*
>
> *Yours most sincerely,*
N. E. H.

I realized years later what a tremendous effect my mother had on me, teaching me lessons which would be immensely useful in business. In those years after the Depression, and during World War II there was enough money to keep the family going but no extra. When I would tell mother I wanted something, she would invariably say, "When you don't have what you want, make do with what you have." Mother abhorred waste, and would caution me with, "Waste not, want not," and if she saw that I was not paying attention she would fire back again with, "Willful waste makes woeful want." These instructions were repeated often and left a deep impression on me. She taught me how to work, saying, "Lazy people work twice as hard," and, "Where a good worker has been working, there is no evidence of his work except the job well done." She taught me to be careful with my jobs, and to clean up as I went along. She knew there would be errors, and reassured me, "When you make a mistake, fix it quickly and quietly, and try again." When I was whiny and impatient, and asked why I couldn't do something, she would say with undoubted authority, "Because your mother said so." That was the end of the story for me, and years later I echoed her words within our business.

When people in the firm made requests which I did not want to do, I would patiently explain why. When that didn't work, I would reply, "It's my name on the door, and I say no." These lessons learned at her knee became a part of my thinking, and with them I learned to innovate and not be afraid of making a mistake. I used her thoughts in training and encouraging scores of other people over fifty years in business, and at the Museum of American Finance, as well. I wrote some of these thoughts to my mother in February 1989, "I realized many years later these were the tools of innovation—doing things differently, certainly, but more important, having the temperament to think that things could be different, the real key. These ideas have had a terrific effect on my life, and I don't think I ever told you how happy I am with them and how much they mean to me..."

Bolstered by my family's support, in the weeks following my joining the firm, I thought constantly about how I would do business, and get new retail accounts, as I had been doing at Eastman Dillon. One afternoon while walking in Greenwich Village, I found an antique shop with a stock certificate in the window. It was for shares of New York and Harlem Rail Road dated 1873, and it had an image of a vintage train. It was marked $5, and my thought was to buy it, frame it, and hang it on my office wall. When prospective customers would come to the office, they would see it, think it was interesting, and I would steer the conversation to investing, and hope to open a new account. When I got home, I was holding it and I noticed the signature of the president was William H. Vanderbilt.

In that instant, I knew I wanted to get other such certificates. I immediately became a collector, and sent an ad to *Collectors' News*, beginning a correspondence with people all over the country who had various stock and bond certificates for sale. Then I realized I was writing checks, and I didn't have that much income. I worried about how I would sell these certificates if I no longer wanted to collect. I loved the collecting, however, and I decided to collect the financial documents of the American Revolutionary period, as there was a ready market for the autographs of the signers. This was the beginning of a very serious collection I formed over fifty years, and has led me into many wonderful experiences, most notably founding the Museum of American Finance.

The two private wires we had would call occasionally seeking help with prices of stocks or bonds they couldn't find easily, and this task fell to me. Similarly, one summer while in college I went to the office, and found a handful of old stock certificates in a steel cabinet. No one knew if they had any value, so I contacted the transfer agents or secretaries of state with the hope of getting some information on their values. After weeks of working on them, I discovered one share of Anglo Lautaro Nitrate with a value of $8. I vividly remember going with my father to the company's office at 120 Broadway to redeem the share. While doing this type of research for the private wires, I thought I could do it for anyone, and I began to advertise a specialty in inactive and obsolete securities. This step was the beginning of a very profitable lifelong activity. I now saw how important my trading position limit of $5000 would be, and how my production could grow if there were more inquiries.

Trips to used book stores turned up the reference books I needed which enabled me to save the time I would have otherwise spent sleuthing major libraries. I gradually made shelves for these books all over the office.

The physical discomfort in the office was quite disagreeable. It was freezing on winter mornings, especially Monday because there had been no heat over the weekend, and sweltering in summer, with soot coming in from open windows, it was no fun. The long day was punctuated by Leonard's "Lunch" shriek each day, and then a discussion about what to order and from where. The result was inevitably a corned beef sandwich for Louis ("must be lean") with a bottle of Dr. Brown's celery tonic. For Leonard, cream cheese and jelly and milk, and for my father, ham and Swiss on rye, no mayo and a dark coffee, repeated daily for months. By four o'clock, everything to do had been long finished, and the typewriters were covered up for the night. At that point, my father would ask Leonard for the check book, which he reviewed page by page. Seeing all was right, he returned it for overnight storage in the non-locking safe.

Change was implacably resisted, and my mother was my committed support team. I was greatly surprised one night on the BMT while on the way home for dinner, when my father confided that he had very little imagination. He said he found it difficult to visualize what other people were suggesting. A liberating moment, as I had a creative imagination and could visualize all sorts of things.

One day my mother and a friend stopped in to visit. They were shocked at the appearance of the office, and their visit resulted in a new coat of paint. When the painters left, Norman Asher, my college roommate and I spent hours together on a freezing Sunday cleaning things. It was then I discovered the linoleum on the trading table was green and not black. When people came back to the newly painted office, they were quite pleased with the improvement. But too many hours were spent on these chores, and my production was slow to grow.

From a letter I wrote to a friend on December 11, 1959 but never mailed, there was a summary of my first important months at the firm:

> *I had come to the firm quite naïve, knowing nothing about its business, or about trading. Now having learned a lot, Louis complained when I was absent as he needed my help. Arriving with no understanding of the bookkeeping system, I made all the closing entries for November and the*

trial balance hit perfectly the first time. It was clear that the volume levels were far too low and the firm needed to expand. These epiphanies were the cause of dreadful arguments with my father, and we found it very difficult to agree on anything. One issue we did agree about was the need to go into his private office for these screaming matches, which were no fun for the others. I feel the most irritating frustration I can describe. I am making no money, working much longer for it, getting complete discouragement from Dad, the one person to whom I look for approval, and there doesn't seem to be any way out.

During these grinding days, and during dinners with my parents, we talked about how to expand the business. We knew that retail brokerage was not for us, unable to compete with the large firms like Eastman Dillon where I had been, or many others all over the city. We realized trading would be a far more promising strategy for us. We began to look for traders, and in late 1959, we hired Bud Kassel, who had been with A. G. Becker & Co. He began on January 1, 1960, and decided to specialize in utilities and institutional service. Assisting him fell to me, and he taught me a great deal without realizing it. He spent two years with us, was not very profitable, but did move us ahead. He introduced major institutional clients to the firm. Bud and I would call them in the morning to see if they were looking to buy or sell blocks of stock. It was our job to match their needs with the other side of the trade. When it worked, it was very profitable. While I learned from Bud, his way of teaching was different from my father's. Bud eagerly gave me mediocre explanations of what he was doing, while my father expected me to learn by watching. Bringing Bud to the firm was in fact a big change, and I knew things would be getting better. We had begun the long trip ahead and up.

CHAPTER 6

Beginning the Trek

The addition of Bud Kassel to the firm was energizing as it was not often that we added a new person. He was an enthusiastic teacher, and though he was short on information and preparation, he was always amusing. As the office was very small, everyone's personal conversations were monitored. We all admired Bud's enthusiasm, though it was often misdirected, and he stimulated us all in a curious way. We could all hear Bud and Sheila, his fiancée, planning their engagement and then their marriage. On one occasion, Bud boasted about how they would not have any children for a while, to which our secretary, Mary Lasher, a devout Roman Catholic, replied, "Only God can determine that." Sure enough, she was right, and to Bud's surprise, their first child was born just nine months after their marriage. When the couple's new home failed to live up to expectations, we could all hear their heated arguments.

I watched, listened, and helped. Bud was making a market in Arkansas Louisiana Gas, and was doing an arbitrage between the common and the convertible preferred. I came back from lunch one day to hear how proud he was to have sold the convertible preferred short, and covered it with the common. Whether it was the heated morning exchange with Sheila over the car or the washing machine, Bud had done just the reverse of what should have been done. The arbitrage was to sell the common stock short, and remain long the convertible preferred, so that if the common short position ran up too fast, you could convert the preferred, and not lose any money. But we learned from our mistakes and the successes exceeded the blunders. We did make some terrific trades, one notably with Delaware Fund, placing a block of this same Arkansas Louisiana Gas common stock with them. We got a full commission of about $3,000, and I immediately called my girlfriend to help celebrate.

Bud shared his knowledge and his contacts. His friend Burt Barysh was working at the much larger NYSE member firm Ernst & Co. at 120 Broadway. Burt agreed to install a private wire from his office to ours, in return for our New York Stock Exchange business. It would be our third private wire and our relationship with the established firm not only meant more business, but it also meant we could count on Burt to report hourly on where the Dow was — a great resource in the tedious days before computers. This type of timely, fundamental market information was valuable to the traders and customers of our small firm. Because of this new relationship, a call came one day from Howard Ernst, the firm principal, inviting me to lunch. I turned up at his office early, and he was showing me around when I offered a compliment. I mentioned the fine job Burt had done with the sale of a couple of bonds Ernst had a large position in. The much senior Ernst made me feel like I overstepped when he quickly responded with a cautionary rebuke: "Two bonds don't make a market!" I remembered many times how true that was.

I was also trying to do more and varied business. In 1960, I learned about a self-underwriting of a color photography processing lab on Long Island. A self-underwriting is when a company attempts to sell its new shares to the public directly without the help of a brokerage firm. I called the company, Key Color Laboratories, and they sent me a supply of offering circulars and some beautiful color photographs. I enthusiastically went to work, making calls and purchasing shares from the company on behalf of various retail customers. I also called on a few friends on the Street, encouraging their interest. One call was to E. D. Boynton & Co., and I chatted with Elwood Boynton. He mentioned that I should be careful about the word "underwriting" and what that meant according to the very strict SEC regulations. He suggested I go to the SEC and inquire if everything I was doing was all right. Innocently, I did just that, walking into the New York SEC office where it was recommended that I get a lawyer quickly. I was shocked. My activities were definitely not permitted.

Stunned, I went back to the office, and told my father. He quickly called a family friend who was the firm's only access to the legal fraternity. Our friend directed us to an SEC attorney in Cleveland. I got on a plane to Cleveland where I poured my heart out to one of their attorneys. By this time, I had placed about $40,000 worth of Key Color stock, at the $1 per share purchase price plus a commission, and those transactions were about as large as the entire firm capital. I realized that I placed the entire firm in jeopardy, and that my actions could have put my father out of business after thirty years. This was a terrifying experience at the tender age of 24. I broke down in utter dismay.

I went back to New York, and the attorneys decided that all the Key Color trades should be rescinded at our expense, which meant my father needed to advance about $45,000. Rescission checks were written by my brother who came downtown to help us, and they were promptly mailed to our customers with a letter of explanation. There was some satisfaction when the SEC told us that they had never seen such a prompt and praiseworthy windup to a case. Seeing me terribly distressed, my father was encouraging. He told me not to worry and that once we got our money back from Key Color, this would all turn out to be an educational experience. Writing about this over fifty years later is still difficult, and I see that there is no reference to Key Color in the typed diary I kept, as it was far too painful. I remain grateful for my father's wisdom and sensitivity. He did not criticize me, confident that there was more value in this business lesson than the temporary expense he would bear. He was right. As a manager, I benefited from this experience, especially as the firm was growing, and there were times we did experience big losses. Recalling my father, I encouraged those who had losses to act responsibly, and look ahead to better days.

As father predicted, we did get our money back from the company in a couple of months, and I had a new agenda to work on. The firm needed counsel. One of our bankers made a recommendation and I met with Townsend J. Knight, of Curtis Mallet-Prevost, Colt & Mosle, a distinguished firm which remained our outside general counsel until our firm was sold to Merrill Lynch in 2000. He constructively suggested I take a course at the Practicing Law Institute. My next step was to read the NASD Manual. I knew that we must become vigilant when it came to compliance. We adopted procedures and completed forms to address various requirements. I vowed not to make the same mistakes twice. Armed with a painful experience and new found knowledge, I could field calls from the SEC which routinely came during trading hours. An important element of our later success was our fluency with regulations; we knew them inside and out. When a trader would approach me with an unusual trade opportunity which I knew not to be within the rules, I would say, "It is two years from now, and I am from the SEC questioning this trade. How would you explain it?" Soon the traders knew they should not bother to ask about these problem trades, and that was better for all of us. Compliance became a preoccupation, as markets were becoming much more active, and there were many more opportunities to abuse or ignore the regulations.

In 1961 the market was very active, and we had a lot of volume to process. Leonard Berlinger, our cashier, asked for help. My brother suggested Jim Ferris, who was working outside our industry at Goody Products, the hair accessory manufacturer. Ferris came in one Saturday, and I could tell immediately that he was very competent, good at numbers, and very careful. I offered him a job after two hours, and he joined us shortly after. About the time of his arrival, we switched from a monthly balancing system to a daily one, and that required taking a daily run of all our unsettled contracts, a tedious process in the days before computers. Jim made the transition seem a lot easier than expected. This was a generational advance, and I was happy to have another young person in the office. Jim was part of the great migration from the Midwest to the big city. He was from Traverse City, Michigan, and had hitch hiked east. Toward the end of his trip, he asked a driver where he could get a good meal in the city at reasonable cost. The Automat was the answer, also my favorite place to eat downtown. Jim was tall and lanky, a calm, conscientious worker who thought about things before reaching a decision. He could operate a ten-key adding machine by touch. He was constantly discovering odd and amusing things about New Yorkers, like the way they ordered coffee. In New York, there were endless refinements of light, very light, dark, just a drop of milk, and so on. In Traverse City, it was just "with or without."

My father's excellent reputation on the Street meant we could count on a steady flow of visitors to the office. I met a couple of people from General Economics Corporation ("GEC"), and this soon developed into active trading. I listed their company in the pink sheets, and kept them posted about what was going on in the market for their stock. Their shares had a retail following and the company placed many of these shares. After the company went public, I found that most of the calls I got were from people who wanted to sell stock. I would call GEC and sell them the stock I had bought, earning 25 cents a share commission. This was great for me, but as other people in the office saw what was going on, they grew increasingly uneasy with my role in the recycling of GEC shares. Along the way, GEC handled some initial offerings of companies they had created, and then the pattern repeated. We all became more concerned, and to no one's surprise, there were regulatory problems, investigations and one day General Economics was only a memory. We were very lucky, as we had monitored our exposure carefully and losses were kept to a very low number.

Late in 1964 we hired Len Williams as a trader. He lived near Philadelphia, and made the commute every day, regularly "borrowing" a supply of Kleenex on the way home. Len had positions in several "exchanges" in his trading account. This involved new securities issued in exchange for old ones, sometimes due to a merger or a change in name. These were not risky as they were the result of closed corporate deals and sometimes the new certificates were not yet ready, so we had open contracts on our books. My father counted these as positions, even though they were closed transactions merely awaiting physical certificates. Frequently these situations left Len out of trading money. We overcame this problem by talking it through, and this was very reassuring to me.

When Len came, my father moved into his private office, and when he looked through his desk, he found an early checkbook from 1927. Bank balances then were in the range of $800-$1,200, and this stark reality was overwhelming to me. I felt guilty about being so insistent that we spend money for new services without fully appreciating my father's struggle to stay in business during forty difficult years.

My father allowed me to pursue my ideas and remained open to suggestions. By the end of 1964, my fifth year at the firm, he had accepted a lot of my ideas, and became a lot more willing to try new ones. This would continue.

CHAPTER 7

Change and New Growth

My trip to Mexico in 1961 with Norman Asher was the first vacation I had taken since graduating from Cornell in June 1957. It was on that trip, in the town of San Miguel d'Allende, I saw a beautiful girl across the dining room and decided to introduce myself. I excused myself from Norman, bought a bunch of lilies and presented the flowers to the surprised Diana. I asked for a date for when we would both be back in Mexico City. Diana accepted and Norman was our chaperone for dinner at a restaurant with lovely violin music. Diana flew home the next day, but we agreed to write. Diana's letters were encouraging, and because of that, I asked Norman to look her up in London on an upcoming buying trip he would take for Bloomingdale's. I was pleased to learn they had a memorable visit.

Our exchange of letters continued. Our second date was a week exploring Venice. Diana then returned to Germany, where she was attending university in Freiburg. I took the Trans-Europe Express train via Domodossola to Paris to meet some college friends, before flying home. When Diana planned a visit to her parents in Montreal, she came via New York. She invited me to meet her parents, and sample her cooking. I was on my way. Our next meeting was in New York, when we visited a friend in Patterson, New York. We walked in the beautiful woods around her house, I proposed—and Diana accepted! I was very happy. We were married in October 1963, and saved a lot of travel expense.

By the Spring I had discovered how valuable Diana was as a confidante and consultant. She understood my lingering disappointment over time wasted at Cornell, and encouraged me to get a master's degree, advice which proved invaluable in many ways. She came to the office to help when someone was absent, and learned what our business was like from the inside. Her suggestions for changes were constructive, and demonstrated her deep understanding of human relationships and social interaction, which overcame her limited knowledge of business.

Diana took charge of our cultural lives and we did splendid, unforgettable things. She was everywhere in my thoughts, and would remain there for a lifetime. Her encouragement and reassurance at difficult moments were crucial elements in my maturing, and in the progress of Herzog & Co. She gave me the confidence to pursue my interest in inactive securities, which began to pan out. My production involved very low risk and high returns, of which a good portion was taxed at favorable long term capital gains rates.

Other traders were not faring as well at the time as I noted in my diary. Bob Manghir had shorted 1000 Industrial Timer rather casually just before a bullish announcement. He confided to us all that on the subway he had read his horoscope and the message was "full possession of all facts in faraway places would be beneficial to you." Convinced that his horoscope was always correct, Bob went short. Despite Bob's faith in astrology, the stock opened three points higher for a big loss. Len Williams had markdowns of $3000 at the same time, but persisted in complaining about not having enough position money to trade effectively. The markdowns erased profits he had made of about the same amount.

From my diary: "It is as though traders want to take risks, and eagerly look for ways to do this." Whether at Barings, or JP Morgan's "London Whale" we often read of rogue traders searching for unrealistic gains who fail to accurately gauge risk and lose discipline. Those who handle risk well do so with careful analysis. They control their emotions and rarely seek profit in the stars.

The first overall firm photo was taken on April 2nd, 1965, and it tells a good story. There were twelve of us in the picture: Paul Adelsberger, a friend of my father's from the Josephthal days, where Paul had lost heavily arbitraging German marks, Hugo Knight, a sub-tenant trading as Sherry, Maloney & Co., and Ed Dorosh, who had just liquidated his company and joined the firm. At this point, the firm was listing about 90 stocks daily in the pink sheets. The average age of the people in the picture was 43, and that average would drop as the firm moved ahead. Men from the "old days" of the Street furnished perspective to the younger people in the office. This was extremely helpful since the next generation was just beginning to discover Wall Street, and they didn't have any idea of the history, just an eagerness to make money. Our trading volume was low for the number of people we had; we were conservative, and moved deliberately. We would never jump into a new situation just because we heard a tip.

When it came to new initiatives, I was still having difficulties with my father. But I remained patient, knowing that it would take some time to overcome my own lack of confidence and gain his. My patience was a virtue. Before a vacation in Spain, I gave him some ideas and problems in writing, and he was not openly averse to them. I had suggested a mailing to banks about inactive securities, sending them a tabbed card with contact information. My father did not immediately reject the idea, or remind me of the $800 legal bill from Townsend Knight that "wiped out all our profits so far this year." By the time I returned from Spain, my father had fired Len Williams and Ed Dorosh. Father was in a far better frame of mind, but best of all, he told me he had missed me. I returned refreshed and ready to begin again with new ideas.

Louis Weingarten officially retired on June 15, 1965, cigar smoke, Helmar cigarettes and all. He had great old-time charm, and was a good trader, with a good sense of value. He would caution me, "Never make a bid unless you want to buy the stock," and he was rarely intimidated when one of his positions became oversold, lessons that have stayed with me for many years. I missed him, but he was very tired, and it was a step into the future for the firm.

As I saw the firm changing, I began to think it was time to write a history of the firm. To get some perspective, I thought I would visit and compare Herzog to some of the other trading firms. John J. Meyers & Co. was a surprise — small, unpleasant and disorderly, with three thirty position turrets. Frazee, Olifiers entire office was about the size of our trading room, and not air-conditioned. H. J. Weinberger & Co. was a very small one-man office, and this investigation gave me renewed confidence in Herzog & Co., and we began to explore clearing for other firms.

One of the problems we faced if we wanted to clear trades for other firms was the signature guarantee issue. To achieve "good delivery" of physical securities to another brokerage firm, the signature of the owner must be present, and it must be guaranteed by his broker and the endorsement of the broker must be guaranteed by a member firm of the New York Stock Exchange or a commercial bank. I had been referred to Amott, Baker & Co. and I suggested we give them our stock exchange orders in return for guaranteeing, and in February 1966 they agreed. This was very important as they were located close by at 150 Broadway, which made the work very easy for us. We could then take a more aggressive posture regarding clearing accounts, which we did successfully.

I was doing business with Peter Toczek, who had been at Salomon Bros., where he was responsible for a large loss. My father and I talked about that, and he said "anyone who can lose a lot of money can also make a lot." Peter was now at Merkin & Co., and he began sending me some broker's broker trades, quite lucrative for me. Then there were trades he designated for his own account, and this made us anxious. We had trouble getting delivery instructions, and they were always late. When we finally delivered some Keuffel & Esser to the National Newark & Essex Bank, the stock was taken in and paid for because the senior clerk, who would have rejected the delivery, was on vacation. We were very lucky! When I told my father that I was not going to do any more business with Peter, he said, "Don't be so hasty. Now you know how he operates, and with that knowledge you can protect yourself if you do more business with him." This was good advice from someone with a lot of experience. I was wary, but I did continue doing business with Peter, and it was very profitable.

The Rosh Hashanah service at the Brotherhood Synagogue featured a sermon on "Morality in Business." I listened and I found the sermon to be meaningful and relevant to the problems of the day. It helped me form the foundation for my future in the business. I would always maintain a respect for rules and the employees who were a part of the business experience. This foundation has served me well and benefitted the firm. I expanded on it in a diary entry from October 1965 which reads, "It is absolutely to emphasize the desirable, the progress, and the positive in business, for to dwell on the disappointments makes business a very dreary pastime, whereas it should be a wholesome and rewarding exercise of ingenuity and hard work."

By May 1966, things were indeed looking skyward. Business had been good for the year so far, and stock prices had gone up, especially my positions in inactive securities. U. S. Manufacturing was quoted about $4, up from pennies, Vista Industries up from one cent to 1¼ and Geoscience up from four cents to 1¾. I was very pleased. My work at NYU was going well, and Professor Arthur Svenson said he was very excited by my work, which he asked me to prepare for publication. He told me my paper on innovation contained material for three articles, and approved my firm history project as a thesis topic.

Against this background, Diana learned from Mother that my father was unhappy with things downtown, and complained about several small items which I had earlier tried to ameliorate unsuccessfully. This came at a time when his concentration on business issues had waned and his trading was not profitable and prone to errors. I realized during a longer conversation that my father was questioning his usefulness at the firm, and was uncomfortable with aging and the new environment. He didn't want to miss a day at work because he knew things would be done well in his absence. A difficult and tricky transition began and ended later with his move to West Palm Beach, where he and Mother spent very happy years. This coincided with the fortieth anniversary of the firm, and my parents, Diana and I went for dinner at Emke Hungarian Restaurant.

It was the end of September 1966, and my father and I were talking on the corner of Cortlandt and Church Streets. In that moment in a passing gaze, I was shocked to notice how much he had aged. It had been a bad month for him trading, and he had taken a large markdown, by his own admission a mistake. I suggested he leave the trading desk, and I would take over his situations, and he reluctantly agreed. I acted on this the next day, moving his personal things from the trading room into his office. Later in the day, he seemed relieved, and I was pleased. After seven years with the firm, I had gotten to see the ups and downs and managed to survive them. I knew now that responsibility for the firm was on my shoulders, and I took that obligation seriously. I also felt great satisfaction that we had gotten to this point together, mutually respectful, with the deepening love we shared overcoming our misunderstandings. We were one of the very few father and son teams on the Street that had succeeded, and we were both very proud of that.

CHAPTER 8

R. M. Smythe & Co. Joins the Office

The October market was slow and discouraging with too much time for talk. Jim Ferris joined us on the trading desk, but my father was not happy as Jim was "sitting in my seat." I hated to see my father sad or resentful, and I felt rather callous, but we proceeded. I realized that making decisions was relatively easy, but managing the outcomes of these decisions was far more difficult, requiring skill, patience and understanding. Diana's counsel at times like these was especially valuable, and I began to realize the special talents women have for resolving tense situations.

The fortieth year of doing business as Herzog & Co. was just about over, and a great deal had been accomplished. I knew there was a lot more to learn, and that I needed to pay attention to avoid mistakes. As 1966 was ending, I got a call from my friend at National Quotation Bureau who said he heard that R. M. Smythe & Co. was for sale. This was exciting news for me, as I had known about the firm ever since discovering Roland Smythe's 1929 book *Valuable Extinct Securities* five years earlier. I had visited the firm a year before, after the death of partner Walter Brown. If I could buy the firm, I would own a venerated Wall Street name that dated back to 1880, and along with it all their records and a large library of reference materials. I was ecstatic, and called for an appointment with Godfrey Bligh, the head of the firm. At that time, the firm consisted of Godfrey, his brother Fred Bleibtreu, and their secretary, Mrs. Cohen. The price mentioned was $26,000, which I thought was high, but I kept listening. Fred was to become the American broker for several European banks, and he was to join our firm as a registered representative, so there would be revenue, as well as a way to get exposure in Europe. This first meeting was a good one, and I returned to our office and began to make notes and take measurements.

If we could close the deal, Godfrey agreed to come along and continue working for Smythe, and he was quite spry for 83. I came to know him during the purchase conversations, and trusted him from the outset. We made good progress, and at a point I asked Jerry Mulligan, a young attorney with Curtis, Mallet-Prevost, to have a look at Smythe's corporate records. He gave his blessing. My purchase of the firm was done, without the benefit of any due diligence - as though I even knew what that might entail, and I never saw a tax return or had any real understanding of the revenue and expense of the firm. I knew there would be less rent to pay, and I knew I wanted to do the deal. My father was against it from the beginning, but I was stubborn. He said, "You don't need another company, you have one!" And when everything was done, he taunted me about how much I had paid for the company, saying, "Easy come, easy go." I was determined, confident and energized, and in words from my diary, "walking on air."

The deal closed in early January 1967, and the next task was moving them from 79 Wall Street to our office at 170 Broadway. The movers came on a Saturday morning, and by one o'clock everything was in our office. Then I started to arrange everything. With the wooden boards taken from their office, I needed to re-make the shelves required for all their books. This was real work, but with careful planning it came out well. I remember feeling an intense sense of ownership of all these physical objects, something I never felt before about anything at Herzog & Co. It felt terrific. The library and reference material was very impressive, and over time, proved to be extremely valuable.

When people came in on Monday morning, there was surprise, but the overall reaction was constructive. My father described the scene as a "second hand furniture shop." He countered my determination by avoiding any spoken word with Fred Bleibtreu and Godfrey Bligh. It was an awkward start for us all, but I stubbornly and confidently moved ahead, certain that the deal would be beneficial.

This was a very important step in my Wall Street career. I found the opportunity, negotiated the terms, handled the physical requirements, and used my own money to do it. I learned a lot, and I was eager to forge a success of my own doing. As things turned out, my dreams were not nearly as exciting as the reality. The first order of business was to assure my father that Smythe would not do any trading, though the firm was an SEC registered broker-dealer, so I quickly terminated their registration. In return, Herzog & Co. would not do any research. I remember very clearly when the first batch of mail arrived, forwarded from Smythe's old address. There were half a dozen checks for $20 payable to Smythe for work I was unsuccessful in finding for our firm at $4. A big opportunity came along when *Finance Magazine* decided to write a feature story with Godfrey and me as central characters. There were many favorable comments. Herzog & Co. benefited as the Street learned that there was a lot of life in the firm, and that the services Smythe offered were quite useful. Many inquiries came in, with many trading follow ups for Herzog & Co. In my inactive securities department, I now had the research resources to make intelligent bids for many more stocks and bonds. This activity allowed me to have conversations with brokerage firms and banks all over the country. My initiative helped pave the way for many new relationships.

My small collection of old stock and bond certificates, started in 1959, began to grow, with great finds showing up in the mail all the time. Smythe's capabilities at specialized research were later recognized by SIPC (Securities Investor Protection Corporation) and during Michael Mullan's tenure as Manager, we helped the agency liquidate twenty-three firms, among them some large bankrupt brokerage firms, including McDonnell & Co. Because of our growing reputation in this area, we won the New York State Abandoned Property account. This was not only lucrative for both firms, but there were marvelous worthless certificates which found their way into my collection. We kept the account for three years, providing the State numerous improvements to their systems, which may still be in use today.

Diana joined the firm when our children were in school, and together we developed and nurtured our collectibles business for forty years. As the old stocks and bonds hobby, "scripophily," began to grow, we received profitable inquiries from Europe. To further these, I took a trip to Frankfurt to meet the bankers who were publishing *Freunde Historischer Wertpapiere* for hobbyists, and that trip resulted in the new magazine, *Friends of Financial History*, published by Smythe. Soon after, the first Smythe auction of antique certificates was held at Fraunces Tavern, where we sold some American Revolutionary War bonds. This grew into later auctions of autographs, photographs, books, and ephemera, and valuable contacts were made across the collector spectrum. Smythe's auctions were trusted, and the firm received consignment leads from the largest auction houses. Smythe underwrote the first reference book on loans issued to raise money for the Revolutionary War, *The Price of Liberty* by Bill Anderson.

One of the people we came to know over the years was Douglas Ball, a lifelong numismatist, and nationally recognized expert on Civil War subjects. He brought the opportunity to acquire NASCA, the Numismatic Antiquarian Service Company of America, which resulted in his coming to work at Smythe, along with Stephen Goldsmith, a lifelong coin dealer. This acquisition put Smythe squarely in the numismatic auction business. Smythe began to hire traders in the numismatic field, and that activity grew into a lively retail business. The firm attended numismatic shows, notably the annual June show of the Memphis Coin Club. When the stock and bond dealers needed a less expensive show in the winter months, Smythe created the Strasburg Event in Pennsylvania, where dealers from all over the country and Europe came and traded. There was always an auction during the show, and it was at those auctions that the Penn Central obsolete certificates were first offered. The Strasburg Event grew to be the largest show in that field for about fifteen years. The firm provided leadership to a new collecting field.

After Herzog Heine Geduld was sold to Merrill Lynch in 2000, I joined Smythe full time, and by 2008 it was clear from changes in the field and the aging of the firm generally that a sale would be advisable. The business was sold to Spink in London, the oldest collectibles firm in the world, established in 1666. During the last year of Smythe's operations, 2007, the firm's auction revenues were $6.5 million and gross retail sales were $14 million.

The experience in collectibles has been rewarding, filled with innovation and travel to meet interesting people in many parts of the world. I worked with Diana in a business she understood. She excelled, and distinguished herself as president of The Manuscript Society for several years, and a senior officer of the International Bond & Share Society, addressing the Society's needs in the United States. We were proud to have trained many people, and they have mostly remained in the field, establishing fine careers. And, we had a lot of fun.

CHAPTER 9

An Improving Market Environment

It was now eight years since I had joined Herzog & Co. and I felt confident and well informed about all aspects of our business. The Smythe deal greatly enhanced my self-confidence and it helped me in our trading business. The market environment had improved and our business was thriving. There was no better time for me to plan our first ever Board of Directors meeting on January 27, 1967. We met over dinner in my parents' apartment at 70 East 10th Street, site of the former Wanamaker's department store.

My mother and Diana were there, as they were both intimately involved with the business and their insights, opinions and suggestions were crucially important on many occasions. We followed an agenda. My father voiced his criticisms, most of which concerned me. When he did so, he addressed Mother and Diana unemotionally. I responded and received an objective hearing, and on most issues, Mother sided with me. One very important issue raised unexpectedly by Mother was a sale or gift of some of the firm stock to me. Here, Mother was increasingly sympathetic toward me. She cried while telling a story about her father who always told her that what he had was hers, except when she wanted to borrow $500. We continued talking and learned that my father's concern was his expense allowance which he enjoyed and feared losing if he gave up stock. We addressed my father's concerns objectively, as directors and as a family bound up in the success of the business. The love that we all shared was complicated by resentments, competing agendas, and recalcitrant attitudes about relinquishing authority and responsibility to the next generation. When consensus is elusive, confusion often results, decreasing chances that good decisions will emerge. But as our first attempt, I felt the meeting was a success. Diana agreed. We all remained calm and objective, pleased that we resolved some issues and found a way to deal with the problems our business was facing.

There was more activity on the trading desk, and volume levels were rising. We needed more help. In April 1967, I called the New York State Employment Agency, and we hired two trainees who started at $75 a week. One man had been at Florida A & M for a semester studying music, and the other was from Detroit, living at the YMCA. Both did well on the test we gave every candidate. Training was supervised by our cashier Jim Ferris.

Saturday work was often necessary, and being in the office alone again convinced me that finding and training skilled help was the key to successful growth for the firm. This is easier said than done, but I have always spent a lot of time coaching people in the office, with good results. Counter to these efforts, my father's work habits were declining noticeably. He was 66 and showing signs of fatigue after a lifetime of work. This affected me. The issue of succession recurred in my dreams. Discouraged by my inability to resolve it, I asked Mother for help. I thought that her input at the Board meeting on the issue of stock ownership was indicative of her desire to help me with father, but she was not terribly helpful.

I spent another Saturday at the office catching up with higher volume levels. Working in operations was physically tiring, but mentally invigorating. We needed to complete the processing of 151 trades, the biggest day since 1959 when I joined the firm. Returning to my apartment on Horatio Street at 8:30 that night to unwind, I realized that this weekend work was a blessing and the fatigue was a well-earned reward. It helped ground me following a week of profitable trading.

As the market became more profitable, young traders would find each other socially, and I had opportunities to start new friendships with men my age who did what I did. But I was hesitant, and avoided peers who made meeting for a "drink after work" part of their routine. Having wasted my time at Cornell, I needed hard work. Diana wisely suggested I go to graduate school for a master's in a field related to the business. I was accepted into NYU's Masters in Management program. This was stimulating and valuable. It provided a source of mature advisers who gave me perspective on many firm problems. It was a way for me to become more self-assured.

We had done some business that year with V.S. Wickett & Co., one of the newer firms. After a recent trade, I got a call from one of their traders, Irwin Geduld, who suggested we meet. Irwin was happy to talk as we took long walks to Greenwich Village. He seemed genuinely interested in Herzog & Co. and asked a lot of good questions. He respected my efforts, and complimented me on several occasions. As a trader, he was good at the short side of market-making, something we needed to be doing. The only experience I had with this was with Bob Manghir, and when Louis Weingarten sold 1000 shares of Bzura Chemical short at 5 and had to cover at 14, for a big loss. That reinforced the popular wisdom in the firm that short selling was very dangerous. It is interesting to note that much more money is lost marking long positions down than on short positions which don't work out. After several conversations, Irwin asked if he might come to work on our trading desk. I was flattered, and gave it serious thought. I discussed this with my father, who had met Irwin on several occasions, and he was quite pleased to move ahead.

Irwin was about my age, had married his high school sweetheart and they had already started a family. I found him straightforward, honest and reliable. We talked a lot about where our business could go, and I shared my ideas with him. Irwin decided to join us before the summer. It was a good time to get to know one another as the summer months were quieter, with less trading activity. Irwin's younger brother Buzzy had begun to come to the office to sit with him as he had completed his Army reserve requirement and always followed the stock market. Buzzy wanted to learn to trade, and Irwin was teaching him. But the summer days were not active, and Irwin had a family to support, so he decided to leave the firm and return to the donut business which he and Buzzy had begun. My father encouraged them both when they would visit, and we proceeded slowly.

Conversations with my father revealed a continuing resentment about some things I had done at the firm, about Smythe, and about additional expenses which found their way into our operations. This was discouraging, and with profits of $20,000–50,000 each month, my decisions were proving correct. I was depressed by his complaining, and I was not alone. Leonard Berlinger complained about my father, and this was very unusual, as they had been working together for over twenty-five years. Diana learned that my father had not spoken to Hugo Knight for a year after he gave up his firm, Sherry Maloney & Co., and moved in with us, but when he finally did, they became friends. I became increasingly aware that my father's attitude influenced everyone's experience at work. I needed to help the business advance. To lead I needed to set an example, and adhere to a standard that would work for the many successful years I planned for.

Yom Kippur is a time of great introspection for me. While in synagogue, I wrestled with a thought. Perhaps I was not as open-minded as I might like to be. I can show fast acceptance of ideas that agreed with my thinking, but was I fair with those who brought ideas that conflicted with my own? Perhaps not. Open mindedness requires objective attention, and careful examination and somehow on that solemn day I gained a revelation. Ever since, I have always been ready to hear a new suggestion, however strange. Though my reactions can be swift, I have avoided thoughtlessness and demonstrated respect toward those who wish to make contributions.

Diana meanwhile was managing two jobs. She worked as a guide at the New York Chamber of Commerce, showing people around for their 200th anniversary. She was also teaching English as a Second Language at the New School. It was not a coincidence that a few of her best students interviewed for positions at our firm. During the summer, Diana and I did manage to get away for a trip to Israel, and I returned with the idea that we might start trading Israeli stocks and bonds.

1967 had been a solid year and we had every reason to believe that the next would be better. We confidently jumped at the opportunity to add another 500 square feet of space to our offices when the suite next door became available. I remained guardedly optimistic. It was my responsibility to remember that not long ago we struggled to do a few trades per day, making only a "sixteenth" on each share.

The increased business was a blessing, but the result was too many back to back weeks of 60 and 70 hours, not only for the staff, but for me as well. And as the burden increased, so did the errors, costly and time consuming to correct. A trade that went through as a purchase rather than a sale could cost hundreds of dollars if not discovered and corrected quickly. Due to the heavy volume, there was a paperwork crisis which jeopardized the entire industry. In response to widespread reports of failed trades and insurmountable mounds of paper, the Exchange decided to close each trading day at 2 P.M., and suspend all trading on Wednesdays. I looked for solutions in every small area of the firm.

In the 1930s, IBM correctly concluded that small businesses would need computers to handle increased paperwork, but not all businesses could afford to buy or rent massive "mainframes." They had a division called the Service Bureau which offered a solution: computers which could be rented when needed with software packages geared toward specific needs. When I met with an IBM representative, I described how we were processing trades. We knew that three part forms and window envelopes would not allow us to cope with the trading volumes we were experiencing. I saw that computers were here to stay, and I became the IT department, operating alone without technical experience or advisers. It was said then that technology was dominated by two types of people: those who understood what they do not manage, and those who manage what they do not understand. I encountered both types.

By joining the National Over-the-Counter Clearing Corporation, we benefitted from an industry-wide effort to use technology and standardized practices to improve operations efficiency and reduce errors. The robust market helped our profits and we continued to innovate with quick fixes. At about this time, our experienced Cashier, Jim Ferris, decided to leave the firm, making me even more anxious. We were very fortunate to find Robert Meli to replace him.

Bob Meli was a very unusual man, and by chance almost perfectly suited to our opportunity. He had lived in Egypt for many years, and had worked in a management position for an important commercial firm in Cairo. He was Jewish, and told an amusing story of his work in Egypt. When he was required to enter the ages of the women on the payroll of his firm, they were quite reluctant to give him that information until he reassured them that by writing their ages in Hebrew, only he would know. He was mature, and married to lovely Esther. They had no children. He was put in jail during one period of political turmoil, and when released, he and Esther went to Israel, and then on to Italy en route to New York. Bob's resettlement was aided by the Hebrew Immigrant Aid Society ("HIAS"), and it was through HIAS that we found him. He was older, disciplined, and hard-working, more experienced than I was. While he was observant, he would still come to work on Saturday when necessary. Seeing the needs of the business, he quietly enrolled to get a degree in accounting, telling me of this only when he was very close to graduating. He took responsibility for many areas, and he performed beautifully. He became the Human Resources manager, and the employees grew to respect him greatly, though he could be very tough. Occasionally, he would stand at the front door of the office from 8:45 until 9:15 with his watch in view and a pad to record the time each employee reported to work. Bob and I and our wives became dear friends, and this relationship was very important on many levels. Years later, he gave me an article about the Automat, where I had conducted his interview. He wrote: "Just for reminiscence, November 1967, where the interview was held which changed the face of Herzog & Co. and its future. All my respect for your accomplishments, John. Love, Bob."

As this important year ended, I made some notes about major accomplishments. My trading gross for 1967 was an impressive $110,000; we began trading inactive life insurance stocks; the firm began advertising in the *Security Dealers of North America*, the industry handbook. We also ordered new telephone equipment with six 30 line turrets, a necessity as we set many new volume records, with an average of 200 tickets per day. We got part-time help to ease the labor problems, and the firm grew to twenty people. Fred Bleibtreu's Swiss business began and we got our first check for $800. We installed an international telex machine to save on European trading expense and there were substantial additions to my reference library found on forays to Fourth Avenue book dealers. I finished writing my Master's thesis for NYU while I completed two courses.

Like many firms, we were weary and overworked, trying to cope with trading volumes we never anticipated. Exhausted people can't do their jobs well and there was simply too much for me to manage alone. I had been thinking about these issues for a while and the idea of having partners seemed logical. With early closings, we gained precious time to do settlement work carefully. There were strict new rules. If a firm fell behind in any way, there would be restrictions on the firm's ability to trade. We were never subjected to restrictions, and free to do all the business we could.

Late in February I got a call from Irwin, and he asked me about coming back to our firm. This was big news, and I was reminded of my father's experience with people returning. Irwin and I met, and we talked at length about things that had transpired at our firm during his return to the donut business. He wanted to have a meaningful position in the firm, and would not be satisfied to remain a trader without some sort of management interest. My father had encouraged me and this seemed like a logical way to go forward. Irwin came back to the firm shortly afterwards.

Volume levels continued to rise, so again I looked into data processing during a series of meetings with the Service Bureau. I remember describing our system and the many elements that made our operations as efficient as possible for the time. They responded to my many questions in a way I understood. They explained, "You will move your furniture into our living room, and if some of it is the wrong size, it will have to be changed." This explanation made me pause, but I remained open-minded as I didn't have any other workable plan. I felt anxious but determined and prepared for the new technology.

The decision to go with the Service Bureau proposal was painful for me. We converted to what was called a "computerized batch" system. I knew little about computers, and very little about the system, but I was hopeful. This was dangerously optimistic of me, as I didn't have any idea how we would manage output from the new system. It was late in the spring, and I thought that some enthusiastic college students employed for the summer would help us make sense of the system and provide an idea as to what our permanent staffing needs would be in a future filled with technology. Diana sent over some of her New School students and we hired a few of them. They were excited to be part of this ambitious project and we put together a very capable and hard-working team. They were bright and diverse and visitors referred to the office as a "small United Nations." With the help of our summer staff and Bob Meli, we worked through frustrating problems, had some fun and found the new technology exciting.

The market helped our bottom line, and on April 25th, we achieved another volume record with 260 tickets, 100 more than our previous best. In addition to the challenge of the Service Bureau conversion, it was imperative to stay ahead of the growth with problem-solving and labor-saving ideas. We ordered basic supplies, and made sure we did not run out of the printed forms we still used, but now in ever greater numbers.

I was still spending a lot of time in operations. The firm now had twenty people on the payroll, plus the traders, and the weekly payroll had climbed to $2,500. There was a lot of concern about the bad days coming back. My father cautioned, "1929 will be back again, and values will melt away like sand goes through your fingers at the beach." This was scary but well-intentioned and very valuable advice, what later became "inter-generational instruction" being passed on. Irwin and Buzzy were mindful of this advice, and they too were close to their father. We always tried to reduce risk, and if things didn't look right, we figured out why, and stopped doing that business. This training saved the firm from disasters on several occasions.

For the first time, the firm took a table at the STANY Dinner at the Americana Hotel on May 10, 1968. This was an important "first" and we were there with a new generation of traders who were eager to make friends and do business. Soon after the dinner, the summer people came to work, and the results were rewarding. They adjusted quickly, and enjoyed the work immensely. We made new long term friends, and managing these new hires was well within Bob Meli's skillset.

At the end of August, the summer people headed back to school. I met one many years later at an NYU Stern School Christmas party. Suzie Kleinman, the first woman on the firm's trading desk, became an important senior manager trading government bonds at Carrol, McEntee & McGinley. That summer had been wonderful experience for everyone. I enjoyed the time I spent in operations, and was very pleased to have had the opportunity to teach the new hires something about the business. They had learned enough to qualify for part-time jobs when they went back to college, and I wrote several reference letters. I heard from many of their employers years later and took pride in how pleased they were with their hires.

Before a well-deserved vacation, my last task at the firm was to have a meeting of the Planning Committee, consisting of Bob Meli, Gil Druckman, our cashier, Sam LaMantia, the head of data processing, Irwin and me. I outlined each person's responsibilities and what I expected of them. The meeting went well, and this group gradually evolved into the Managers Group of later years. We celebrated these accomplishments at the end of the summer taking everyone to an off-Broadway show followed by a party in our apartment, where my father cut a special cake with IBM decorations. It was kudos for all. I joined Diana in England at the end of the summer after I turned in my Master's thesis.

I returned from England after three weeks, and found things were in order. Our processing of trades had improved. Gil Druckman could now provide us with correct balances for our bookkeeping systems, and each morning we had reports and accurate figures that we could depend upon.

New opportunities continued to present themselves. Irwin's friend Michael Levine became interested in joining the firm after a few conversations. He had been at Herzfeld & Stern on the retail side, and we reached an agreement with him in mid-October 1968. He would do some research and bring retail clients. We also made a deal with Bob Albright, who had been working at Brager & Co., to handle the stock record. He also had experience trading Israeli securities and bonds. After our trip to Israel the previous year, I thought it would be good business to support the growth we saw there, and this seemed a reasonable way of doing that.

By December of 1968, we were doing about 400 tickets a day and had 30 people on the payroll. Mike Levine helped add some more volume. The data processing work was under control, and we were all feeling confident. I needed to review our arrangement with Bob Manghir. Bob suffered from the malady that a lot of traders catch in a roaring market. He not only thought he knew more than the rest of us, he also thought he alone was responsible for our success. He agreed to a reduction in his split, and I wanted to temper his over-confidence and self-aggrandizing attitude which can often lead to excess risk and big losses. The first new personnel announcement ever made by the firm appeared in *The New York Times* of December 9th on behalf of Michael Levine, whom we named Director of Research.

Soon it was Christmas bonus time, and when Leonard Berlinger received his bonus for the year, he let me know he was not satisfied. He told me that he would be taking his vacation in the coming weeks, and that he wanted to retire afterwards. This was the first we had heard of his plans. My father and I spoke at length about how the departure of our most senior person with almost twenty-five years at the firm would impact us. We concluded that the firm could easily move on without him and my father was content to simply let him leave. I disagreed. Out of loyalty, and good business, I thought it appropriate that we provide some pension to Leonard. I suggested that we pay him $200 monthly for a year and some lesser amount for up to three years. I was pleased that my father agreed to this. When I told Leonard what we planned, and added a cash bonus of $650 to his unpaid but accrued commissions, he broke down. Leonard struggled to tell me how much he loved the firm and that it was always his desire to be helpful. I was guilty of taking advantage of Leonard in some of our dark days, but I was pleased that later we formed a genuine bond. In the late 1960s what we did was meaningful to him, and I felt fulfilled that we could do it. We parted with tears and on the best of terms. I felt we had done the right thing, and was pleased that my father agreed.

1968 would close as a very significant year for us, one not easily forgotten. We did more business than ever, earned good profits and enjoyed the goodwill of our dedicated staff. We handled our operations problems with a successful conversion to data processing. Our outlook was optimistic and some barely perceptible changes proved crucial to our future.

I cannot overstate the importance of Irwin Geduld's joining the firm, along with his brother Buzzy. His business, especially his contribution of short-selling, became an immediate and integral part of our market making. Mike Levine was another positive addition. With good hires, growing volume, and an automated back office, it appeared we knew what we were doing. I formalized what we did and created a firm Procedures Manual which let everyone know what was expected of them. It all added up to a banner year. We were traveling well in a good direction.

CHAPTER 10

Confidently Moving Ahead

The market remained active, and we were very busy. A rude awakening occurred when I received a call from the wife of one of the operations people at 10 o'clock at night, asking why her husband was not yet home. I was shocked by this, and called a meeting of the operations managers to talk about it. At once, I made a rule that no one was to work more than ten hours each day, and further that it would drop to nine hours as soon as some adjustments could be made. We decided to get a safe in the office with an alarm, and that would likely save an hour each day, eliminating the need to go to our rented vault at 120 Broadway. Once mastered, our new, improved bookkeeping system would save time. The "blotter" was a summary of the previous day's trades, and each day it required review and "balancing," a matching of buyers and sellers. I had been able to balance the blotters we received in the initial days, so I knew that it was a straightforward task. I looked over each task and responsibility, re-structured many, and devised useful changes. I began to streamline everything I could, and saw how even small changes to a growing number of transactions saved a lot of time.

That year, 1969, my birthday present from the company was a bank balance of $1,018,000, the first time it exceeded a million, an all-time record. This milestone made me feel important and genuinely integral to the firm's success, just as I did knowing I had earned $100,000 the previous year. My inactive stocks had been performing well, as many issues thought to be near-worthless were now worth real money. I met a competitor, Bill Bromson from Tyche Securities, and he told me that a couple of years before, he had invested $150,000 in stocks listed on Canadian exchanges selling at less than 15 cents a share. He was very pleased to tell me that they were worth two to three times as much now, but this was a fraction of what I had accomplished with my inactive stocks. This specialty was attracting attention from some larger, well-known companies.

News that Hoit Rose & Co, another trading firm, was going to close brought Theodore J. Widenski, Jr. to our attention. We reached agreement that he would come to work on our trading desk. He brought his ideas and experience, having worked on a very active and well respected trading desk. His suggestions streamlined procedures on our desk. He was an enthusiastic deep-sea fisherman, and shared many of his adventures. The steps we took to contain hours and handle increased activity were working. Our new telephone turrets were installed, and we upgraded to eight positions, each with thirty lines. By early April, the bookkeeping system allowed us to balance all the accounts daily. The new safe was protected by Holmes, and operations were more efficient, with greatly reduced overtime. We then decided to join the National Stock Exchange, a big step ahead.

Diana and I vacationed in England, and when I returned to the office, I was pleased at the way Bob Meli handled various issues with thoughtful leadership. Meli's conservative thinking and creative problem solving gave me confidence. We were adept at recruiting and training, and when we made a mistake, we dealt with it, learned and moved on. We reduced our Israeli trading desk. This business turned out to be more complex than Bob Albright or I had anticipated, so we cut our frustration and losses. By chance, my father met Nathan Engel of Brager & Co., where Bob Albright had previously worked. We met for lunch and learned there had been some misunderstandings between Albright and his former firm. We cleared these up to a good result—business from Brager & Co.

Our new data processing system turned a year old. We were delighted to see a perfect Trial Balance Recap for July 1st. The system worked, and the operations people knew how to use it. Training and frustration yielded to self-confidence and reliability. Much of this is due to the diligence of Don Cone, who came to the Service Bureau during the year. He was experienced, careful, thoughtful and very sensitive to the needs of his clients. We spent meaningful time together, and became friends as well as business associates. We heard harrowing stories from the Street about the cost of errors associated with new trade processing systems. When we tallied up our cost attributable to errors, we came to a figure of $3000, a modest sum. Our cost per ticket at this point was a competitive 62 cents.

One of the attractive elements of the new system was the Inventory Average Cost Report (IAC), which gave each trader a recap of every trade made the previous day. It enabled traders to review the previous day's transactions and identify any errors. We enhanced the report constantly over the years, making it more effective with each revision. By mid-summer, we had converted to a new IAC report with excellent results. We were adding new clearing accounts, and this began to represent a meaningful portion of firm income. Summers were ideal for reviewing operations with daily volume running about half our normal 500 tickets. This respite gave us time to think, review and plan. In evaluating staff, we noticed that our problem employees were found mostly among those we had hired from other firms, where training had been poor or inconsistent. This encouraged me to hire people who could pass our interview test but knew nothing about Wall Street. We did this over and over with excellent results.

I was surprised one day when Irwin told me that he was thinking about going into business for himself, with his friend Brian Greenman, with the promise of a partnership if things worked out. I did not think this was a good idea for Irwin, and I spent several hours with him talking about the business. I thought it would be difficult for him to succeed in the venture. Father and I spoke privately. We came up with a strategy to keep the brothers with the firm. We countered with an offer to sell Irwin and Buzzy 45% of our firm for $225,000. They considered the offer, and responded that they would "still be working for Bob and John Herzog" and decided to decline. We considered this to be a lucky break, and we agreed we would be far better off on our own. Irwin's talents as a trader could be replaced, and by the beginning of September, Irwin had gone. I was greatly relieved, and rejoiced in our continuing independence. After Irwin left, we were still listing 215 stocks in the Pink Sheets. Without Irwin, others stepped up and took a greater interest in our activities, notably Mike Levine and Ted Widenski, who added additional private wires on our new turrets. Privately, I felt the loss of Irwin and his contacts, and wondered whether I had done something to alienate him. I was hurt by his leaving, but got over it quickly.

After Irwin left to join Greenman & Co., Buzzy wanted to talk to me. Buzzy was beginning to trade in a very small way. He became quite interested in new issues, a market he had been following in the trade papers for some time. A. P. Montgomery & Co. was the leading firm in that specialty. The quoted markets were often quite wide, with big differences between bid and offer in the initial trading days for a new stock. Buzzy felt that was an opportunity for new talent. We went for a walk together, and we ended up in the churchyard of St. Paul's on Broadway and Vesey Street. We sat together for a long time, sharing ideas and hopes, and at the end of that conversation, Buzzy committed himself to the firm, and I was very pleased to hear that. I told him I would talk with my father, and get back to him soon. I did not fully grasp the importance of this development at the time. It would assure the firm a talented man of integrity with ideas for growth, and no aversion to hard work. And this had happened apart from Irwin, now at Greenman & Co.

Only two months later, Irwin called me to say things were not working out for him. He wanted to return to Herzog & Co. He echoed Mike Levine when he said there was something special about working at the firm. I would hear this time and again. We quickly reached agreement on many issues, but one could not be immediately resolved. Irwin wanted to become an owner of the firm. My father and I knew Irwin and his capabilities, but this was more than a personality or business issue, as there were balance sheet issues and tax questions which would need to be explored and addressed. I could certainly understand the interest Irwin had in ownership, something I had taken for granted for years. The firm, or some part of it, was my birthright and I knew that it would happen at the right time. My father and I agreed to let Irwin know we would try to do what he asked, and we began to investigate the issues. After a lot of thinking and conversations with lawyers and our accountant, we agreed to recapitalize the business, and remove a large portion of the equity value by allocating it to a preferred stock, and that was to be owned by my father and me, 75% and 25%. This was workable, but there were difficulties. My father needed the dividend income from the preferred stock, as his trading production had declined greatly. The preferred stock dividends were not tax deductible to the corporation, and in some years that might be a hardship.

At this time there was a lot of distress in the Street. Respected old line firms like Gregory & Sons were suspended, and Dempsey Tegeler & Co. was restricted, and we were all concerned when the NASD came in to do a comprehensive audit of the firm. After many days in our office, they found one error due to a lost ticket. Our capital ratio was 2.5 to 1, very conservative, and I told them they ought to congratulate us for a job well done! More than eight months later, I was surprised and disappointed to receive a censure and $250 fine for the single missing trading ticket. This was low level bureaucratic nonsense, and I considered an appeal, but decided not to waste my time. We had another high-volume day with 389 tickets, and the National Stock Exchange accounted for 5-10% of our normal volume. Now, Amott, Baker & Co. expressed interest in doing a merger deal with our firm, and that was very flattering. Time passed, and they were unable to give us any credible financial information so we could not structure a deal. They were in danger of violating their capital requirements, and were taken over by Charles Plohn & Co. The experience of this period gave rise to the Securities Investor Protection Act of 1970 which protected investor accounts and aimed to supervise the orderly liquidation of impaired firms as an alternative to dissolution.

The holiday season was upon us, and for the first time, at Irwin's suggestion, we decided to have a party in the Oak Room at The Bankers Club. The day was December 16th, and the party was a success, with over five hundred guests. It was the first event of its kind, like a coming out party for the firm. We had door prizes, too, and happily they were won by just the right people! On the day of the party, an ad ran in *The New York Times* announcing that Irwin had become a Vice President of the firm. My parents attended, as did Abraham and Sylvia Geduld, Irwin and Buzzy's parents, a very proud day for them. The parents shared a table, and Irwin's father told my father, "It is the happiest day of my life." Then he pointed and said, "That's my son Buzzy, the little one. He has fire in his belly. He's going to do very well." The two fathers hit it off well, and they were both proud about what they saw happening with their sons. Abe Geduld who loved me, said that I was honest, good and a smart guy. Buzzy was living at home then, and his parents shared the warm feelings my father had toward him, and Buzzy felt he had a special relationship with my father. Our parents related well and respected each other.

Once the books were balanced, all our employees joined the festivities. I still remember the impressive platter of poached salmon with all the trimmings, and a wide variety of cakes and cookies. Several of our competitors called us to let us know they had heard it was a great party, but now they will be expecting much more from us.

Yearend bonuses were due, and I gave them out on Christmas Eve with a bottle of wine and heartfelt thanks for each person. They were well received, and everyone felt we were generous. We also gave Bob Meli and Gil Druckman signature privileges on the Chemical Bank firm account, and they were both very pleased with this increase in status and authority. They joined the firm knowing nothing about the business, and had become very well informed and effective. This gave me great pleasure as I saw how proud they were of their progress. The year ended on a high note, with 671 tickets on December 30th, as people sold stocks to take advantage of tax losses. We were now trading 375 stocks, an all-time high. We were all breathless upon seeing a $20,000 profit figure on the IAC report for a single day's trading. Little did we dream that on the following day, New Year's Eve, we would write 800 tickets, almost all of which were processed by 6 P.M. that night. I could see how far we had come. We now had well-trained personnel in operations and a fine team on the trading desk, all at a time when there was a lot of distress elsewhere on the Street. We all went home quite happy for the New Year.

As 1970 commenced, we were all eager to get back to the office to see if we could build upon the success of 1969. Almost immediately, as if planned, the "January effect" commenced, with stocks which were oversold in December being marked up once yearend tax selling abated. This was great for us, as everyone started the year with positions that exceeded their limits, and profit opportunities were numerous.

This was still the era of the rotary telephone dial, and I had the idea to send dialing pencils out across the country. These were very well made by the Dur-O-Lite company, imprinted with our firm name and the trading department telephone number. Primitive by today's standards, they were extremely popular. We sent out 7,000 of these red pencils, and we began to get better and better calls, helping trading results nicely. I also decided to go to the Chicago Mid-Winter Dinner of the Security Traders Association of Chicago, the first dinner I had attended since going with Bud Kassel to Baltimore. They had a casino night. I was impressed seeing the craps tables, with lots of big bills tossed around on every play.

Meeting clients gave me insight into how people viewed us, and what our competitors were doing. I could visualize our business from a distance with greater clarity. When I got back to the office, I made some changes which had eluded our decision-making routine. We agreed to concentrate on the business we knew best, and prune several distractions, making the firm more efficient. We had placed an ad in *The New York Times* for clerk trainees, and we got a tremendous response. Unlike other firms, we were still looking for promising novices whom we could bring into the business. Things were going well, and the January gross profit was $200,000.

April 14, 1970 found us at the New York Chamber of Commerce in the Cruger Room for our Officers Meeting. The attendees were my father, now Chairman, myself as President, Irwin as Vice-president, Buzzy as Secretary (a title he never liked, but I wanted him to be part of this group) and Bob Meli as Treasurer, with Diana attending as a guest. More than any other item on the agenda, I wanted the group to know that it was essential for us to be prepared and meet formally every second Tuesday of the month. This meeting was a milestone. We completed the recapitalization of the firm, new common stock was issued, and Irwin joined my father and me as owners. It was a momentous step forward, which would result in an outcome I could not have dreamed. Even after markdowns of $107,000, we still had capital of $700,000, and showed a profit for the month of $5,000.

That year the months in spring and summer brought low trading volume and weak markets, with continuing distress around the Street. The decline in business impacted us. We made more errors, as people became lax in their work due to inactivity. Diana and Mary spent the summer in Bedford Hills in a rented house I had found. I commuted. It was workable but not perfect, and we realized we wanted to be out of the city for summer weekends. As summer waned, things started to pick up. The Friday before Labor Day our volume was 302 tickets, up from a 240 average during the month. We remained confident and decided to take more space on our floor, doubling the size of the office and providing room for new trading desks – including a replacement for the dark green circa 1926 table which my father had bought - and fourteen new turrets, each with 120 lines. We were adding private wires at a rate which even six months ago was thought impossible.

We operated at a profit while others had continuing troubles. There were sixty-six New York Stock Exchange firms in difficulty or liquidation, and our capital was increasing. I felt strongly that success was due not only to trading profit, but also to sound management decisions, and my NYU training. I eagerly returned to the trading desk after six months away in operations, and tried hard to get back to my old production levels. I was lucky to get a 60,000-share order in Hamilton Brothers, and that restored my confidence and momentum. We decided to lower the trading splits again, reducing what we paid out to 40% and 37.5%, and that change was immediately reflected in our profits. As our new space neared completion, we took a step long-planned and added a new partner. Buzzy was issued 3% of the firm stock at book value, with another 3% promised in a year. November 23rd was our first day in the new office, and after 11 years my first day in a private office. The entire project came in under budget with few complaints, I was satisfied.

CHAPTER 11

Difficult Years, Complex Problems

It was now eleven years since I joined my father's firm. It felt quite different from the early days. We were in our new trading room, and I liked my new office. Between my desk and the trading room, there was a plate glass window, and this construction detail quickly became legendary. Whenever I asked one of the traders or another employee to come in, murmurs of "Into the fishbowl" were heard in the trading room. It was entertaining for some but not for those who left by another door for good.

In the early part of the year, Diana, Mary and I moved to Brooklyn Heights. The house at 162 State Street came to our attention by way of my college roommate, Tom Asher. He and his family had been living there for only a few months when Tom assumed the role of Assistant National Marketing Sales Manager for Goodbody & Co. Rumors had been circulating around the firm, and by December, it was known that Goodbody would be taken over by Merrill Lynch. Tom decided to move back to Atlanta, and he called to let me know. I asked him when he would be going, and he said, "As soon as the house is rented." I replied on the phone, "It's rented," and I set about at once to make the arrangements.

It was freezing on moving day and it took about a week for the house to feel comfortable. We loved the house, and spent many happy and memorable years there. We acclimated to Brooklyn Heights almost immediately because Diana was so good at the social scene. She took Mary out in her pram, and we made many friends in the neighborhood. My parents were in their car crossing the Brooklyn Bridge for their first visit on a sunlit Sunday when Mother remarked that she didn't even know the address. When Father told her it was

162 State Street, she said she had a feeling it would be lovely. In Flushing, we lived on the corner of 162nd Street and State Street. We became very friendly with the owners who lived in California. When we signed our lease, I asked for a right of first refusal if they ever decided to sell, an outcome they felt was extremely unlikely.

We also knew we needed a retreat for summers and weekends. We rationalized our purchase of a modest house in Clinton Corners, near Millbrook, New York, as a good investment. We had plenty to do moving things around, and lots of work to do on the house. To shuttle our family back and forth, I bought our beloved dark green Volkswagen Squareback for $2,800 which the firm paid for with Irwin's blessing.

We were settling in at the office and wanted to show it off. Lured by free hot dogs from the vendor who normally parked his cart on Broadway, we hosted parties and attracted many visitors from the Street. We were proud and they were impressed. We began keypunching our own data cards, taking that work back from the Service Bureau. We reduced errors and time loss considerably. We also began clearing in different places as new settlement facilities became available after the paperwork crisis.

Markets evolve in response to the needs of investors and traders. A major flaw was that it took too long to get prices and consummate trades in the over-the-counter market. Clerks working for commission firms like Merrill Lynch were required to check three markets before executing a trade. The process might start with a call to a trading firm like ours to see what the best price would be for their client. It took a lot of time, and if the market for a stock was moving, by the time the clerk called back to make a trade, our market often changed. This delay was frustrating and often the cause of lost business.

One of the important innovations of this time was "Nasdaq," the National Association of Securities Dealers Automated Quotation system, and there was a good deal of debate when it was first introduced. There was to be a terminal on each trader's desk, and on the desks of the order clerks at the commission houses. Clerks could see the market prices entered by all the dealers in real time. This made the "inside market" immediately known to buyers, sellers and traders and the highest bid and the lowest offer could be immediately identified. It was promoted as a great step forward. We were anxious about how it would work once it was live, as it had been pitched as "only a quotation system." There was a lot of reticence about becoming part of it, and there were sceptics who feared replacing human interaction with a computer.

We discussed it at great length and we were not at all sure which way to go. In the closing days before it went live on February 8, 1971, we decided to join, a good decision.

We began using the Nasdaq machines. Early on there was an announcement that a widely-held stock had announced bankruptcy proceedings, requiring it to be delisted from the stock exchange. As a specialist in delisted issues, we immediately registered to trade the stock on Nasdaq. We were all surprised to see how many calls we got right away, from all over the country. Trading was active and profitable, but most importantly, we realized that we had become a national market-making firm, no longer a local or regional firm. This was a great development, and we had many conversations about how to handle this new expansion of our business without impacting our legacy clients or losing discipline with respect to position limits and capital adequacy. Many new opportunities presented themselves, many seemed compelling, and we had to think twice about how to handle them.

Experience and lessons gained from my father came into play with the advent of Nasdaq. We proceeded cautiously, but also tried to anticipate consequences of this new business, and we sensed that compliance and research might also take a leap forward. We issued rules which required our traders to be fully informed about every new stock they wanted to trade. This applied not only to regular stocks, but particularly to new issues and secondary offerings which were becoming our specialty. We relied upon the National Quotation Bureau disclosure forms and began accumulating reports and other information on all issues we traded. Our traders would be authoritative if questioned about any of our stocks. It was a big job but we got many kudos when it was finally done.

Nasdaq very rapidly became the standard. Our Nasdaq symbol was HRZG, and we used that symbol in our advertising, and in other promotional material. Within a short time, we were very happy about our increased efficiency with the new system, and we began to figure out how to use it to our advantage. The investing public could now find daily quotes for 1650 stock subsets of the 3450 stocks quoted in Nasdaq in newspapers along with a shorter list of issues with local interest.

To fill up our new 120 line turrets, we tried to add new correspondent firms to our system. Correspondent firms were the equivalent of our local private wires, but these firms were in other cities. These regional firms could provide order flow which we wanted to see, and try to trade. One of our early success stories was Scott & Stringfellow & Co, in Richmond, a firm my father had visited forty years before. Woolard & Co. in Chicago, Clark and Clark in Dallas, and Stix Friedman & Co. in St Louis became part of our system, and we worked hard to get others.

We were now making markets in 600 stocks writing about 500 tickets each day, with a bank balance near $300,000 most of the time. Trading exposure for the firm was about $1.2 million, the sum of all the risk positions in the various stocks in which we were making markets. The "position money" allocated to each trader had always been a problem. Our traders relied on the axiom that the greater the risk, the greater the return would be. Adequate capital remained a struggle and we did not have enough to remain well ahead of the changes that were happening in the industry and our own business. Markdowns remained a consistent problem. This related to the integrity of the firm's financial profile. If the firm was carrying inventory at levels higher than the actual market for those shares, a markdown "to the market" was required. Markdowns reduced the trader's gross profit and the firm's, so there was a tightrope to walk with aggressive market-making challenging our financial integrity. This could result in the loss of a profitable trader. Traders who felt they were not being given enough position money would seek better opportunities at other firms. Traders recognized our empathy and integrity as managers and, the historic legacy of the firm. We committed to fairness, but despite this, we could occasionally lose a talented trader. Father and I were disappointed when our most senior trader Bob Manghir left to go to Sprayregen & Co., and Mike Levine was not far behind.

Time and again we learned to focus on our strengths, and well-intended departures often proved unwise. We wanted to be in the retail commission business, but we underestimated the perils. We were aghast when a retail client filed a suit against the firm alleging our sale of "unsuitable securities." He was seeking $5 million in damages, an unheard-of sum. We lost plenty of sleep over this, and it turned out to be a costly lesson. We mounted a credible defense, after all, we had instituted a rule about our brokers being knowledgeable on securities they sold, and we were sure that the customer was informed. The truth remained elusive, as the matter became a battle of nerve and endurance. After eight months, we were encouraged to settle the matter for $75,000, but there was collateral damage to relationships, and a loss of business going forward.

We began to have some problems with direction and goals, both long and short term. We could never find consensus, each of us sure that his views were right. As partners, we were each growing headstrong, reaching conclusions based on our private observations. When we tried to discuss them, there were hot tempers, or meaningless silence. From my diary: "I feel that we do have a very real problem of direction... and of working at cross purposes." We would monitor the work of certain trader's day in and day out for months, and come to different conclusions about who should stay and who should go. Our disagreements were rooted in the way we each viewed production, profit, and position exposure.

The market was poor over the summer, and we had to adjust to the loss of Bob Manghir and Mike Levine. We were also disappointed by a couple of the new traders who arrived with promise, but turned out to be slackers. Amid all this unquiet, Abraham Geduld passed away quite unexpectedly, and this was a devastating blow for their family. Irwin and Buzzy were out quite a bit attending to family matters, and business issues just had to wait. The old order, so familiar, loving and reliable, was breaking up. We all knew it, but never discussed it. We were all nervously wondering how the new order would settle into place.

It was during this time that I met the partners of Kahn, Peck & Co., a New York Stock Exchange member firm with a specialist book. A specialist book is a group of stocks which had been assigned to that firm for market-making. They were interested in a merger, and I had several meetings with them during which we tried to figure out what we might do together. We were also negotiating with Lombard Street, an options trading firm. We were considering having them come into our office on some sort of participation basis, so we could get into trading puts and calls.

Mike Levine called us. He wanted to come back to the firm, and we hoped for the best and agreed; though following our recent litigation, we were still feeling very cautious about the retail business, Mike's focus. The industry was still quite weak. M. H. Meyersohn & Co. had reduced operations, as did Singer & Mackie, both direct competitors, shocking us. On the bright side, we did get a wire to Thomson McKinnon, a very large commission firm. My father was talking about buying a condominium on a golf course in West Palm Beach, and I began to feel anxious about his impending absence. I would be alone, and I knew it would be a difficult transition. The new order had not yet settled.

Thinking about his planned move to Palm Beach early in the New Year, my father presented me with an analysis he had made of the firm expenses, the amounts we owed, and his recommendations based on experience and his take on the current state of the business. He summarized his findings in a short paragraph which he gave me while we had a sandwich together, time stamped '72 Jan 10 PM 12:33:

"Borrowing to run a business is the wrong theory. The easier business finds it to borrow the more over extended it becomes and the end results are inevitable at the first reaction. Witness the hundred odd firms that were restricted last year by the Stock Exchange. Plus, the many that fell by the wayside. A major operation is urgently called for immediately. A serious conference should come up with the right solution and implementation." This was his intergenerational instruction. We found consensus and did as suggested in the face of a turbulent market. We cut expenses, trimmed debt, and we ended up with a healthy bank balance.

Business improved for us in the first three months of 1972, and net capital rose above $650,000, a new high. I could sit on the desk again, thinking I would always remain there. But I was the only one who understood all the aspects of the firm's operations, from trading to clearing, to office renovation and corporate records. Any time an alarm went off, I had to leave the desk and solve the problem. This was valuable to the firm, but as a jack of all trades my trading talents languished. When I began with my father, he warned me I would have to do every job, because at any time I might need to fill in for someone else. While this was advantageous, it was at times resented, especially when I came to a quick opinion or dismissed someone else's suggestion. My experience at almost every position gave me insights the others lacked. I could analyze a decision swiftly and this was often mistaken for impatience or closedmindedness. In reaching decisions, I always put the firm's interests first, while others spoke out of self-interest. It was my responsibility above all else to improve operations, control expenses, encourage employees and safeguard the reputation of the firm.

On one of my walks around downtown, I stopped in to see Hanson & Hanson, to say hello. It was a well-respected firm, but their office was very small, old timey, and disorderly. I was invited to have a look around, and in a back room I found the spectacular framed commemorative of the New York Stock Exchange building, completed in 1903. The photo of the new building in the center was surrounded by images of the members at that time, each identified with the name of his firm. As an avid collector, this was a great find for me. I asked if I could buy it, as they were not displaying it. Arnold Hanson said he would think about it, and return my visit in a short time. The next week, Arnold came to visit us, and he was impressed with our office. He then told me he wanted to hire some traders and get into active trading once again. He asked for my help. I told him he was being unrealistic, and when I asked again about buying the Stock Exchange print, the conversation meandered on until we had reached agreement, not for the print, but for their firm. Fortunately, the price was only $5000, and I had a plan.

Hanson & Hanson, about to celebrate their 60th anniversary and well-respected on the Street, was restyled by us as a research firm. Our plan was to create some interesting reports, and advertise them over a fine old name. Then I found a large supply of unused stock certificates from several Vanderbilt railroads, and hired a calligrapher to inscribe each one with the name of one of our customers. Arnold and I both signed each one in sepia ink, and we sent these out to about 1000 recipients. This unique promotion was well received. It was a good example of how my collecting benefitted the firm. It was creative, and we had a lot of fun while generating tremendous goodwill. I ended up with the 1903 Stock Exchange print, which hung in my office for many years.

Downtown, it was business as usual and we were closer to a deal with Kahn, Peck. We took a vote to go ahead based upon a 55/45 equity split in our favor. My partners agreed that they were honest and conscientious, and their exchange memberships would be valuable, as many member firms preferred to execute their over-the-counter trading business with other member firms, a disadvantage to us. The new name was to be Herzog, Kahn, Peck & Co., and I was slated to be president and CEO. Total capital of the new firm would be $2.2 million, and we were positive the deal made sense. But the market was very sloppy, and we were discouraged by September's losses. To move the deal forward, it was necessary for me to leave the trading desk again. Late in October, I went uptown to finish up some details and found a surprise waiting for me. Their business had been very bad, and two of their senior people wanted to leave. Arthur Kahn wanted his $260,000 capital back right away, and their specialist book was falling apart. Another deal I had invested a lot of time pursuing was not to be. We felt some satisfaction in that the weaknesses in their firm were the very ones we had been concerned about, and we were all relieved to have missed the knife blade so narrowly. No matter how much dissention or disagreement we experienced amongst ourselves, we knew we were better off with each other than with anyone else.

We knew there was a lot more business to be gotten, and we worked hard to find it. I was appointed to make a date with a trading manager at Merrill Lynch who could direct trades to our firm. I remember how anxious I was, arriving at The Bankers Club for our scheduled lunch. John Tognino and I sat down together. I took my time telling the story of the firm, and the pitch lasted through the main course. When dessert came, I simply said we'd like to have a private wire installed, and immediately the answer came to, "Please order it." I was elated, and so were Buzzy and Irwin and the rest of the traders. I felt encouraged. My skills went beyond operations. I could effectively represent the firm to its most important clients and prospects. Getting the okay for a private wire to Merrill was big. We all felt we had arrived, and Buzzy's specialty in new issues continued to grow as he attracted better quality calls. Merrill had already given Buzzy a couple of their syndicate bids to work, and this was a very important step. Buzzy was inspired. He tirelessly traveled all over the country to traders' dinners, and got to know the important people in many firms. They liked his straightforward style, and they were very pleased with his work on the trading desk. He was laying the groundwork for far larger business ahead, but Buzzy kept those aspirations private. Our relationship grew stronger during this period.

Nasdaq was gaining respect and participation. It could be relied upon for accurate pricing and firm markets. If an order clerk called a market maker and found the quotations to be unreliable, the trader was said to be "backing away," an unpleasant and damaging result. Market making was entering a new phase, with far more capital required to satisfy the needs of customers. We were young with big dreams that required more capital, but we hadn't been successful finding it yet. By December 29, 1972, Nasdaq hit a new high with 14.4 million shares traded, up from the previous record of 12.9 million shares on February 2nd of the year. Despite weak markets, Nasdaq was growing, and capital needs along with it.

During the last days of the year, following considerable tax and legal advice, my father gave me 291 of his shares in the company, representing 40% of the stock. The day I had long anticipated had arrived, and I was very gratified. I wrote a thank you letter, and posted it to my father at his Palm Beach address. My father replied to me, saying:

Dear John,

I read and re-read your lovely letter and each time it brings tears to my eyes. Your feelings about me are something that every parent strives to achieve and that I hope you will experience with your darling daughters.

Looking back on my life I realize that the good Lord dealt with me very kindly. To reach my age in relatively good health, good family life and reasonable business success is not given to many men to enjoy. You, your family and your success are a source of great joy and contentment for me. I am proud to be the father of a solid citizen respected and admired by all who know him.

It is your intelligence, forthrightness, imagination and perseverance that account for the success of our business. All that I tried to give you was a solid foundation, a respected name, and the benefit of my experience, even my mistakes.

So you see my son, the score is pretty even. I have taken from you as much as I have given. My love and admiration for you and your family is an instinct and a part of me, of which I am proud and forever grateful.

Dad

I longed for the time my father and I spent working side by side. Though my partnership with Buzzy had strengthened following Dad's retirement, I felt lonely in the office. My family and I went to Palm Beach to visit my parents in their new apartment, and it struck me how much they had aged. While we were in Florida, I got a call from the office informing me that a stock in which we were carrying a large long position, Pelorex, had gone bankrupt, and we were short capital. Though father had officially stepped down from the firm, he helped steer us through another crisis, as the only way we could repair the situation was to use some securities that my father had in his safe deposit box. He extended a subordinated loan, which we would need until we could formulate a longer-term solution. This emergency was a great shock to all of us, but I remained optimistic about the business. This crisis reminded us why we needed to have confidence in one another as partners. We each made five year subordinated loans of $25,000 to enhance our capital position, and that solved the problem in the short run. We could continue doing business.

As year-end approached, it was an ideal time to take larger positions. Once again, people sold to take tax losses, and prices fell to attractive levels. I remember going to Chemical Bank to ask for some loan accommodation during the year end period. They were surprised at the request, saying they had no interest in low priced stocks of the kind we traded. We knew this was exactly the time of year to become interested in these stocks, but we went away empty handed, and had to juggle things internally. January helped with markups for these stocks and we breathed a bit easier.

1973 started well. Lombard Securities Co., the put and call broker we had been talking to for a while, finally acted, resulting in our acquiring their wires and registered representatives Paul Sarnoff and Harry Snyder. We were now in the put and call business, and Paul and Harry began steadily grossing $500-$750 each day, a nice addition to our bottom line. They were both experienced and hard-working. Paul was an established author with a wonderful mind for math, capable of solving tricky calculations in his head. Everyone loved that, and when we occasionally checked his results, they turned out to be correct. He began writing a letter with option strategies for customers, and their business grew. We were now executing some trades in the commodities markets, as well.

We hired a new advertising agency, Friedman Rosner Inc. Their creative work was inspired by Warren Lee, who was clever, original and became a close friend. These ads were memorable, featuring original pen and ink drawings by Oni, a very talented artist. We managed to get the firm's name out, and put a smile on the faces of our readers. I oversaw the advertising, with Diana's help.

We joined the Securities Industry Association, which we had previously thought was just for the larger firms, but we realized we had become one and earned our place at the table. But on the trading desk, we still had to deal with the smaller firms, and a few were weak or about to fail. We needed to manage our contra-broker risk. If we made a trade with a risky broker, the firm might not be in business when we went to deliver the stock against payment. The awkward reality of having aging contracts in our fails to deliver or fails to receive accounts increased that risk. We were now doing put and call business, clearing for fifteen firms and expanding our National Stock Exchange business.

Irwin had given me his full confidence by this time, and our relationship flourished. It had been a little more difficult with Buzzy, and I imagined he was a bit impatient with all my strange ideas. He was very focused on trading issues, his strength. I had left the desk and was now working on management issues full time.

Relentlessly, distress continued around the Street with some of the biggest firms disappearing through merger or bankruptcy. It was contagious. If a firm became weak and could not meet its contracts, then other firms who were dependent on that firm were also suspect. I refused to be anything less than optimistic and conservative, and this helped steady those around me. We decided to sell our National Stock Exchange seat, as business there had declined dramatically, and forego that part of our clearing revenue. Late in the year, things began to improve a bit, and exchange trading volume was as high as 20 million shares as the Dow Jones Average managed a string of gains. Our figures were also responding well.

1974 was welcomed as a fresh start. Although we were still watching pennies, we thought a party might stoke some optimism. Diana and I invited the firm to our home on State Street for a "Swing into Spring" party. There were hundreds of daffodils to cheer everyone up, and Diana's usual good things to eat. The party was a great success, and everyone had a fine time, but the palmy feelings of that day didn't last. The market refused to cooperate. I would have hoped for a better time to get a call from the owner of 162 State Street now living in Los Angeles. He reminded me of our right of first refusal, and informed me that the house was for sale. Diana and I would be tested. We analyzed the figures, considering our assets, income and expenses dozens of times, consistently coming up with the same conclusion. We wanted to remain in the house, but we had no margin for error, and business remained weak in early July. When we finally had to give our answer, we said yes with a $125,000 bid on the same day that Columbia Gas was unable to sell its issue. My father gave us $10,000 and I got a mortgage at 7 1/2%, a good rate for that time. This was scary, but we went ahead, and were never sorry. This transaction helped me in the business, too, as the mortgage interest deduction left us with more disposable income, even though my income was flat. The market worsened with losing months and more distress on the Street. Every day on the desk we would hear about another firm that had closed or gone bankrupt, and this went on for months. I began bringing a sandwich to the office for my lunch, saving a few dollars, something I had not done since the market break in 1962.

In our constant search for additional capital, I began talking with John Green, a friend from Clinton Corners. He was interested in small business, and liked what he heard from me about our firm. He suggested that we have dinner together. After a long meal, he said he would consider investing $50,000 in the firm, but he wanted to be actively involved. A Poughkeepsie office was suggested, and things were looking promising until John attended one of our officers' meetings. It was a stormy meeting, and while we would routinely accomplish things while letting off some steam, it was not what John envisioned for his investment. That was the end of another attempt to find more capital, though we did remain good friends.

Before we left Clinton Corners after the summer, we had a yard sale, and were delighted to raise $225 in nickels and dimes, which helped our budget.

Renting out the house for the winter made sense, and we found tenants at $300 a month, relieving us of the various utility bills, and a lot of worry. We retreated to Brooklyn, and made further cuts in our expenses. We knew the decision to buy the house was right, and we set about making it work. I returned to the trading desk, and started producing as before. The Boston Stock Exchange had listed all the former National Stock Exchange companies, and I was awarded 18 of the 44 stocks involved. The Watergate hearings set the stage for the Ford administration, and the new President wanted to address the country about inflation. Peter Toczek explained to me that when the White House schedules a conference on inflation, the problem is depression. The market must have been listening because it slid badly afterwards. It had been another very difficult year, but we had persevered, were still in business, and the partners found comfort in their shared adversity.

It was early 1975 when Peter Toczek put me in touch with Heine, Fishbein & Co. as a potential merger partner. Peter was a good friend of mine. His reputation on the Street was bad at that time and it could not become known that he was close to me, or various important relationships we had developed would be jeopardized. I managed our dealings discreetly. It was a pivotal time, but we were progressing as partners. While we still disagreed about lots of things, we did so constructively, and we seemed to be growing closer on many other issues. We agreed that operations needed to be re-examined, and we would make changes to personnel and procedures. We also saw eye to eye on the Heine Fishbein deal. We liked that they were a clearing Stock Exchange member firm.

As with other market making firms, we had become very concerned with the New York State stock transfer tax, which was costing us far too much money. I had expressed strong views on this issue, and *The Times* published my letter to the editor. We felt the legislators in Albany did nothing, and we needed to respond. Late in the year, we announced we would move to Jersey City. The office would be ready early in 1976, our fiftieth anniversary year. We still had our lease at 170 Broadway, an expense we could not avoid.

"May Day," May 1st, 1975, was the day on which fixed commissions ended. This was a big step, but it wasn't seen that way at first. Peter Toczek called me to tell me that after speaking to several firms, he anticipated a 10-15% reduction in prevailing commission rates. We would see in days to come, that reductions would be far greater. There would also be changes in the way customer's accounts were handled. Commissions receded and some brokers

1914 Armin Herzeg business card

1922 Robert Herzog

Famous Wall Street Tigers.

Andrew Carnegie (1835-1919)
Scottish-born steel tycoon who distributed $35,000,000 in charitable gifts, reflecting his passion for scientific research, education and peace.

Herzog Heine Geduld (Est. 1926)
Market makers in 4000 over-the-counter stocks.

Andrew Carnegie

Call us. We mean business.

Herzog Heine Geduld
Established 1926.
Members: New York Stock Exchange.
26 Broadway, New York, N.Y. 10004. (212) 962-0300. WATS: 800 221-3600.
Institutional traders: (212) 908-4132. WATS: 800 843-4845.

1980 Andrew Carnegie ad

Bull and Bear of Wall Street, New York; Tiger of Herzog, Heine, Geduld, Jersey City—at the Cleveland Summer Outing—discussing prospects for peace in the Middle East.

Herzog Heine Geduld
(212) 962-0300.   WATS line 800 631-3095   SIPC

1981 Cleveland Outing ad

1981 Operations Department. *Left:* Tony Geraci, John Herzog, Donna Connolly, Robert Meli.

1934 Robert Herzog with father, Armin Herzog

New York City **NEW YORK** New York City

Brokers and Dealers in

GENERAL MARKET SECURITIES

Reorganization Securities
Real Estate—Public Utility—Industrial—Foreign

Stocks and Bonds

HERZOG & Co. *Est. 1926*

Members New York Security Dealers Association

New York 7, N. Y.
170 BROADWAY
Tel. WOrth 2-0300

Bell System Teletype—NY 1-84

HERZOG & CO.
(*) (n) (SD) [1926] 170 Broadway (7)
Dealers & Brokers in Foreign, Industrial, Public Utility, Real Estate & Municipal Bonds & Over-the-Counter Stocks Specializing in Securities for Dealer Distribution
PROPRIETOR—Robert I. Herzog
MANAGER—Morrison Gilbert
TRADING DEPT.—Ben Grody, Mgr.; Robert Z. Block, Louis Weingarten, Leonard Berlinger & Hugo J. Weinberger
CASHIER—Morrison Gilbert
CLEAR THROUGH—Trust Company of North America
WIRE SERVICE—Bell System Teletype—NY 1-84
PHONE—Worth 2-0300

HESS, WALTER W.
(*) 30 Broad St. (4)
(Offices of Auerbach, Pollak & Richardson)
Floor Broker
Phone—Whitehall 4-6280

HESSE, STANLEY
(*) [1944] 60 Beaver St. (4)
(Offices of H. Hentz & Co.)
Floor Broker
Phone—Bowling Green 9-8420

HETFIELD, RANKIN & CO., INC.
o (*) [1938] 30 Broad St. (4)
Dealers & Brokers in Over-the-Counter Stock & Bonds Specializing in Inactive Securities
Officers—Monroe V. D. Towt, Pres. & Treas.; Charles M. Grundy, V.-P. & Sec.
Clear Through—Underwriters Trust Co.
Phone—Whitehall 4-3830

● Do retail or institutional business; many of these firms engage in other phases of investment business
(*) Member National Association of Securities Dealers, Inc.
(n) Principal or Employee a Member of National Security Traders Association
(SD) Member New York Security Dealers Association
(*) Member New York Stock Exchange

1947 Ad in *Security Dealers of North America*

1983 26 Broadway trading room

1984 Max L. Heine

Founded in 1926, Herzog Heine Geduld, Inc., a member of the New York Stock Exchange, trades over 3,500 stocks and bonds. "In the brokerage industry, there is a continuing pressure to increase commissions, revenues and trading spreads," says John Herzog, President and Chief Executive Officer. "Enter Stratus with a very strong transaction processing capability, fault tolerance, and a wonderful maintenance record. Those capabilities are the tools that enable us to meet those pressures and to solve those problems."

1984 Stratus Computer annual report

1960 A trader's position record of Genral Box Co (+ = Long, – = Short)

1965 Herzog & Co., Inc. *Standing:* Len Williams, Lynne Feuer, John Herzog, Bob Manghir, Jim Ferris, Paul Adelsberger, Ed Dorosh, Hugo Knight, Jonathan Schwartz. S*eated:* Leonard Berlinger, Bob Herzog, Louis Weingarten.

1991 David Bostian at the White House, to left of President Reagan

1992   Buzzy Geduld on cover of *Equities*

1970 170 Broadway trading room. *Standing:* David Maroko, Irwin Geduld.

DELISTED ISSUES

When a major stock exchange suspends trading in an issue, call us for a market. We'll try to answer any questions you have with the most current information available. We've always specialized in situations with marketability problems, whether a few shares or a large block. If you would like a list of the 400 active stocks in which we make a market, please call Irwin Geduld, our Vice President in charge of trading.

Herzog & Co., Inc.
ESTABLISHED 1926
MEMBERS: NATIONAL STOCK EXCHANGE
NEW YORK MERCANTILE EXCHANGE
170 Broadway, New York, N.Y. 10038
Telephone: 212-962-0300 Telex 620703 HERZOG

AF-GL   B&S 1942   Proof 1   5-12-70

1970 Delisted Issues ad

1994 Trading room at 26 Broadway

1995 New trading room in Jersey City

1996 Stockholders at 70th anniversary party

2000 Deal cake with "Merrill Lynch Pierce Fenner & Buzzy"

1973 John Herzog

began charging a fee for managing their customer accounts, a fundamental change in the basic business of many firms, creating distress and opportunity. Some firms were conflicted, unwilling to change and cope with deregulated commissions.

In November, we began merger discussions with Troster, Singer & Co., one of the great trading names. Soon M. S. Wien & Co. joined these conversations. It was suggested that one operations department in place of three would save about $150,000 each year, but these discussions were sporadic, and we decided to go ahead on our own. As partners, we were executing more smoothly. More than ever, I respected Buzzy and Irwin's pragmatism, and their efforts to help me focus whenever I became distracted.

In December, I went to visit Harry Donald of Donald & Co. who was then 84. During the visit, Harry told me about my father's difficulties in 1929 after the market crashed. Harry also had an account for the person who had reneged on the trade in Chase Bank "when issued" shares. My father had gone to see Harry after the Crash and told him that he was unable to consummate his contracts, and asked him for an extension of time. Donald & Co. was making a lot of money at that time, and Harry offered my father more time. He told my father to "just forget it," while characterizing the customer in the most uncomplimentary terms. This was a stunning revelation as I was unaware of Donald's connection to my father's early career. Donald's decades-old generosity was a grand gesture, and my father's struggle to meet his obligation all the more admirable. Donald & Co. was considering clearing through our firm, or becoming a registered representative of ours, but neither of these came to pass. I was amazed to learn all this from someone whose connection with those early days had never been suggested, and this made me realize that those observing the things we do are more numerous and more secretive than imagined.

We had made some important decisions, and as 1975 ended, we focused on our upcoming move to Jersey City. It was a time of some confusion in the trading room, and capital was still very difficult to get.

CHAPTER 12

More Change and Bigger Growth

The early months of 1976 were taken up with building the office in Jersey City, and a conversion to a more advanced data processing system with Automatic Data Processing, "ADP," a decision we weighed for a long time. For the new office, we took a construction loan of $200,000 from First Jersey Bank. We finally moved in at the end of April. There was tremendous upside to working in a new office in a new building. Some considered moving to New Jersey, to save on taxes, but few did.

Despite promises of a smooth transition, shifting our data processing to ADP from the Service Bureau was messy, and reminiscent of our 1968 problems. The chaos we experienced was only quelled through superhuman efforts by the Operations Department, under Bob Meli's inspired leadership. Our books finally got into balance by the end of April, coinciding with the completion of the move. We were lucky, as it was just in time for an audit by the NASD in May. My father reacted well to these changes, as evidenced by his decision to give me all but ten shares of his common stock in the firm.

I had hired my first secretary a year earlier, and after sixteen years of doing everything myself, it took me a while to learn how to use her time effectively. This was difficult for me, as I was accustomed to doing whatever was needed in less time than it would take to teach someone else to do it. My inexperience revealed itself in the incompetence of my first assistant. She was a poor choice, and lasted little more than a year. At this point, we had about seventy-five people in the firm, quite a big jump from 1959 when I became employee number five.

Our office seemed more like those of the larger firms, the result of a better and more sophisticated data processing system, and a shift in our management style, especially when it came to recruiting. Earlier, we had great success bringing novices to the firm. We found it easier to teach the ways we wanted things done, rather than breaking people of bad habits learned elsewhere. Now we had less time for training, so we brought in more skilled and experienced Wall Street workers, losing some distinctive and unique attributes which contributed to the firm's culture.

By the end of July 1976, one-year-old Herzog Commodities Corporation under the direction of Paul Sarnoff had contributed $25,000 to profits. We applauded his efforts which included guiding the account of a coffee trader who parlayed a small investment to over $1 million. That story was written up and circulated and Paul's skill came to the attention of Continental Grain. He left us to accept a very lucrative position there. Harry Snyder kept things going, doing a small commodity business. Unfortunately, our stock trading partners never understood the commodities business, so that part of our business progressed very slowly.

The data processing conversion had finally settled down, but it was tested by the move and the high volume we were experiencing. High volume gave us our biggest profit day on record on February 23rd, $47,490, and there were others of that magnitude that followed. We first thought the computer had miscalculated, but the profits were real. Growing volume led me to retake my seat on the trading desk, and I used a head set and foot clicker to keep my hands free and take more calls. We were getting great respect from the Street. Buzzy had made a big success of our new issue business, and his trading account had become very profitable. He was asked to address a syndicate managers' convention at the Greenbrier Hotel. Our hard work traveling and entertaining was paying off handsomely.

On July 4th, there were many celebrations of the bicentennial of American independence, and one of them was the "OpSail" event on the Hudson River, which attracted splendid square rigged ships from all over the world. We decided to have a party that day, as the new office offered views of the river. We held a baking contest, and the winner presented a sheet cake in the image of an American flag. It was a festive event that was talked about all summer.

As the dust settled after the move, I heard from Tony Geraci of Heine Fishbein. He suggested we restart talks about a deal. Tony was the Heine Fisbein manager of operations, skilled and knowledgeable, with many friends he had cultivated at the Stock Exchange and throughout the industry. We began meeting regularly. I showed the new space in Jersey City, and discussed the possibilities for reconfiguring our old space at 170 Broadway. One of the problems was that Heine Fishbein would need to reduce its concentrated positions in railroad bankruptcy securities, the specialty of Max Heine and Hans Jacobson. Max spoke to me and urged me to buy some of these bonds, with assurances that they would be worth a lot more soon. Irwin, Buzzy and I considered it, but we didn't know Max well then, and we knew nothing about these securities. We told Max we wanted to stick with our low-priced stocks. This turned out to be a classic error of ignorance, as the bonds became far more valuable very soon afterwards, while our stocks remained low priced. Tony and I worked out most of the key issues concerning the possible merger. We envisioned the combined firm as a clearing member firm with competent margin account supervision. The trading operation would be enhanced with the additional capital supplied by Max Heine. Their retail department would fit neatly into our space at 170 Broadway. The form of the merger took shape and the elements appeared to be mutually advantageous. Tony and I began to outline the details, but people on both sides seemed far less interested. We would need to overcome that hurdle.

Work moved forward and late in the summer, we brought the deal to a vote. With measured enthusiasm, we voted to acquire Heine Fishbein & Co. I learned afterward that my partners voted in favor because they knew I was so totally convinced it would work. We had a deal, and Tony and I were very pleased. There were the usual delays with the lawyers and the regulators, but on November 18, 1976 our name appeared on the Stock Exchange tape welcoming us as members. The capital of the firm had been increased by $400,000 plus the value of the contributed Exchange seats. We gained some significant additional production and a genuine specialty in railroad reorganization securities. We acquired an experienced member firm clearing department with many valuable contacts. With the added capital, we could increase trading position exposure meaningfully. Our trading call improved greatly and our customers responded as the market improved. As operations manager, Tony handled personnel issues, including the voluntary departure of some of his former associates who didn't see a future with the larger combined firms. With Tony we gained a recognized expert on regulatory issues. The new firm, Herzog, Heine & Co., Inc., moved ahead confidently.

Adding and integrating Heine Fishbein required a lot of time and energy. There were internal issues to reconcile and no shortage of regulatory approvals to obtain. We needed to learn about our new associates and make room for them in Jersey City and at 170 Broadway. Several new personalities joined the Executive Committee meetings, held each Monday at 7:30 in the morning. A couple of the new people were quite forceful, and unafraid of confrontation. There were some unpleasant meetings at the beginning, but we all soon gained respect for one another and learned to work effectively together.

One of the very good results of our Stock Exchange membership and the member firm clearing capability was a change in our banking relationships. Before the deal, we had not been able to borrow from banks on our trading positions, which impeded our market-making. After the deal, Tony Geraci and I went to visit a couple of our banks, and when the banks heard that we had a full margin department, and would be needing margin loans, they were quite happy to have our trading positions as collateral. This made a big difference on the trading desk. With our new clearing capability, there were important improvements making it easier and faster, with reduced contra-broker risk. We finally had the important foundation for substantial growth.

We had all learned a lot going through this process and we were constantly reminded that negotiating is very tricky business. Once combined and significantly larger, we remained a family firm, but we had gained another family. Max's wife Lotte became part of the negotiating team late one night when the closing was taking place. I had to call Max to discuss some details of the capital calculation, and I was surprised to hear Lotte's voice cautioning me not to bother her husband, and I realized she had been listening to the whole conversation. She earned a lasting reputation on that call.

Things were shaking down well, and we were still ahead about $350,000. We prayed the up market would continue, enabling us to learn the newly acquired business lines and remain profitable. We guarded against impulsive decisions. Buzzy saw the emerging big picture, and his input showed a new level of commitment to the needs to the firm. Nothing could compare to the satisfaction I experienced a year later when my partners came to me and agreed, finally, that Heine, Fishbein had the earmarks of a terrific deal. This was a big moment, but a far bigger story was about to unfold.

CHAPTER 13

Bright New Days Dawning

Dec. 27, 1977

Dear Arthur,
    I have set myself the formidable task of clearing my desk completely before the year ends, and with that deadline firmly in mind, I have the great pleasure of answering the letter you wrote March 1976, which in its own indefatigable way has been reminding me all this time of my frailties.
    Your letter arrived at a time when, for a change, the sky really was falling. Chicken Little had to move the office from the old Broadway location to a newly built one in Jersey City. We all dreaded the trip, but it turned out to be much closer geographically than psychologically, financially or emotionally. Naturally, that was a surprise for which we were not prepared. We moved April 2, a day which was a culmination of six months of agonizing, planning, and haranguing, and as well the start of a completely new set of management problems which came upon me like thunder. I found that we suddenly were a three office company with high fixed overhead, personnel problems, production problems, and personality differences which seemed to be exacerbated by these changes. I again found myself working awful hours and feeling that I was accomplishing little.
    At just about that time, a firm we had talked merger with a year and a half earlier approached us once again, and since we were just then more painfully aware than ever of the shortcomings of the firm's long term capital position, we started talking. When I left for England in early June, we had all decided to think about it. Talks squirmed along all during the summer, and

I know that if I had not persisted, everyone else would have stepped away in delight; I did, though, since I was convinced that my perception of the thing was correct, and on November 18th the deal was effective and some much larger, far more complex problems found their way into my lap. In the deal, we acquired certain assets – all except a few, and no lease liabilities — in return for 20% of our stock. While we remained in control on paper, we found ourselves outfoxed lots of times, and we were unable to pull ourselves together for many months. Incredible differences, petty problems over small dollar amounts inuring to the benefit of certain partners over others, and a general acrimony filled our lives for the first five months, until April 1977. All this time, business kept going, data processing conversions yielded astronomical differences in the records, and tempers were short. By April, operations began to settle down, and we finally saw the reduction in expenses begin to materialize. I had by that time completely rebuilt the old 170 Broadway office vacated a year before for a retail sales operation, and moved the new group into that space. Old and trusted employees on both sides were let go, and you could cut the anxiety around the place with a salad fork.

By the time the fiscal year ended last July 31, we realized that we could have good partner's meetings, we had operated quite profitably, paid off the tremendous legal bills, dealt with countless tedious problems, and, to make a long story shorter, made a go of it. In addition, we found ourselves with a $1 million tax loss carry-forward which has already had a significant effect on the balance sheet.

The capital base we constructed as a result of the merger has enabled us to remain highly competitive and grow, so that we are now among the top three firms in the country in our business, with correspondent firms in 13 cities, and making markets in 1500 stocks. Fortunately, it worked, and it was some tremendous gratification to me that my perception of the thing turned out to be correct.

In the process, however, I became so uncomfortable with everything, with the cajoling, convincing, compromising, and so on, that I realized I was doing the personal thing wrong. Time after time, when I felt I knew what I wanted to accomplish, I would go and make a terrific mess of it. I became shy and lost my confidence, and reached the point at which I was truly at a loss for the next step.

At just about that time, my office manager/controller, who is like a brother to me, and sensed my discomfort and malaise, happened to make *a remark during dinner one night to the effect that he takes great pleasure in observing how other people handle situations. Overnight that percolated in the old bean box, and the next day I visited the behavioral science department at GBA cold, and sat down to wait. The next free person happened to be Richard Friedman, who I guess is about my age, and who agreed to listen. I only had about fifteen minutes, as I was, as usual, late for another meeting, but I realized in that time that this was just what I needed, and he, too, said that he felt he could help. We made a dinner date, and aided by some good food and red wine in a place on 57th Street, I articulated what I could. He was excellent, and rearranged the jumble in my mind so I immediately felt more at ease, and as well achieved a far better and more important understanding of the whole context in which I was working. The whole concept of different people's agendas, timing, and lots of other simple things became a lot clearer. I worked with him for about two months until we were both off for vacation. From then on, it was a lot easier. At one time, after hearing a few hours' worth of narration, he said to me that it was lucky I could tolerate ambiguity, since if I hadn't been able to, he felt there wouldn't have been a business. It's one of those statements that sounds very impressive, but it is difficult to analyze. Anyway, I know he understood the difficulties I was having, and his advice was extremely useful.*

After the summer, and the completion of the audit, problems began to dissolve, and for the first time in what I realized had been three years, I found myself with some time to catch up, and to think more comprehensively about things. I started working through my backlog, and now, I caught up, and am working ahead again. Our operations are smooth and efficient, business is good, and I take very little work home to do at night. It is a wonderful change.

It has been a very exciting, scary, instructive and broadening experience. I got to feel sometime in there that I was dealing with business problems, not just the problems of my firm; I felt as though I could tackle another business, not only our business. Anyway, now it appears that I will have a lot more time in the next six months to attend to my areas of production, and that is very interesting to me as I have missed that a lot.

In the Smythe firm, I had a problem with the principal player, since his personal needs had outgrown the firm's ability to compensate him, a fact which I saw long before he did, and which led to some unpleasant discussions. There a very lovely change has finally taken place. Largely at my urging, Diana began working for them in November, as both children are now in school (Brooklyn Friends) until 3. She is there 9-2 each day, and has surprised herself, I think, by enjoying the work a lot. Mike meantime left to go to the American Stock Exchange, a wonderful step up, and thus the entire economics of that firm have changed. I am delighted that Diana is there (in the 170 Broadway office) and of course my interest in that business is alive once again, and all is well, and that business is developing nicely.

Arthur, I have thought of you so many times, and wished that you were around. It was a great treat to hear from Dorothy, and your trips sound wonderful. I hope everyone is well, and once again, we urge you to consider this hotel on some jaunt north. The food is better than the company — Di supervised 28 for Christmas and on Monday my principal afterthought was that we must have been nuts, but it was one heck of a good party, and the children were completely spaced out. Tomorrow we expect my cousin from Charleston with her two daughters, 8 & 5, like ours, for a few days. A good holiday season I call it.

To fill in some of the blank spots, the country house has become more a part of us all than ever, and the scene of some great events. My organic gardening continues to thrive, now with 60,000 honeybees which yield about 35 lbs. of honey a year, apples, peaches, currants, the old gooseberries, and so on. We have just completed a renovation which added a screened porch and doubled the size of the kitchen, and we did all the painting and decorating, finishing Thanksgiving weekend. Di's parents were here for a month at the end of the summer for a wonderful visit, her father's first to either of these houses. He is a wonderful person with dozens of interests. We went all together to Martha's Vineyard for the first time this summer, and it was very good. We also had trips during the year to Chicago in January, Washington in April where I was stunned by the 1876 exhibition, Boca Raton in October. I have been doing a lot more work on an industry level for the NASD and the Nat'l Security Traders, and I find that very challenging, too. By the way, after Boca, we went to New Orleans for the weekend, and we were able to see the King Tut exhibition, which is excellent.

The children are really cream puffs, and I often find myself thinking about them and chuckling quietly. Di complains that I wake her up *chuckling in my sleep, but there are just so many nice things going on all the time. Mary's teacher bought half a dozen fertile chicken eggs for the class last January, and three of them actually made it right straight out to lay eggs for the class cooking projects in May. It was quite a sight to bring her to class and see three chickens flying around. The program at Friends is excellent in my opinion, and I feel very close to it, since it's the way I learned the things I know which are really important to me. Sarah made a good start this fall, and it turns out a lot more was happening than we realized, and she is doing well also.*

So there, we are, and you are caught up to date. Many thanks for writing to us, even though we haven't always written back; we love to hear from you. I still remember that afternoon at Alfred very well, playing tennis and then talking on the lawn. How is Leigh? Carro and Barry? Where does Peter live? And finally, we want to wish you the very best for the New Year, one of health and happiness, and hopefully one in which we can see each other again. With our fondest regards,

Sincerely, John

I wrote that letter to Arthur Svenson, my former professor at NYU Graduate School. It neatly captures the feelings and sums up the events of these times.

When 1977 was born, we were ready. Mike Levine became a partner on January 1, after some apprehension and lots of discussion. A few familiar faces of old had departed by year end, and "Tony Geraci's men" had filled their places. Our Operations Department was far more professional than it ever had been, and the stock exchange element was a big benefit. We were doing things more efficiently, especially on the trading desk, where hesitancy of every kind was erased from our clients' minds. I was anxious to see if my creativity would result in more business for our larger organization.

My job at this point was to supervise all the paperwork and regulatory requirements at an emerging national trading firm. There was a new stockholder's agreement to complete, and special attention was paid to avoid any of us discovering a deceased partner's widow had become our new partner. There was need for a comprehensive insurance review which took many weeks, and finally, there were changes to the profit-sharing plan which had to be written, voted upon and put into practice. At this point, I had been on the

NASD Options Committee about a year and a half, and was then appointed to the NASD District XII committee, the STANY Options Committee, and the NSTA Options Committee. All these were new to the industry and I looked forward to staying involved and contributing.

These changes came rapidly, and I was too busy to notice their impact upon me. This realization came painfully. When my discomfort grew, I decided to get some help, and I quietly began a series of meetings with a behavioral psychologist at NYU Stern. We had several meetings, and he was very helpful explaining how the new relationships might work to my advantage and how I might reorganize my responsibilities to make them more manageable. I readily adopted some of the recommendations, such as: containing my thoughts, focusing on them later, and thinking more about the other person's problems and what he or she might be thinking. He said it was a good idea to suggest fewer, but more well-developed ideas, and rank their relative importance versus other pressing issues of the day. He recommended I resist advancing an agenda simply because it was mine. By modulating my responses, he said I could encourage discussion and gain a better understanding of my associate's views.

This was all valuable when it came to working with the Heine Fishbein people. Until the deal, I gathered that they never had organized meetings, and their main concern was what to do when the talking stopped. This was dangerous. I learned to be less sensitive when my own ideas were critiqued, and to use humor to diffuse hostility.

Buzzy, though not schooled in psychology, also taught me a great deal about people. He always seemed to know exactly what he wanted to accomplish, and he patiently listened before he spoke. From Buzzy I learned about the need for closure and resolution before proceeding to the next issue. He showed me that timing was all important and that there was nothing worse than sharing an idea before it was fully baked. And if you're trying to build consensus and support, the idea is just half of it. If you are looking for buy-in, have an idea as to how to get it done, in other words, the "who" and "how" required for implementation. I realized that at meetings I had to lead with the proper emotional tone.

I was the boss, and that meant I needed to manage the supervisors and let them manage the staff. I couldn't be a part of any particular group. It was lonely. It was my responsibility to lead and be a role model and foster self confidence in my managers. Relying on my creativity, I moved the firm ahead in small steps. I took all the regulatory tests and passed them, did committee work outside the firm, and participated in as many industry events as I could. I strove for quality and maintained an acute awareness of all that was going on. I saw the expertise of others as being beneficial to the firm, and not as a challenge to me. We were bigger now, and unlike the earlier days, I realized I could never become an expert in all our areas. I embraced those who had the skills we needed.

By the fall, I was feeling better. I was dealing with issues and people more effectively. Relying on some good advice and my inner strength, I began to change numerous things I was doing and steadied myself emotionally.

In one of the 12 file boxes holding the records of the firm, I found some interesting data about where we were in the spring of 1977. It was in a FOCUS report (Financial and Operational Combined Uniform Single Report) for the quarter ended March 25, 1977. The figures were a source of pride at the time. Our Cash was $174,000, Fails to Deliver $3,438,000, Cash and fully secured accounts of customers of $7,618,000, long positions in corporate bonds $244,000, long positions in stocks $2,357,000, the Demand Note from Max of $400,000. Value of exchange memberships owned at cost, $80,000, and memberships contributed for use of the company at market value $120,000. On the Liability side, there were bank loans of $7,377,000, Stock loans of $587,000, and fails to receive of $2,146,000. The Net Capital computation came to $914,094. Impressive, but the numbers provided no clue as to where we would be a few years ahead.

The fiscal year end ritual was once again upon us in July of 1977, and while we progressed, we were happy knowing that this demanding year of progress with its problems and dislocations would soon be filed away. I was happy to spend more time with Irwin. Our discussions, personal and sincere, benefitted us both. He left to manage the Miami branch later in August, happy to embark on the next phase of his career with reduced anxiety and malaise. About twenty of us celebrated his contributions at a party at Christy's.

On August 12, 1977, Governor Carey signed the "STIF" bill into law (Stock Transfer Incentive Fund) effective October 1, 1977. A year and a half after we had moved to Jersey City to avoid the stock transfer tax, the State of New York saw the light. While the tax-induced exodus to New Jersey would largely abate, the entire tax would not be off the books until October 1, 1981. This was great progress for New York, and we thought immediately of the day we would be able to move back to Wall Street, but we still had a lease in Jersey City in the Ukrainian National Building. Several people had made plans to move to New Jersey to avoid New York State income tax, but most of the firm had not done that.

With Irwin in Miami, Buzzy and I spent more time together. We tried to have dinner together every few weeks. We were becoming more effective as partners. During one of these conversations, Buzzy raised the issue of the firm name, suggesting that Geduld be added. This was a big step, but when I thought about it, it seemed both natural and fair. I knew the contributions that Buzzy and Irwin had made, and would continue to make to the firm's growth and success. Buzzy was now the manager of the trading room, where he patiently made changes that were well thought out and effective. I respected his ability. It was an easy decision and I agreed to his request. We began to design new logos for the firm and the official change in name came early in 1978. I was very proud of this change, but no more proud than Buzzy and Irwin.

In the latter part of the year, more than twelve months after the Heine Fishbein deal had been closed, we finalized a new stockholder's agreement, a milestone. Diana and I invited the managers and traders to our Brooklyn home for a Sunday lunch and conversation. Bob Meli was celebrating his tenth anniversary with the firm, and we took the opportunity to present him with a gold watch, and he shared a few heartfelt words. The party was a great success. I have always thought that getting together in a social context was a good way to start and maintain constructive workplace relationships.

As the organizational problems settled down, we were all able to spend more productive time on our substantive work. One of the new activities was doing business with Mutual Shares Corp., the fund which Max Heine was managing, now nestled comfortably in the firm. In January 1978, Michael Lipper from Lipper Analytical Distributors wrote to Max to let him know that Mutual Shares was the top performing fund in the country over the five-year period ending December 31, 1977. Mutual Shares also gained more than any other fund of similar size and objectives over the last ten years. Wonderful news, certainly, and the fund continued to grow. Max's assistant in the fund was Michael Price, a highly competent and creative young manager, and his record would stretch far and wide over the coming years. Another young research person, Seth Klarman, was also with the fund, and we were able to offer his research to our retail clients. The firm's relationship with the fund was beneficial, and it was a credit to the firm that the fund was associated with us. It made a big difference on the trading desk.

The firm had grown in personnel after the merger, and there were now just under eighty employees. Like the larger firms, we provided a pension and profit sharing plan and employees were content and enthusiastic about the things they saw happening around them. The aggregate balances of all employees in the profit-sharing plan at the end of the fiscal year, July 31, 1978, was $215,000. It seems small now, but it was meaningful at that time. Departing employees bought homes and started businesses, paid for educations and prepared for a rainy day.

As our trading call improved, we became more adventurous regarding entertainment events. We hosted an event at the very fashionable Studio 54 in August 1978. A couple of hundred guests attended, and it was talked about long afterwards. Fortunately, there were now several people in the firm who had insight into our customers' preferences, a skill which eluded me.

We decided to take a booth at the first "Money Show" in the Coliseum. We displayed a large banner which proudly announced our membership in the New York Stock Exchange. There was also a tiger in one of the early iterations of our logo, this suggested by Warren Lee, from our advertising firm. He was a very creative thinker, and at an officers meeting he said that Merrill Lynch had a bull, Dreyfus had a lion, and we should have a tiger. I was surprised to learn that Buzzy had always been interested in the large cats, and he liked the idea right away. The rest of the officers thought it would be fun, so now we were seeing all sorts of different presentations using the tiger theme. The tiger was doing well. We ended 1978 with a book value of $2,823,271, a material increase from $1,609,415, eighteen months prior.

In November, we had a long-term planning dinner meeting just before Thanksgiving. We talked about the businesses we were in, market-making, retail, and clearing, and reviewed our firm liquidity figures. At the meeting, we also discussed moving back to New York City, since the stock transfer tax was declining and it would soon end as scheduled. We occupied 4,000 square feet at 170 Broadway and 6,500 square feet in Jersey City, and we anticipated growing. If we moved, we would look for 15,000 square feet. This proved conservative, and we grew far larger over the coming years.

My efforts at classical management procedures were not always popular, but they were tolerated. I was trying hard to put my NYU training to work, but others felt they knew better. Buzzy and I were forming a very effective partnership. He did see value in what I was doing, and I grew to appreciate his thoughtful, methodical and determined ways. Moreover, he showed leadership abilities and management skills. We learned how to disagree without raising our voices, and we had an unspoken agreement about how we would handle differences. If one of us felt that a decision was going to be problematic, we just agreed not to pursue it. This relieved us both of the normal anxieties which plague many partnerships. We thought ahead, trying to spot trends and recognize opportunities. At our meetings we considered opportunities in London, Canadian stocks, gold stocks, corporate finance, and discount brokerage.

Good markets continued, and as in the past, the year-end was a good buying opportunity for many stocks under pressure for tax loss selling. I had been asked to serve on the Board of the National Securities Clearing Corporation ("NSCC"). This was a wonderful step for me, and for the firm. NSCC was a tremendous advance for the industry. A little history is useful here. Under the NASD rules, our firm, as a market maker, was obliged to trade with any other NASD member who called us. It was very easy to become an NASD member, and some of the firms we did business with were not well capitalized, a risk we understood, but couldn't avoid. We were often in the position of having to make trades with such firms, even though we had information that the firm in question was not good for its contract. This is referred to as contra-broker risk, and it meant that when we delivered stock to complete a trade, we might not get paid or the check might bounce. Losses could mount when prices fell below the level of our failed trade. NSCC changed all that. It created a continuous net settlement process, which included netting of all the contracts submitted to it by its members in each of the individual stocks. This meant that when we sent NSCC our trade information each night, they netted our trades against all the other submissions, and then returned to us a net settlement figure for the number of shares we were to deliver to them, or receive from them in each stock we traded. And the best part was that when we got that information, our contra party became NSCC, and not a brokerage firm. This eliminated contra-broker risk and made our business far less risky. I was only one of twenty directors on the NSCC board, and it gave me an opportunity to meet senior officers of firms from all over the country. None of our competitors was represented on the board, and my access to NSCC officials was helpful whenever a related problem arose at the firm.

At the fiscal year end, we had seventeen traders in New York and nine in Miami. For each trader, we calculated the percentage return on investment, the position exposure taken, and the estimated net capital charge for that trader's positions. This analysis enabled us to evaluate risk and rank each trader's true profitability. As we grew we needed to improve our analytics. Data was the best tool when it came to measuring and controlling risk. Tony Geraci was one of our best when it came to spotting danger and avoiding it. The year had been a good one, and shareholder's equity had grown by $859,000. We were feeling confident and self-assured.

In the fall, we began to execute trades on the Cincinnati Stock Exchange, as we continued to explore new opportunities. Pricing disparities was an important issue. Despite improvements in communications, surveys showed significant differentials in quotes from city to city. NASD rules required traders to execute customer orders at the best price, but it was not always easy. These were the days of industry discussions about the National Market System, as improvements in communications revealed inconsistencies in the prices for the same stock in different cities. This influenced where firms would execute customer's orders to achieve the best price, as NASD rules required. There was a great deal of discussion about this issue, various white papers were circulated, and certain industry figures like Don Weeden of Weeden & Co. made this issue their own. Technology helped resolve the issue and helped bolster confidence of investors in our market.

CHAPTER 14

Onward and Upward

The decade began with a feeling of accomplishment. We moved past the difficulties that came with partners coming and going, new offices and the ever-present need for additional capital. We digested the acquisition of Heine Fishbein and emerged a larger, smoothly running firm. The antagonism that greeted the new members of the Executive Committee dissipated, and the combined group learned that more could be accomplished by speaking plainly and curbing emotions. Tony Geraci was a tough boss, but he was what we needed in operations. The quality of the trading calls continued to improve and the result was increasing profitable business. Our 26 traders excelled at our specialties: new and secondary offerings, and railroad reorganization securities. Our retail business was solid, but not yet of meaningful size. Batch processing solved our data processing woes, and our clearing for other firms grew profitably.

Our staffing stabilized, and we continued to see the benefits of our years of in-house training. Our people were highly regarded, and they were often asked to participate in industry committees. This was not only gratifying, but it also led to business. We had correspondent relationships with 18 firms around the country, a national presence, and a growing reputation for dependability and service. Shareholders' equity exceeded $6 million. We were prepared for the new decade, anxious to show the industry how serious we were.

In the *Wall Street Journal* and *The New York Times*, we announced that the firm had five new stockholders and a new Vice President. This last addition, Robert A. Mackie, was especially notable as one of the founders of Singer, Beane and Mackie, a long-time competitor. We continued to promote the firm in trade ads which featured our tiger. In an ad created for the New

York Money Show, our mascot was talking to a bull and bear while referring to a small loose leaf remarking, "Now, here's our plan," and then he went on describing our 54 years of experience, exchange memberships and our four offices. The tag line was: "Call us, you'll find we mean business." The tiger was getting noticed as he showed up in various situations. We had as much fun with him as our audience.

To mark the start of our specialty in trading Canadian issues, we dressed the tiger as a Canadian "Mountie" and he asked our new French-speaking traders, "Voulez-Vous trader nette?" He let those traders know that we had a telephone number dedicated to French speakers. Luckily it never rang! The tiger peered out from a background that included the Liberty Bell and Independence Hall to announce the opening of our Philadelphia office, which we turned over to Bill Feather, a well-known trader assisted by several other experienced people from the area where I had worked 20 years earlier.

We concluded the 1980 fiscal year with 23 correspondent firms and 23 shareholders. It was part of my strategy to offer these skilled, dedicated and experienced individuals not only the opportunity to achieve competitive current income, but also build wealth by sharing in the success of the firm. I took pleasure in amending the capital structure of the firm and our shareholders' agreements to accommodate new partners.

We did not pause, and by October we were operating in Dayton, Ohio and boasting of our new membership in the Philadelphia Stock Exchange, our nation's first. Our tiger was working hard, and we showed him carrying a cub in his mouth to let people know that we specialized in trading new issues. Two more stockholders were added by the end of the year and Charles Padala became a Vice President. While there was much that was new, old traditions were continued with every employee starting their holiday season with a Thanksgiving turkey, our gift. With the stock transfer tax ending, plans were well underway for our return to New York City. Concluding a tremendous year, we sensed that the next would be even better.

We raced into 1981, and in the first two weeks we added another correspondent - Schneider, Bernet & Hickman, Inc., of Dallas. There was no rest for our tiger. We promoted the new office in Boston by standing him on a ladder in front of a chart with a line going sharply up and to the right, with only his feet and tail visible. The headline read, "Wonderful city, Boston. Great place to do business." And the ending was, "You'll find we mean business. In Boston." We were then making markets in 1500 stocks, and as the ad conveyed, we were eager to do more. At this point, we were placing a full-page ad in each of the 17 issues of the *Investment Dealers' Digest* scheduled for 1981. Warren Lee was doing a great job with the ads, and the over-sight of the advertising activity was taking more and more of my time. Warren and I spent a lot of time together, and our families became close. The Lees came to our home in Clinton Corners for weekends in the summer, and sleigh rides in winter. We talked about different advertising ideas, with Diana actively participating in these conversations. Our tiger appeared in the Dayton ads with a Wright Brothers airplane and a jet fighter moving through the clouds.

I felt strongly about the need to have a well-rested staff and the need to promote balance between work and home life. I was convinced that the best way to sustain loyalty was through recognizing and respecting the need for personal time. We liberalized the vacation policy, providing three weeks off after five years, and a day off for every month worked for the new people. I was never disappointed. I recall an operations person dropping in to let me know that she would be working late, and why. Buzzy and I felt confident that operations were going smoothly, and that the employees were happy. I did everything I could to recognize people's efforts. This meant being a good listener and offering praise when warranted. The managers group which paralleled the executive committee had a weekly meeting during which anyone could speak up about any subject. I would always participate, and make sure that people could let off steam in a sympathetic environment. I got a lot of satisfaction seeing our managers' growth and development. We would have meetings in different places, not always the firm conference room. One of the favorite places was the McDonald's on Broadway and Maiden Lane, where they had a ticker tape and a pianist and an upstairs conference area where we could meet privately. I planned these meetings carefully, and made sure that breakfast was on the firm.

I was shocked to learn how many of our people were burdened by crushing debt on their high interest rate credit cards. I initiated a policy to address this problem. We offered to pay off their debt, if the employees would agree to repay the firm through deductions from their paychecks with no interest. This was a popular benefit, and widely used.

Financial results were moving in the right direction, and the figures for February 27, 1981 showed shareholders' equity of $9,836,000, again a new high. This pleased the new and old stockholders, as they could see their wealth increasing. The possibility of becoming a shareholder was a very important reason to have a career at Herzog. Buzzy and I would ask different individuals if they would like to purchase a share or two in the firm, while others hoped they might one day have a chance. We proudly compared our net worth figures to our major competitors, and at mid-year they were: M. S. Wien $5,503,565, Mayer & Schweitzer $2,588,479, Sherwood Securities $7,938,490, and our own at $6,511,000. These figures made the rounds of the executive committee.

My birthday is in March, and Harry Snyder decided to write a poem for me, to be sung to the tune of "The Thing:"

John — you celebrate today
The date you were born.
And since that most important day,
The mustache you have worn!
You always seem so dapper
And are always in command!
You have that certain quality
That marks the "Leader of the Band!"
We wish you nothing but the best
That you yourself desire
That every stock you buy or own
Should suddenly catch on fire!
Good health to always be with you
And long life you acquire
And work your magic — so that we
See our paychecks moving higher!

Harry wrote things like this for several people, and he had an enthusiastic following. This one reveals a lot about Harry, and the attitudes of the people around him. It was no small feat. The feeling in the office was good and people liked to come to work. It was apparent to all who visited.

Our progress and maturity became clear when we experienced the inevitable hiccups, those unforeseen events that were costly. Earlier I referred to a crisis we had over Pelorex, a stock we were carrying which suddenly became worthless, and how we had to scurry around to find capital to avoid a deficiency. We had subordinated loans coming due, and we managed to pay them without any difficulty. We put our loss in perspective, contained the damage, and did not let this influence the rest of the business. I instinctively remained optimistic.

My optimism has always been important to the firm. When someone had a bad day, or lost a large amount, or had a bad error in operations, I was able to encourage them, and they were grateful. I would accept the loss and try to understand the mistake. I found a longer view and a sensitive response to be the best reaction to those moments.

Our plan to move back to New York was fully formed. Our estimates of moving costs, tax benefits, and construction indicated that we could save about $100,000 a year by moving back to New York. We started the formal planning process in 1979, but it wasn't until March 1980 that we were approached by a real estate broker, Martha Burton, who located some space at 24 Broadway. We engaged Ted Moudis, our architect, and we began thinking about the layout of the space. By July we had negotiated rent, which would begin at $10 per square foot and escalate to $13.50 for the last five years, low by today's standards. Our sometimes stormy relationship with Constitution Realty Corp. commenced September 1, 1980 when I signed a lease for our space at 26 Broadway in the Standard Oil Building.

Ted Moudis configured the space, and while still in the planning stages we could add some contiguous space in anticipation of continued growth. There were trips to the new space, and meetings over the plans, with lots of details to consider. At the same time, there were new demands upon us, in the form of increased SEC oversight. Compliance became a priority for me, as I dreaded being unprepared for a regulator's visit. To stay focused, we kept asking ourselves: "What business are we in? Is this something we want to be doing?" This question helped us to remain focused on the markets, and the needs of our customers.

The tiger continued to help us tell our story. In one of our ads, our tiger, in a vest and repp tie, was the central figure between a similarly dressed bull and a bear with the caption, "Bull and Bear of Wall Street, New York; Tiger of Herzog Heine Geduld — at the Cleveland Summer Outing — discussing prospects for peace in the Middle East." It was all good fun, and the customers loved it. Our tiger was still on his ladder in the Security Dealers of North America ad that year, which read, "In short: things are looking up."

The fiscal year had ended well, with shareholders' equity at $11,087,000, and total assets at $76,175,000. These were formidable numbers, but we never lost sight of where we came from. Whenever I saw these numbers, I would think back to the early days, when overall capital was $40,000 and we were writing four trades each day.

Our institutional call was important, improving, but not yet what we wanted. An institutional call is an inquiry from a bank or asset management firm, but unlike a typical trade of 500 or 1,000 shares, an institution might be interested in moving 5,000 or 25,000 shares. For us, this was tricky business. It was hard enough to cultivate these major institutional accounts, and when we did get a call, our traders were easily frightened. They needed to be nimble, especially when it was a large sell order in an issue they were already long. This is where Buzzy excelled. He could tell the institutional order clerks what to expect, and then he helped our traders with the market-making once we got the order. There were often real losses on these trades in the early days, but gradually, with experience, the confidence of our traders grew with Buzzy's patient and nurturing leadership. He helped us build a beautiful call. Our tiger reinforced this message, as he was seen with a compass, leading the bear and the bull through dense underbrush with the headline, "This way, men, we're gaining on it..."

We had taken the space above the new office on the small second floor of the adjoining building. One of our first sub-tenants there was Bond Richman & Co., the firm of Stanley Morgenstern. Stanley was a deal specialist and Buzzy's good friend. He completed several small underwritings while he was with us in that space. He also loved to cook, and had a stove installed in his office. His favorite Italian specialties, heavy on the garlic, made lunch hour a very fragrant event for his immediate neighbors!

On September 1st, the National Security Traders Association sent a letter to its 4600 members about a trip to Washington taken by their Executive Committee in June. They had met with Senator Alphonse D'Amato, newly elected, and Chair of the Senate Committee on Securities. They attempted to familiarize him with the over-the-counter marketplace, and invited him to visit some Wall Street trading rooms so he could see things first hand. They said he appeared eager to learn, and responsive to their comments. They also met with the Federal Reserve, the SEC, SIPC, the NASD, Representative Tim Wirth, then Chairman of the House Committee on Telecommunications, Consumer Protection and Finance, and finally, Representative Dan Rostenkowski, Chairman of the House Ways and Means Committee. These trips brought attention to the changes the industry was experiencing.

It was during this month that M. S. Wien & Co., a major competitor of ours, ceased doing business, a very shocking development which resulted in our adding some of their trading talent. In October, we sent a press release announcing our move back to New York, and I was quoted: "Nothing beats person-to-person contact. We want to be near the people with whom we do business; we want to be back in the city." We called on our tiger to prepare people for our arrival with a full-page ad. Our mascot was depicted with text patches telling all about the firm's attributes. Perched on a ladder, beside his chart, he was wearing a herring-bone suit and tie looking very self-assured as he casually uttered, "As we were saying..."

In the November 9th, 1981 edition of the *Wall Street Letter*, a headline story began: "Herzog Leaves Jersey City for NYC. After shifting operations to Jersey City in 1976 to escape the New York State stock transfer tax, as did nearly a dozen other firms, Herzog Heine Geduld has moved its trading operations back to New York's financial district at 26 Broadway. The move is expected to save the firm over $500,000 per year in interest costs on overnight loans, since the proximity of the National Securities Clearing Corp and Depositary Trust Co. will enable Herzog to clear trades faster, President John Herzog explained. Herzog makes markets in 1800 over-the-counter stocks and provides correspondent services for 31 other securities firms around the country, he added. "The move also was prompted partly by phenomenal growth since 1978 and partly by a desire to consolidate all the 56-year-old firm's activities—portfolio management, retail sales and options operations—under one roof," said Herzog.

In the same issue of the *Wall Street Letter*, it was reported that NYSE large block volume, trades of more than 10,000 shares, had increased by 34.4% for the month just ended, further evidence of the influence of institutions in the market place. This confirmed the growing importance of our institutional business which Buzzy was skillfully handling.

The move was well executed, and the new offices were superior to Jersey City, with a desk for everyone, and ample expansion space. Moving day was exhausting, but I was joyful when the movers finally left. I found myself alone in this very large, newly built space overlooking Bowling Green in the heart of the Wall Street financial district. I remember going around straightening things further so that when the employees came in, it would look as pleasant as possible. This all felt wonderful to me, exhausted as I was, and I loved every minute of it.

And then our ads hit the newspapers. The final design was a vertical image 18" tall and 4" wide, and against the background of several of the buildings near the new office, our tiger was standing up in a convertible car, license plate HRZG, our Nasdaq symbol, with arms outstretched, jacket open, tie flying in the breeze. The headline read: "We're back! And we're delighted to be home again. Herzog, Heine, Geduld, Inc. has moved all its financial services to one new location. At 26 Broadway. Here's what happened in the meantime: In 1976, we left the city with 40 employees; we're returning with 260. In 1976, our net worth was $1,000,000; at our last fiscal year-end, it was up to $11,500,000. Back then, we made markets in 800 stocks. Today we make markets in 1,800. Call us. Over-the-Counter Market Making (212) 962-0300. WATS line — 800-221-3600. Retail and Exchange Services — (212) 908-4000. We mean business. And how does it feel to be back? Just great."

The ad ran in the major papers, and several magazines, including *Forbes*. We were courted for additional advertising, and in time Diana and I received an invitation to take a ride on the Forbes yacht during the next SIA convention in Boca Raton. It all did feel great! We ran a follow up ad which told more of the move story.

"We are here at 26 Broadway. Home at last. The walls are up, the flooring is down, the phones are in... And all's well with the world. (As well as can be expected.) There have been stories about the difficulty of moving a large organization into new quarters. But naturally, we think ours are better than others. For example, we moved in on October 5th, but the carpet people had not finished their work; we tread lightly upon bare floors. When we moved in, the plumbing had not been turned on and despite all our planning, we still did not have a front door. (The other doors were working nicely, however.) And to top it off, just before lunch one day, in a section that had been pronounced completed and habitable, the ceiling collapsed. For those that were there, it was the Great Crash of October, 1981. Still, despite all, we are here; we have settled in. The traders are all hard at work. The correspondent wires are all working nicely. The same reliable service is fully operational. And we expect to have a new front door any day now. Call us. We mean business." It was one terrific year all right.

CHAPTER 15

Back Home in Town

When the lights were turned on in our beautiful new space, the few punch list items were taken care of, our spirits soared. We loved the new surroundings, and the building itself. The former Standard Oil Building at 26 Broadway was well known and very handsome. There were great places to eat, and all the departments of the firm were in one place making it very easy to talk with one another. We invited people to the office to show off, and they were enthusiastic. We were feeling confident and eager to be doing business, happy to be back in the city at the center of things. It was a heady time. Buzzy had an impressive office right behind his desk in the trading room. Business continued to be profitable.

We continued to ask ourselves "What business are we in?" We tried to refine all the elements of what we were doing. We knew the markets were changing, but we could not tell how rapidly it was happening. Nothing had changed more than telecom and we needed a consultant to show us how complicated things had become. He catalogued sixteen different telecom systems, and twenty-six common carriers, equipment and service vendors! We were advised that things would get more complex, but it would provide opportunities to combine communications with data processing technologies, and that we would benefit. We needed to learn more, so we thought we might create a new specialty for one of our employees, or continue to use a consultant. We decided on a combination, and we began to get better informed. We discussed these issues internally at the Executive Committee, and in the Manager's Meetings.

We continued to advertise, and the *Investment Dealers' Digest* was the preferred place. We were then running an ad showing our tiger explaining to the bull and the bear what was coming next: "Now, here's our plan," and it was very popular. As usual, the January issue of *Stock Market Magazine* had a piece on what would happen in the markets in the year. Their columnist, Marvin Hollander, wrote that 1982 should be a good year for the market and for the economy as well, contradicting the gloom many felt at that time. The editors did not agree, however, citing 10 million unemployed, high interest rates, and other drags on the economy. It was same old, same old.

As new members of the Securities Industry Association, we wanted to become more active, and I decided to attend the May meeting at The Homestead, in Hot Springs, Virginia. These gatherings were still new to me, but we felt the exposure would be good for the firm. My goal was to meet new people and pitch our market-making abilities. The speaker at one of the panels was John McCarthy, senior strategist at Lord, Abbett & Co., investment managers since 1929 with assets under management of about $1.5 billion. He was a good speaker, and I took notes. He spoke about factors which might turn the market, like the 10% tax cut coming in July, the improving picture in the Federal deficit, and President Reagan's policies aimed at lowering inflation. McCarthy felt there would be big changes in the stock market, and that we were in the late stages of high interest rates. He thought it was a good time to be buying equities, with book values and earnings set to grow at a quicker pace than any time since WWII. He anticipated possible rises in the Dow Jones Averages to the 3000 area with downside risk of only 10-15% to the 700 level. In closing, he asked the audience what they were now recommending for their clients. He guessed that most were probably in short term high yield investments, and this would likely be the wrong sector, as usual. I thought this was an excellent presentation and it coincided with my own traditionally optimistic view of the future. I then took my notes, summarized the talk, and had it printed on a wrapper for the July issue of "Friends of Financial History," a Smythe publication. I was always trying to use whatever assets were at hand to promote our business, and this turned out to be a worthwhile effort.

In June, I received a letter from Walter Raquet. He enclosed his resume and asked for an appointment. His resume indicated 14 years of diversified financial services experience with heavy administrative responsibility in operations and computer systems as well as long term planning, reviews, and personnel evaluation. He had been with Paine Webber since October 1980, and had directed the Corporate Controllership function including accounting services, financial planning, budgeting, financial statements, and regulatory reporting. He was a C.P.A. since 1969, and had studied computer science and finance at the graduate level. Anticipating further growth based on the telecom and computer changes we planned, he was someone we needed to talk to. Buzzy agreed. We interviewed him for the first time several days later. We had a series of meetings, and I checked his references. The president of Paine Webber praised Walter's creative skills and his innovative way of thinking. A senior officer at Morgan Guaranty Trust was also complimentary, adding that Walter was imaginative, knowledgeable, and good at "the business of business." We did come to an agreement with Walter and he soon began as Treasurer of the firm.

By July, Robert J. Flaherty, Editor of the OTC Review, described the markets according to Charles Dickens in *A Tale of Two Cities* as "The best of times and the worst of times," referring to weak brokerage firms, and those who were optimistic, buying stocks at what some called historic lows. On July 30th, Michael Price, Max Heine's colleague at Mutual Shares Corp. was the guest on Wall Street Week with Louis Rukeyser, talking about bankruptcy securities, a highly specialized field requiring study and patience. Things were moving along just fine, and Dickens was half right when, in August, totally unanticipated, a bull market began that was to last just short of twenty years. We were well positioned and our call on the trading desk improved due to our careful preparation. We had a strong operations capability, a new office, and our trading department well managed by Buzzy and several lieutenants. I was handling administrative issues and public relations. For the very first time, Diana and I attended the SIA annual meeting in Boca Raton. The highlight was sailing on the Forbes yacht, a reward for our big ad budget. And it all felt terrific.

I look back over the past from this very comfortable vantage point, with advanced years to help me. I see a different picture than I had originally thought. As young men and women, we were eager to do the right things. We kept our eyes on the essential elements and avoided distractions. We made decisions and followed through and executed. We built the firm from the inside with better management techniques, and strong operations. We increased capital, and stayed informed and conservative about what we were doing. My father's advice guided and remained timeless. We invested in our own employees and earned their loyalty with fairness, and praise when deserved. We went to weddings, bar mitzvahs and other events as we were asked. I never asked any employee to do anything that I was not ready to do myself. We couldn't wait to get to work on Monday morning, and that was a great feeling.

Our transaction volume had reached 3,000-4,000 trades per day. We had been thinking about how this kind of activity would be handled, and Walter Raquet became a valuable contributor to these discussions. We were getting to know each other and as always, there were precarious moments. Walter had completed the office we allocated to him with high priced furnishings, and that was not popular. He had also looked at executive compensation. He told me I needed to have a larger salary – as it had not been adjusted for years. That was more popular, at least with me. In discussions about computers, we decided to ask the software firm that had been working for us, Femcon Associates, to sit down and share their views of the near-term future. As the weeks went by, volume again rose, and suddenly we were writing 9000 trades each day, making the computer decision a lot easier, and far more crucial. We needed a real-time trading system that could keep up with the growing volume. Femcon was experienced, having worked for the Boston Stock Exchange for years, and they also suggested Stratus fault-tolerant computers. They had installed the first one, at a company near them in the Boston area.

The initial cost was $600,000 but Buzzy and I knew it would be more. Femcon set to work, and company principals Paul Femino and Craig Conti became regular fixtures around the trading room. In four months, the first beta terminal was working, and the reports were quite good. By Christmas, everyone in the trading room was equipped with a new COLT terminal. COLT was an acronym for "Continuous On Line Trading." It was the first real-time trading system, and an instant success, and within months, we offered it to other firms. Goldman Sachs was the first firm to take the system, and that enabled us to recoup some of the money we had spent on development. This new system would help us immensely, and we began to suggest enhancements for the software. Femcon obliged and everybody loved the results. Our clients could get into the system remotely, give us an order, and get an execution guaranteed at the inside market in ten seconds. On our side, the trade was reported to SOES, the new Small Order Execution System of the NASD, Nasdaq, as well as our internal departments, and the necessary clearing corporations. A celebration was in order once all the COLT units went live, and the project was complete. It was on time, and the traders were enthusiastic, and we were not surprised when the final cost came in at about $1 million. Femcon and Walter were praised. We boarded a Staten Island Ferry and watched fireworks marking the centennial of the opening of the Brooklyn Bridge.

COLT was the major project of the day, but there were other things happening. We needed to do some planning, as Bob Meli began discussing his retirement plans after years of tireless effort on the firm's behalf. The wonderful friendship Diana and I enjoyed with Bob and Esther would continue, as would his relationship with many of his co-workers.

We hosted 700 during STANY week at Dish of Salt on West 47th Street. Talk was split between the COLT system and the coconut shrimp. Our correspondents agreed about the shrimp and the speed of COLT, as they could now get execution information with COLT faster than trades on the Big Board.

We had decided to retain a professional public relations firm to help promote what we were doing, and Mount & Nadler was chosen. Alan Mount was creative and had a terrific sense of humor. Hedda Nadler was wonderful at controlling details. In June Alan and Hedda organized our first press luncheon, which we held in our conference room just a short walk from the trading room. Attendees were from *Business Week, Investment Dealers' Digest, USA Today*, Research Institute of America and *Barron's*. To start, Hedda and Alan explained that we had a story to tell, and then I shared a short history of the firm, and where we thought we could go in the future. Buzzy was just a bit reticent at the early meetings of this sort, but he quickly saw that these events were crucial to our growth. He spoke with conviction, and his detailed knowledge of the trading process made him quotable. The press people left satisfied and impressed. We had a few of these, and as a result, both of us became recognizable financial industry media personalities. This was very useful for our trading call, and we could begin trading more stocks, and expand our operations further. Mount & Nadler formally announced the COLT system in June, and shortly afterward, I received a letter from the London Stock Exchange with an invitation to speak about our new system at the first "Computers in the City" conference. London was in the midst of a tremendous change in the way they did business, and there was a crucial need for trading systems.

We enhanced our capital position with internally generated subordinated loans from employees to the tune of $1,171,000. Our annual shareholders meeting was held in early October 1984 in our own conference room, and the reports were excellent. Shareholders equity had increased to $16,271,000, another record figure despite extraordinarily high expenses.

Following our rollout of COLT, there were reports of ambitious plans for competing computer systems. A favorite hobby horse was the 24-hour trading day, which could be easily accommodated by COLT. All we would need to do was send the "Book" to London, or even Tokyo, and have it circle back in time for the open of U.S. trading. It gave the media plenty to write about, but it never materialized.

John Phelan, Chairman of the New York Stock Exchange was featured on the front page of *The New York Times* of Sunday, October 14th. He said that he was looking for new business, and I sensed he was looking overseas, and this was about a month before the Computers in the City conference, which would have a tremendous impact on things to come.

The Conference was a very big event. Held at the Barbican Centre, 20-22 November, I had been asked to deliver a paper during the program segment, "Competing in High Activity Markets." I suggested to the organizers that they might like to have Craig Conti speak, and they were receptive, adding him on Thursday under the heading of "Planning for Round-the-Clock Reliability." This was an exciting opportunity, as we had heard that the London firms were very worried about reliability. I took notes. Before teatime, John Gutfreund, CEO of Salomon Bros, Inc., characterized the markets of that time as, "a poor business to be in." My talk was well received, with a lot of follow up questions. Some attendees asked if they could come to see us in New York.

I was thrilled to receive an invitation to dinner at the London Stock Exchange. It was a night to remember, evocative of the splendid state events we have all watched on television. The Brits know how to do it right. When I got to the dinner, I received a personalized menu and seating plan, with a diagram of the large table with every person's name, firm and country on it. There was a red star next to my name making it easy to find my place. The dining hall was lit by candlelight from tall silver candelabras. Waiters in tails served smoked salmon, followed by roast pheasant. We concluded with Grand Marnier Soufflé en Surprise. It was quite a show! I was seated next to Mark Ferguson from Pinchin, Denny & Co., and a friendship developed. Diana and I brought the girls to their home near Winchester, where we watched young lads play soccer and had our first experience with duck egg sandwiches.

On Thursday, Craig delivered his talk late in the day. It was well received, and a bit of a bombshell, as he mentioned that the COLT system was available for the London market. We began to get inquiries for COLT. With Craig's work successfully concluded, we were both tired and elated. We left the Barbican to find a place to eat dinner. It happened to be Thanksgiving at home, so we called numerous restaurants trying to find a turkey dinner, but the closest we could find was roast duck at a place on Beauchamp Place. We picked up a couple of other people, and we had a festive end to a productive conference. Reviewing my notes, I found lots of people to follow up with and several "Possibilities." I was convinced we needed to be in London, and there were options. We could open our own office in London; open an office within the office of another London firm, or form a correspondent relationship. With the latter, the major contender was Laing & Cruickshank, where Barry Olliff planned to discuss the idea with his managing partner.

My attendance at the conference was pivotal. Several people I met there became very important in the years ahead, and personally I found the opportunities and challenges invigorating. My visit made it possible for others from the firm to visit, and create the trading relationships which became so profitable. COLT was also a winner, and it became the choice of a consortium of five large London firms, which meant Craig would be frequenting London. COLT became a byword. In early 1985, some of those who expressed interest did come to New York to see how we did things. "Big Bang," the deregulation of UK financial services, was coined to describe the abolition of fixed commission charges and of the distinction between stockjobbers, what we would consider to be specialists, and stockbrokers, who represented clients.

At the London Stock Exchange, it also meant a change from open outcry to electronic screen based trading. The big day was scheduled for October 27, 1986. For us, it was back home for the Christmas rush, with a holiday party at our home on State Street.

CHAPTER 16

A Rapidly Changing Milieu

In January I received a letter of praise for our real-time trading system, with apologies for being too busy to write sooner. It was not from a client, but from a professor at the Cornell Business School. He understood most but not all of what we were eager to accomplish, not bad for an academic. But he didn't seem to get the importance of our knowing each trader's position in real time, as well as our positions in the aggregate. The professor suggested several rather arcane data points which he suggested would best be studied at Cornell. We politely declined.

Recently, Craig Conti wrote me with his recollections of the COLT phenomena:

"The original London COLT firms were Barclays Capital, James Capel, Dresdner Kleinwort Wasserstein, NatWest Stockbrokers and Cazenove (later Schroders). The London system had all the features of the US system with real-time position keeping, risk management, trade reporting, etc. Additionally, it had the ability for multi-currency and multi-settlement systems. It was much more global than Colt US. It was reported that 80% of all equity trading following Big Bang was done on Colt systems running on Stratus Computers. Later, we added Smith New Court and Salomon (both London and then US) and Andelsbanken (Denmark). U.S. firms for Nasdaq market-making included: Goldman Sachs, Donaldson Lufkin Jenrette, Salomon Smith Barney, Alex Brown, Credit Suisse, and Wertheim Schroders." (Conti Email 12-8-14)

With offices substantially newer than those of our London counterparts, our visitors were impressed, and Buzzy was very receptive. The visitors always reminded us of the pressure they were under to get things sorted quickly and accurately. One of our more perceptive visitors was Nick Roditi, who recently recalled:

"It is 30 years ago now. At that stage I was working for J Henry Schroder Wagg. It was the time of Big Bang in London and we were charged with looking at what happened in the US. Actually, it was a time of great change in the City of London and the London Stock Exchange and in a way your firm influenced our thinking. I was then charged with establishing Schroder Securities, which became a member firm of The London Stock Exchange and lots followed from that." (Roditi Email dated 12-9-14.)

After his requisite tour, I recall that Nick decided to stay on, asking me if we could chat further. We did, and our conversation went on for a couple of hours. I was greatly impressed with his advanced understanding. When I visited London again, I contacted him and got a tour of a very impressive trading room, obviously influenced by what he learned during his visit. Our friendship developed, and Nick became an important source of news and ideas about the London scene.

As we contemplated a future requiring us to have call on greater amounts of capital, we had some thoughts about selling our firm. We began a couple of conversations. One with Merkin & Co. would have valued the firm at the industry standard, two times book value of our firm, just under $40 million. Subordinated loans would be paid off by the acquiring firm. The proposal went nowhere, but we ventured on knowing the capital we needed was a multiple of what we were adding through our operations.

In March, we published a "Specialists List" to assist people in finding the firm members they wanted to talk with. My name appears on the list for international questions and Buzzy's appeared under the heading, "24-hour trading." We identified seventeen specialists covering thirty subjects. Word of our rapid recent progress spread with the help of Mount & Nadler who helped us get a feature in *Fortune* on June 24th titled "Hitting it Big Over the Counter." The article detailed our trading in 3,000 stocks and 6,000 trades each day requiring $35 to $50 million in risk positions. Buzzy was pictured with the caption, "'Despite 16 years at the trading desk, Geduld says, 'I can't wait to get to work.'" Mutual Shares Corp. (Assets: $652 million) under Max Heine's direction was also recognized by the magazine. They said our firm was as good at picking stocks as we were at trading them. People noticed, as Mutual Shares had the third best performance over a 15-year period among funds tracked by Lipper Analytical Services.

The agenda for the June 25th officer's meeting was serious. It included 33 pages of comprehensive reports narrated by several officers. Year to date revenue was $45,524,452, a staggering increase. These meetings generated good discussion. Around that time, Buzzy came into my office to chat. He was serious and very happy to tell me that trading inquiries for 5000 share lots were now routine.

No sooner had 5,000 share inquiries become routine, when we began to get inquires for 10,000 to 25,000 share orders. This was very encouraging to us both, as we had applied ourselves to improving the institutional call for some time. Our challenge was to help traders overcome the fear they had taking positions of this size. When it occurred, Buzzy took over, and the trader was liberated from anxieties that would divert his attention from the rest of his positions. As more investment managers began including Nasdaq stocks in their portfolios, these calls increased. We had 34 correspondent firms, and our institutional call was becoming more and more significant.

We finalized a correspondent relationship in London and it allowed us to mimic our experience in America. I was fortunate to have been introduced to Laing & Cruickshank through Barry Olliff, an investment manager who was working at the firm. Discussions early in the year following the London conference led to several visits, first mine to London, and then theirs to New York. We announced the agreement on November 21st with appropriate fanfare. We needed something to put in the hand of many of our new contacts. The result was a very effective firm brochure, beautifully executed with the help of Mount & Nadler. This was given out with other information about our operations capabilities and Mutual Shares literature, a neat package.

The subject of fairness, or lack of fairness, in the execution of over-the-counter orders, especially for rapidly moving IPOs, was discussed widely. Trading IPOs had become important for us, and Buzzy had established a very good reputation for us in the specialty. Our firm was the destination of choice for a growing number of IPO orders. The Nasdaq market was still evolving, and the concept of a "national market system" in which every order in every stock found the best price for execution was still new and developing. John Wall, Nasdaq Executive Vice President, promoted the fact that more issues were finding multiple dealers on Nasdaq, indicating deeper markets better able to absorb sell orders during market declines and financial strength that exceeded the capabilities of specialists on the exchanges. At this time, our share of Nasdaq daily volume was about 9–10%.

Invitations to speakers for the second Computers in the City conference in London went out, and I was on the list for a talk on "A Dealer's Experience of Automated Trading." I was also asked to chair a discussion group on the "Trader's Workstation," desktop trading systems.

Another conference organizer asked me to speak on "Nature and Timescale of an Electronic Trading System." Diana came with me for the conference days, and afterwards we decided to attend another conference at Templeton College, Oxford titled "The Changing World of Financial Services." We loved the idea of study at Oxford, despite sleeping in sparse student dorms in uncomfortable beds with the bathroom down a long, frigid hall. But the conference was well-attended by many big name firms.

We ended the year with our usual treat for our clients. We were trading Republic Pictures Corp. and we got the idea to send videos of two of their movies in which we added a trailer describing our firm. The films were "It's a Wonderful Life" and "Flying Tigers." Republic was pleased, and our customers were delighted. It was a lovely way to say goodbye to a solid year.

CHAPTER 17

More Exposure and Greater Opportunity

As we began the year of the firm's sixtieth anniversary, it felt as if we had arrived. It brought to mind a trip I took with a friend from Milan to Venice by steam train. It was on the day most Italians took off for their summer holidays. We had train tickets, but there were no seats for the long ride. It was hot, so we stood between the cars, hoping to catch a breeze. The breezes were infrequent, but we did get a grimy coating of ash as it spewed from the locomotive. We arrived in Venice after dark, exhausted, hot and dirty, needing to find a place to sleep. We left the terminal, and walked outside to see the Grand Canal, gorgeous lights twinkling, waves lapping. We were exhilarated and no longer tired. That is how this momentous year began for me.

But old problems we couldn't shake were still with us. We considered subordinated loan proposals from several institutional accounts, and we carefully developed a crisis management plan so that we would be well prepared to handle customer assets under SIPC guidelines if there was a financial shock. In tedious meetings, we monitored our stock loan exposure, planning for the worst and hoping for the best. In all, the management group tracked 23 different risk measurements. But we were not without good news. We received a letter from Donna Connolly, the head of the accounting department, who was out on maternity leave for her third child. Donna told us how much she appreciated our support, and that she would soon be back. Donna could multi-task. She was up to date on every number in her department. My birthday in March prompted another poem from Harry Snyder, by this time self-appointed "company poet."

We had been anxiously anticipating our 60th for many months, making plans, sharing ideas, and taking stock of our legacy. Celebrating began with anniversary stickers and moved on to party plans and gifts for the shareholders. I ordered handsome scrapbooks from Italy, and I filled them with a brief pictorial story of the firm. We reserved the Carlyle Hotel for a June 15th celebration. There were invitations to design, menus to plan, seating charts, and endless details to trifle over.

The round of celebrations began with a luncheon for the Manager Group at Windows on the World on May 21st. We invited important people from outside the firm to join us. Each person found a sparkling Tiffany decanter at his or her place setting. I spoke first, acknowledging the difficulties we had overcome as a responsible, competent, committed group of professionals. I reminisced, noting the difference between the old days and the firm we all knew now. I stressed the promising outlook for the future. I thanked the operations group, which seldom received adequate praise for their sacrifices. I assured everyone that in our firm, we knew that operations excellence was the key to real success. I expressed my personal gratitude for having had the opportunity to work with them all. I spoke of the pride I took in their growth, and I urged each person to work towards the realization of their full potential. I meant it. It was all I could ever hope for. I let them know that when my father started the firm in 1926, he wanted to build a firm that allowed others to achieve their ambitions. When I finished, I invited others to share their sentiments. It was unanimous, as a firm, we felt we had done the right thing, and done it well. We moved onto the popular 60th Anniversary baking contest. Tony Geraci and I gained a little weight that day!

Many of our retail customers called to offer congratulations and we were grateful for their loyalty. We decided to have some fun with this, and we developed a giveaway to promote the celebration and build goodwill. The American Telephone "breakup" case had been settled some years before and I was able to get a quantity of obsolete AT&T stock certificates which had been discarded. I sent them to a jigsaw puzzle manufacturer who turned them into a puzzle and prepared them for mailing. We created an ad with a picture of the puzzle certificate with several pieces missing and sent it out to clients. The headline was "Call us. We'll help you put it all together." We let clients know that we could handle financial plans, self-directed IRAs and Keogh plans. We stimulated interest in the 4,000 stocks we were trading at that time. The return label was a big puzzle piece. These were popular, and we sent them all over the country.

The June 15th anniversary dinner followed, and the Carlyle Hotel was beautiful. It was a time for visiting and remembering, and people from the other offices had a chance to catch up with old friends. Before dinner we took a photo of the shareholders and my father was seated in the center of the first row, a moving moment for him and his partners. In all, 36 of the 38 shareholders attended, four women among them. Each shareholder received a Tiffany clock engraved with an anniversary message as well as the special menus we had created for the event. It was a fitting celebration of the collective efforts of those gathered, and we savored each course.

This was a significant moment for me, and I repeatedly fought back tears. We were ending an era and starting a new one. The evening was so much more than a dinner. It was a ceremony which marked the passing of the firm from my father and his generation to the younger generation, a moving and momentous event witnessed by my mother, my brother Bill, his wife Carol and Diana. I was the first person to speak, and I began by saying that everyone in the room, except my father, had begun working for the firm after me. The young people on the desk had been born after I started, in 1959. I had interviewed most of the people in the room, but none of those interviews was as short as mine, nor were any of them less well prepared for the opportunity than I had been. I had an ace up my sleeve, however, and that was Diana, and she had always been immensely helpful. For the first time publicly, I shared the story of my misstep with Key Color and how I had almost put the firm out of business. I emphasized that by maintaining high standards of integrity and soundness, we could come to work each day without anxiety, confident that the firm would endure. I told them how Louis Weingarten had shorted 200 Bzura Chemical at 5, and covered it at 14, making short selling prohibited until Irwin joined us. I made some comparisons with the past. Employees then 5, now 366, capital $25,000, now $20 million, stocks traded then 40, now 3,500, trades then 4, now 6,000 a day. I recalled how Irwin and I had gone to our first STANY dinner and sat in the back of the room, not knowing anyone, and how now, only a few weeks ago, we had a table in the center of the room. I gave credit to them for making me a hero. I told them of my well-established reputation as a dreamer, and how with their help, I could remain that way. I remarked how proud I was to see them each progress from apparent anxiety to self-confidence, self-reliance, and achievement. I was deeply thankful. I let them know that their success was a great gift to me. I hoped they would enjoy the scrapbooks, and urged them to look back and learn about the firm they had built. I called the books a gift to and from my father, a celebration of the seeds he planted in 1926 that had flourished, and brought satisfaction and accomplishment to so many people. This was a gift from a grateful son to a loving father, in trust for all of us, a tremendous idea that grew to become an enterprise that was now bigger than any of us. I said thank you, and sat down, to big applause as everyone stood up.

My father stood, and thanked everyone, praising their efforts. He was deeply moved, and with his remarks and blessing, the firm was passed on to the next generation seated before him. He received warm applause. I felt very sorry that Abraham Geduld was not with us that night, but his wife Sylvia was there, as was her daughter Eileen Zaglin. It was emotional and heartwarming.

There was also good news when Mike Price was the subject of a beautiful piece in *Forbes*, and the firm was mentioned in a complimentary manner. But we remained preoccupied with the need for firm capital and the need for a buffer for unexpected eventualities. Very quietly we had engaged Goldman Sachs to represent us in finding a suitable acquirer, a decision we reached with difficulty. Their original pitch book about the firm was dated December 1985. During the first half of the year, Goldman identified a prospective buyer, Smith New Court in London, the Rothschild firm. Negotiations quickly moved forward and by November, it was time for a face to face meeting in London. There were five on our team, and we prepared diligently. Discussions carried on over several meetings, with a purchase price of two times book value, then about $50 million on the table. We were pleased with the number, but we tried to be good poker players. When we thought there was general agreement, they started to question some of our numbers. At first, we thought it was just a minor misunderstanding.

As drinks were poured, the hour grew late and some personalities flared. We could not satisfy their concerns with some of our numbers. The deal tanked. We went home empty handed, except for some continuing education in the art of deal making. We learned from the experience, and kept making markets as before.

A major surprise awaited us. The NASD had been monitoring quotations entered into Nasdaq, and they were questioning several entries by one of our traders. We responded with all the information they requested, and then went to Washington with our counsel for a meeting. They were unrelenting, and it was apparent that they wanted to make an example of a leading firm, and send a message to the larger trading community. We were that firm. Succumbing to personal financial pressures brought on by family problems, one of our traders had, in fact, entered fraudulent prices for one of his positions to avoid markdowns. This allowed him to draw money from his account. All this came out, and the NASD insisted on making this infraction public. They said to me at the meeting: "We expect a higher standard from a firm like yours." I had no choice but to accept their assessment. They held us in high regard, and this was the first regulatory criticism the firm had ever received. I was bruised, but I understood what they meant, and took it as a compliment. On the plane home from Washington, thinking about this situation and the remark they had made, the necessity of an Annual Compliance Review was born. We asked each department manager in the firm to prepare for questions from me and Tony Geraci, our Compliance Director. This proved successful and remained a part of the firm's activities for the rest of our business life. We could uncover problems before the regulators found them.

October also brought the unexpected news that Max Heine had decided to resign as Chairman of the Board of the firm after ten years in that position. This meant a change for me, as I would become Chairman, and Buzzy would become President. This was well timed and the transition was popular with everyone. After nearly thirty years, I was comfortable with this. One beneficial result of our near sale in London was my renewed appreciation of Buzzy's loyalty. He unfalteringly looked after my interests throughout the negotiation. Our relationship had matured. We were a good fit with no rough edges.

Thanksgiving turkeys were given to every employee shortly afterward, and the year seemed to be headed toward a quiet conclusion. It was not to be. We got a call from the NASD informing us that they would be publicly announcing the news about our fraudulent Nasdaq quotations shortly. We had previously alerted the firm with a letter explaining the problems, and when the news finally came, it was received with understanding, which was a relief.

It was a challenging year. We worked hard, and stayed true to our principles. We had not achieved all the results we desired, but we were satisfied with our honest efforts.

The torch was passed, and it was clear that the way business was done would be changing dramatically. It was the year of insider trading scandals, with Ivan Boesky paying $100 million in penalties and fines, a figure that produced gasps of disbelief. There was also much more activity with Glass Steagall headed for obsolescence after Goldman Sachs made a deal with Sumitomo Bank, challenging the rules which prevented banks from engaging in the securities business. Responding to new competition from Nasdaq, the New York and American Exchanges implemented rule changes that would make them more attractive to issuers. London went ahead with Big Bang, which meant that fixed commissions were abolished, and all members could act as brokers and principals. An electronic system similar to Nasdaq was adopted, very big steps. The SEC prepared for globalization, as many predicted that companies might list their stocks in London, forsaking American markets. Index arbitrage was quite new, and there were many theoretical issues to be resolved about new products, and whether these synthetic securities would help the markets. Many firms were shopping for capital, trying to make deals, knowing that to survive, they needed assets beyond the resources of the old-line partnerships. Kidder Peabody & Co., one of the old American houses of issue, sold 80% of its stock to General Electric. Morgan Stanley named its first female managing director. Drug use was proliferating at every level on the Street, and many firms initiated drug testing for their employees. Dillon Read & Co. was acquired by Travelers Corp. for $157.5 million. The highest capital prize for the year went to Salomon Bros. at $2.32 billion, when they agreed to a buyout from trading firm Phibro, yielding outgoing Salomon Bros. head John Gutfreund $3.1 million in compensation. In Washington President Reagan convinced Congress to lower tax rates and eliminate some loopholes.

CHAPTER 18

The Year of the Crash of 1987

The New Year began, and we remained busy. The good news was that the January trading profit was a record, $7,551,000. It was a nice way to start the year. Then old concerns came back, and we discussed them at a stockholders meeting at India House on February 4th. We analyzed the Smith New Court Deal, and we affirmed that it was a great learning experience. We concluded that we would not compromise when it came to price and the resulting loss of independence. We remained open-minded and the consensus was that we would agree to a deal to obtain access to capital, gain international connections, and monetize the value of our computer capabilities. We were sure that other deals would come along, and that we would act when terms were best for the stockholders and the firm. We talked about the impact of program trading that had contributed to recent confusing market swings. Insider trading rumors were proliferating and the Stock Exchange was becoming more vigorous in trying to prevent abuses. We discussed the best ways to avoid entanglement and vowed to be vigilant and faithful to the principles which had served us well. We redoubled our efforts in this area and I made sure that everyone understood that we would do everything necessary to adhere to the basic NASD requirement to "create, maintain and enforce" proper policies to protect the firm and its customers. I expected perfection in this area, and I made it understood that if there were questions, a senior manager needed to be consulted immediately. As we predicted, volume levels remained far higher than many expected and we saw the impact in increased block trading activity.

Buzzy gained a second presidency, this time of the Security Traders Association of New York, and we made several new officer appointments at the firm. At this point, we employed 400 and did about 9,000 trades each day of which 2,500 were fully automated through Auto-Ex, where we were the leaders once again. We then decided to upgrade our systems to handle up to 15,000 trades per day with 5,000 automated. On the heels of our biggest trading month ever, we remained cautious, raised the prospect that bad days would come back and made sure we were prepared. We continued to build the firm carefully, aspired to be bulletproof, and prepared for whatever the future held.

In mid-February, there were arrests by the U. S. Attorney at Goldman Sachs and Kidder Peabody, and these proved unsettling to the Street on several counts. It was as much the way the arrests were carried out as the allegations. The media feasted on the sight of the ritual "perp" walk as traders flashed handcuffs below their English cotton shirt sleeves. It was riveting, stunning and so out of place on the Street. We watched in disbelief, and it reinforced what we had talked about at the stockholders meeting, sharpening our obsession with compliance in every aspect of our business. As a National Securities Clearing Corporation Board Member, I gained insight into developing problems before they became generally known. We were not alone in planning for the unexpected. We joined other firms in creating "What if?" scenarios, except now we were speculating about events that were once considered remote. I challenged the firm to consider the possibilities. How did risk trading positions relate to capital? What were the clearing business problems, and how could they be handled in a crisis? We formed a small credit committee that began to evaluate new accounts, and measure the risks in new products we were contemplating.

I had developed a relationship with Bob Bishop, a senior vice president at the Stock Exchange in charge of Regulatory Quality Review and Long Range Planning. My conversations with him gave the firm a big head start in many areas which were to quickly become important. By April, our crisis planning committee developed a robust agenda of scenarios, and we crafted responses to each possibility. Reports of our position exposure by trader were scrutinized by several people. We discovered that the unrealized profit in arbitrage positions in the trader's accounts was 67% of the firm's total unrealized profit for the first three months of the year. This was excessive, and we began to liquidate some of these as opportunities came along.

As STANY president, Buzzy had been working conscientiously. He shared comments after the annual dinner in April, and with 2,700 attendants his audience was the organization's largest ever. His demeanor was statesmanlike and his remarks fitting for the time and climate. He brought attention to the fact that traders served not only the markets, but each other and the investing public. He inspired the membership to pursue higher standards of fair dealing and initiatives that would increase transparency. Buzzy's remarks resonated as did Kenny Loggins' tunes that provided the evening's entertainment. Letters of congratulations swiftly followed as did reservations for the following year's event. I was proud of my partner and the firm.

Our story was reaching not only the financial press, but also general interest publications. These efforts clearly echoed the conservative point of view of my father, and this was a good reminder that in the trading business, the risks are always there, through bull and bear markets alike. We lived with those fears, and as partners we had all benefitted. When *Institutional Investor* published their list of firms ranked by excess net capital, at $9.9 million the firm rose to the 79th position up from 91 the previous year. This was a national ranking, and an important indication of financial strength. Then our automated execution system was chosen by Citicorp's "Streetsense" division, and we were delighted that "Auto-Ex" was in the spotlight. I was quoted saying prophetically that "Ongoing evolutionary changes in the industry required that all firms remain on the cutting edge of technology." In June, Buzzy and I were featured in a story about our new titles in *The Market Chronicle*, with additional reporting on Buzzy's expansion of institutional order flow. *Crain's* of June 29th carried a story about our plans to open an office in London, with a photo of Buzzy and me in the trading room. *Forbes* carried a major story about how the over-the-counter market had come of age, and Buzzy and I were quoted generously. This exposure was well earned. It validated our hard work and we aimed to increase it. As my grandfather used to say, "It is easier to live up to a good reputation than to live down a bad one."

Despite the good press and our continued progress, I recall this was an unnerving time, and most Americans joined me in this opinion. Companies re-structured at the behest of corporate raiders, at times in opposition to their managements. Our great industrial cities found themselves bereft of jobs and the tax base they relied upon. Globalization became a buzzword and there was a general impatience. Time frames suffered from compression as investors sought quick gratification. In the trading community, talk of a trading account passed around the world each day got a lot of attention, but the normal skepticism soon placed this idea on a back burner. It all felt strange, and there was an unexpressed anxiety about financial news. The markets proceeded but the storm clouds went unnoticed.

On Friday October 16th, I had been asked to speak to a meeting of the board of The Knox School in St. James, Long Island, where our daughter Sarah was a student. Despite my anxiety and mindful of my audience, I shared my optimism about the near-term future. Following lunch, I headed back to Brooklyn and the news was not good. The Dow-Jones was down 108.35, 4.6%. I wondered what they thought of my talk now, given the news of the day. How could someone supposedly so knowledgeable be so wrong? The markets were already down from their August highs, so the big drop seemed excessive. I was wrong.

The weekend passed uneasily. On Monday, prices opened lower as pandemonium gripped the trading room. Every light on our turrets was lit, and it was impossible to answer all the phones. Traders were overwhelmed with sell orders, and everyone was yelling, trying to get meaningful price indications from traders on the other side of the room. It was grueling, exhausting and unprecedented with disbelief yielding to relief only after the lagging tape indicated that trading had closed. The damage was inconceivable with the Dow down 508, or 22.61%, a spectacular figure, with the closing Dow Average standing at 1738.74. Nothing approaching this had ever happened during the lifetimes of most who witnessed the carnage.

My father's words echoed prophetically: "1929 will be back, and the values will melt away, the way sand goes through your fingers at the beach." It was harsh, unexpected, a breath-taking blow. Totally unexplainable, a humbling failure of control, it was a dreadful uncontrollable loss. On the day of the Crash, my friend from London, Barry Olliff, was in New York, and he came to our office. While in my office, he told me that an underwriting his firm was to complete that day would not go forward, as the buyers had stepped away, and no longer wanted the stock. Barry's firm, however, was committed to their client, and this led to a substantial loss which had ramifications for years afterward. I joined Barry in second-guessing. Was this debacle something that could have been foreseen and hedged, or dealt with in some more conservative way than a standard underwriting agreement? Perhaps, but no one saw it coming.

October 19th is our wedding anniversary, and months before I had made dinner reservations at The Quilted Giraffe, a very fashionable restaurant of that time. I went into Diana's office, still reeling from the trading room environment. She gazed at me and said she didn't think I looked like someone who would appreciate a fancy, expensive dinner. I agreed. Then she told me not to worry, that she would call the restaurant to cancel the reservation. When her call was answered, she explained that her husband was a broker, and because of the market crash, we would have to cancel our reservation. The voice on the other end then said, "Don't worry, lady, all our reservations have been cancelled!" It was peanut butter and jelly with tea for us that night, the quietest anniversary of our long marriage.

The culprits were quickly identified: the sudden meltdown, an unintended consequence of new program trading techniques, and something called portfolio insurance. Both were innovative and gaining popularity. These strategies were conceived to curb excess risk, said to be the fault of misguided traders. Now we would be guided by algorithms and automation, but they were too popular. When positions had to be liquidated, the exits were overrun with massive imbalances adding to the excruciating selling pressure. Once the damage was done, commentators could explain the danger, but none saw it coming. Economist Lawrence Summers urged us to consider the budget deficit and the high value of the dollar, but we were unconvinced. Neither of these was new or logically the cause of a single day loss in value of 22% of all listed stocks.

The damage for us, at over $1 million, was material. Undaunted, Buzzy's leadership was calming and encouraging. Without denying the magnitude of what had happened, he remained steadfast, and did his best to make us feel better. This was very important and effective. He made us feel at ease in a difficult situation. All around there was a lot of anxiety, but we kept on making markets and worked stubbornly to meet the needs of our customers. I called Jim Tobin, our subordinated lender, to let him know what had happened with us, and not to worry. He told me later that we were the only borrower who had thought to call, and he was grateful for my consideration. He mentioned this again over twenty years later.

On a personal level, I was plenty anxious. My father's stern warnings reverberated in my mind like a giant headache. I slept uneasily and woke the following morning to the voice of a National Public Radio announcer informing the public about the yen-dollar relationship. I was stunned. The yen-dollar relationship was complex, cryptic and as a rationale for recent events, surely beyond the grasp of any audience outside a graduate business school. It brought to mind an idea I had been thinking about for some time. From my industry experience on committees, and personal observations over many years, I realized that Americans did not understand the capital markets, despite their impact upon every aspect of our lives. Finance is a mystery to most of us, and given recent events, that mystery was giving way to fear.

For me, it was an old idea that suddenly became timely. There should be some place for the public to go to learn about these things. My old idea gained greater clarity following the Crash, and I began to explore the possibility of a museum dedicated to the study of American finance. There was a need for a museum that would celebrate the importance of the capital markets and provide education and context to the morning's business news. I had been a collector of historic documents since 1959, especially those issued to finance the American Revolution. I knew Americans had never had an opportunity to see them, and knew little about those directly responsible for creating America's financial infrastructure, starting with founding father Alexander Hamilton. My thought was to display select, curated objects from my collection within accessible, but historically accurate exhibits authored by leading financial scholars. With trained docents and teaching resources, we could make these stories compelling and relevant to current events.

A friend introduced me to the person in charge of the Custom House, the beautiful Beaux Arts building at the bottom of Broadway, recently restored by the federal government. We had a meeting there during which I shared my idea. When I had finished my pitch, I got the answer: "All right, Herzog, we'll give you free space for three months, and you can see if anyone agrees with you." I wasn't expecting anything so positive or definitive, or immediate, and I realized this was something I would have to think about carefully.

It took me months to work through the issues, calculate the expenses, talk with people more experienced about museum work, and generally get used to the idea. At the end, one question kept coming back to me: Assuming the cost was reasonable, and the effort manageable, how would I feel in five or ten years if I passed on the opportunity? I decided it would be better to try it and get the dream out of my system. If I failed, I'd move on knowing that I tried. I notified the Custom House representative that I would go ahead.

The exhibit venue was to be the handsome Collector's Office, and the first exhibit of the Museum of American Finance opened in January 1989. It was a retrospective beginning in England, coming to the American Colonies, and moving through the years to the Liberty Bond drives of the First World War. Objects for the exhibit were borrowed from the Federal Reserve Bank, the New York Stock Exchange, Depository Trust Company and several brokerage firms. About 1,000 people saw that exhibit. I was very pleased and my anxiety about the museum's future dissolved quickly. The exhibit and the origins of the new idea were covered in the media. People said it was well executed and worthwhile. When it was over, people encouraged me to continue, and some meetings were held which led to the first exhibit ever to commemorate Alexander Hamilton and his establishing America's financial infrastructure, the envy of the world. The museum continues, a story for later pages.

We were lucky. The recovery from the Crash was rapid, and we continued to progress. Our net worth figure on December 31st was larger than it was on September 30th, so we had repaired the damage done by the Crash and strengthened our capital position. Thinking this formidable performance might sway Smith New Court to reconsider, we reached out to them again, but there was no interest. We would lack a suitor and a poet laureate. Harry Snyder passed away.

Our Managers Group meeting on November 4th had plenty on its agenda, including 750 uncompared trades to consider. These were trades where we could not agree with our counterparty as to the precise terms. The NSTA had also been busy, and a special meeting with the NASD staff was held on Saturday, October 31, at which several important decisions were made. It was decided that capital requirements would be raised for market makers. They moved to hasten completion of the ACT system to provide same day comparison for trades, and mandated that all National Market System participants be members of NSCC, greatly easing settlement procedures. There were other actions taken with respect to various Nasdaq procedures designed to expose more orders to the system.

The SIA reminded members that the industry needed to keep pace with settlements in spite of the 2.3 billion shares which changed hands during the week of the Crash, double the volume of the week before, which was also a record. Delivery hours were modified, and there were some Saturday openings of various facilities to help operations departments, and they were told to expect to work overtime! The QT problem (Questioned Trades) had risen to 60,000 from a normal daily average of 15,000 for all firms. NSCC daily transaction volume during this busy week went to 2,500,000 from an average of 700,000. By the end of the month, things were getting back to normal, but all sorts of upgrades to systems and computer power were slated for early 1988.

A story about Buzzy, "Trading with a Passion," appeared on the front page of the *Security Traders Handbook* on December 8th. Buzzy was quoted,

"Stocks have entered a new era, and the market we see today is different than we've ever seen before. I'm hopeful that the worst is over but who can say for sure." He spoke about the excitement of trading, and how he remained calm during the worst days of the Crash. "He's a very customer oriented person who has always put the needs of his customer ahead of his own personal goals. He firmly believes that's the only way to do business. And based on that, he has built a reputation over the years that is virtually unmatched in the industry," commented Hugh Quigley, OTC Trading Manager at Merrill Lynch. It was gratifying to have our clients read this, especially after the strain of the Crash. We braced for the volatile markets that would follow.

CHAPTER 19

In the Aftermath

As the New Year began, people were still catching their breath from the Crash. There were many questions to be answered, and no shortage of industry experts, committees and reporters trying to make sense of all we witnessed. For us, it had been a confusing and scary time, but we knew there would be more change. We tried to prepare ourselves, and the first thing we did was take stock. At this point the trading department was functioning but volume was down. Other basic elements of the firm were intact. We had 25 clearing accounts, and things were as close to normal as possible in a post-Crash world. Business continued in our other specialized areas. Employees seemed content, and glad to still be working. We decided not to sacrifice our trained workers just because volume was down, and this allayed anxiety. Keeping with our practice, we awarded thirty bonuses for perfect attendance in the form of a week's salary. This was well received around the firm and helped to maintain a high degree of commitment.

The Street was placed under a magnifying glass by many experts, politicians and regulators anxious to advocate for the small investor and eager to identify those factors which could be blamed for the downdraft. It was as if identifying the culprits would not only avoid a repetition, but somehow restore customer account values. President Reagan quickly convened a three-person commission under the leadership of his future Treasury Secretary Nicholas F. Brady, who served as CEO of Dillon Read before entering public service. The Brady Commission commenced as fearful public investors shied away from the market. Prices meandered and volume decreased. Villains emerged, but they were faceless. Fingers were pointed at new technology-enabled trading strategies and undecipherable transactions which employed futures and options that turned mere sell-offs into routs. The public responded by staying away. Volume decreased, and prices remained at uninteresting levels. Talk of inflation competed with concerns about deflation and the result was confusion. Trade figures were also bad, and in May, during a two-day period, the Dow Jones was down just under 57 points, enough to prompt Robert A. Mintz of Mintz, Wolff & Co. to comment, "The pessimism's pretty thick."

STANY captured the impressions of traders by videotaping their personal views and several taping sessions were held in Buzzy's office. These interviews were the basis of a feature on the OTC market in *Traders Magazine*. Mount & Nadler helped us prepare for these sessions by writing questions that would be used to stimulate discussion. Several traders spoke of the fragility of the marketplace, and the need for automation and capital commitments in excess of levels previously contemplated. Traders sensed that retail investors were uninformed, and pointed to the surprising number of buy orders from the public during the day of the Crash despite the absence of reliable pricing. Questions were raised again about the carrying value of positions, and how "haircuts" should be determined for capital calculation purposes.

Two news stories of note appeared in *The New York Times*, "O-T-C Issues: New Wariness" by Leonard Sloane on November 28, 1987, and "Let's Reform the O-T-C Market" by Muriel F. Siebert, November 27, 1987. This prompted my unpublished letter to the editor of January 20, 1988 in which I attempted to explain recent events from an OTC insider's perspective.

The calamity helped us in a way. Since we were intact, we could expand by recruiting brokers from firms which had problems, or ceased operations. By weathering the storm, our importance and credibility advanced. I advocated for OTC firms at the Stock Exchange as a member of the Regional Firms Advisory Committee, where an "over-the-counter view of life" was rarely voiced.

Bad news came to us all when we learned of the tragic death of Max Heine who was killed in a traffic accident while vacationing in the southwest. This loss added to the general sense of uncertainty many of us felt at the time. Operationally, there was a smooth transition to his capable partner. Mike Price assumed Max's responsibilities at Mutual Shares.

Another important step forward for the firm was the recognition of our need for a general counsel. We brought Charles "Chris" Christofilis into the firm in April after many years in private practice. Chris was very effective and helpful from the start. We could reduce legal bills and decrease response times on many issues.

As volume and profits decreased, we formed an expense committee to analyze every expense line to see where we might make some savings. This worked, and we realized savings which would have been overlooked otherwise. In September, we had a mandatory four-day work week, which allowed us to avoid layoffs and terminations. We targeted monthly savings on the order of $55,000, and we also looked to change the arrangements we had with certain traders. We didn't stop investing in marketing and promotion. We designed special brochures for our clearing and execution services and updated our retail and corporate brochures.

Correctly, traders concluded that the typical public investor was uninformed and emotional. When invested during a sudden rout or prolonged swoon, they quickly became discouraged. Some would respond by selling everything and steering clear of the stock market. Others were numbed by losses and remained inactive, licking their wounds and puzzling over what to do next. Expert opinions rendered the morning after did not help the average investor cope with losses. Investment professionals had weathered these storms before, but the industry could not convince the public to stay the course, find values and think long term. It was no different during the periodic updrafts when cautionary advice would find deaf ears. The industry was always left holding the bag after such events. For a firm to survive it needed to be nimble.

In August, the NASD published a survey, "Investor Attitudes in the spring of 1988," based on interviews with 1,000 individual investors in a nationwide sample. The work was done by Opinion Research Corporation. The report characterized individual customers as being confident about their own financial prospects but more guardedly optimistic about prospects for the stock market. Half of the respondents had made new investments since the Crash, and said they were pleased with the performance of their brokers. They were only casually interested in supporting proposals to reform the markets, probably because they really did not understand them to begin with. They revealed that they were confused by the array of investment products like futures, options, new issues and the smaller growth oriented companies which they saw as risky. The survey predictably indicated that the Crash led people to alter their investments from what they felt were riskier to more conservative holdings. It is well accepted Wall Street wisdom that retail investors always react this way. It takes time for the painful memories to subside and for enthusiasm and confidence to return anew.

On December 15th, Mike Price led an event he planned to commemorate the life of his late partner. The reception, at the Stern School of New York

University, honored the naming of Professor Edward I. Altman, the first Max L. Heine Professor of Finance. This was a grand event with remarks by Mike Price and a gracious acceptance by Ed Altman, who many of us knew from his visits to the office. This tribute was a fitting way to keep Max in our thoughts, and the Chair has been very successful, owing to the great erudition of Ed Altman.

I scheduled an important managers meeting. Borrowing from lessons learned while pursuing my Master's degree, and an article I read in *Management Review*, I tasked each manager with completing a self-evaluation they were to bring to the meeting. My goal was to have the group address the need to cut costs and refine operations for maximum efficiency.

We reviewed the corporate officer lineup. Outside of the trading department there were 29 officer titles, and one of them was a woman, Donna Connolly, our Controller. In the trading department, there were 26 Assistant Vice Presidents and 6 were women. We monitored the progress of all our officers, and our longer-term plan was to give them the opportunity to become stockholders.

In April, Mike Price spoke at a conference on bankruptcy. The conference was sponsored by the Max L. Heine Chair at the NYU Stern School, with Ed Altman moderating. He remarked that that the study of bankrupt securities had become "a serious, analytical endeavor." This event was very well attended, and Price's presentation served to further strengthen the firm's reputation. There was more good news when we announced that the group of institutional professionals trading under the name of duPasquier & Co. would leave Moore & Schley and join our firm. Some of their people worked in New York, but the larger group was in Paris. This was our firm's first branch outside the United States, and it was a high quality addition. We felt very comfortable with this group, as they were experienced, having begun in the early 1950s. This had been a highly profitable business for Moore & Schley, and Dorothy Moran, their manager in New York, was superb. I was asked to go to Paris with Dorothy to meet the firm.

As knowledge of our success with the COLT system spread, there were requests for more information, and Walter Raquet was the main presenter. He had worked tirelessly on the system and on making modifications which allowed automated order routing. Our expertise enabled us to utilize COLT for proprietary purposes which saved time and made our traders more efficient. Walter spoke at The Technology in Trading Conference organized by Arthur

D. Little & Co. in April. Walter remarked that improvements in trading technology in the last five years had far exceeded improvements accomplished during the previous fifty years. He predicted far greater changes in the near future.

Our Annual Meeting of Shareholders was held at India House on May 16th and there was a lot to report. Speaking first, I summarized the year's important developments. There was no shortage of anxiety, but we were making solid progress, notwithstanding a widely-read front page article in *The New York Times* of Sunday, May 7th headlined "Why Wall Street's So Topsy Turvy." We operated profitably and our excess net capital was understated at about $38 million. We had maintained our overhead at the previous year's level and added new computer interfaces with six firms. Our compliance and legal areas had been greatly strengthened, and we had opened a new Short Hills office where Mike Price worked. Our retail production was increasing nicely, and we added 14 new producers since the Crash. We had 7 new clearing accounts and our involvement in Paris was an "ooh la la" with $70,000 income in our first month. Our institutional department now had 400 accounts and it was growing. There were 412 people in the firm, and we were just three years past our 60th anniversary. Diana and I had been to Tokyo, where I visited Yamaichi Securities, and made stops in Hong Kong, Bangkok and London.

Firm members served the industry, attracting attention to the firm and themselves. Buzzy was on the boards of STANY, the Security Traders Association, a member of the SOES Users and Review committees, the OTC Trading Committee and the SIA Institutional Committee. Tony was on the Uniform Practice Committee of the NASD, the Buy-In, ACT, Special Projects for the NSCC and an NASD Arbitrator. Walter was on the SIA NY Area Firms, Regional Firms, and spoke at various conferences. Donna gave her time to the SIA Firm and Industry Analysis Committee and the NYSE 15C3-3 Committee, and Chris Christofilis was on the SIA Federal Regulation Committee. We had a place at every industry table. We were in demand and our contributions and counsel were sought. I made sure we gave back to our industry.

Donna then gave her financial report. She had become very skilled at hitting the important figures in an interesting way. She kept it brief and took several questions. Harvey Wacht, manager of our retail business, reported on the performance of our Profit and Pension Plan investments. They surpassed expectations. Then Buzzy took the microphone. Visibly proud though always reserved and cautious, he described the progress in the trading department. Just recently, the Autex share execution volume standings of all firms were published and our firm was again in third place. He was confident and self-assured. He was president of a firm bearing his name and a leader in the industry. He was given a well-deserved hand.

In May, on Kentucky Derby day, we attended the wedding of the daughter of one of our senior traders, Charles Padala. It was in eastern Long Island and Diana and I were having drinks at a local place overlooking the ocean. I vividly remember the Derby running as the waves crashed on the rocks below. Buzzy had a summer home nearby in Quogue, and he invited us to stay overnight after the wedding. This was the first time we had been houseguests of anyone in the business.

We tried to pay attention to employees, and we let each of them know that they were appreciated and vital to our business. Miles Sawyer was no exception. He was a messenger for years, and before joining us he worked on transcontinental trains, Miles was especially proud of his rail career, notably on the train that took the king of Sweden across America. His 85th birthday was coming up, and we arranged a visit to the Stock Exchange floor followed by a party back at the office. The celebration made an important statement to all our employees. Each employee imagined him or herself as an honoree. During the celebration, Donna announced three promotions in her department, two of them women.

The Management Group met in late October and they reflected on a day on which we processed 18,000 trades, three times our normal volume. This was exactly what we had been planning and working towards. All systems worked well. By this time, 45% of our trades were automated. I commented that the market had an increasingly international aspect, something to be wary about. I liked this new business, but I knew laws and practices in other countries were not like those in America. Our firm was now ranked number 20 in the Autex ranking of "ordinary shares," a foreign term for common stocks, and we believed our rank would rise. We were number 15 in the list of ADR (American Depositary Receipts) brokers. Efforts to enhance our trading systems were paying off. We reported to Nasdaq that we had processed 2.75 price changes per second during the heaviest volume periods. Market realities were changing rapidly and some said that the ability of central banks to influence the markets had begun to diminish. Amidst all this change, the public remained poorly informed.

Supporting our retail division, we published "A Selected List of Growth Companies in the Over-the-Counter Market" and it was popular. The Dow

Jones Average was still unsettled. On October 13th, "Black Friday," it was down 190 points. This was troubling, with the financial press blaming the collapse on the United Airlines deal. But we benefitted from the volatility. On October 19th, our one day trading profit was the highest ever, at $817,000. Sometimes things work out just the way you imagined. This was a fabulous figure. My thoughts were of my father and how he might have responded.

Sad news followed. My mother passed on October 29th. It was a terrible blow for me, even though her health had not been good for some time. She suffered from a heart condition, which came with all the prohibitions of activities and foods she enjoyed. One day during a visit to the doctor in which we both anticipated the sad outcome, the doctor told her to "enjoy herself, and get a corned beef sandwich," a pleasure she denied herself for years. She took the advice and relished it. She taught me a great deal, especially about how to manage, which she did so well. She taught me about antiques and collecting, and sharpened my enthusiasm and curiosity, gifts I've enjoyed every day of my life. She also taught me about people, and ways to help them quietly and sensitively. She taught me that giving was a privilege. She taught me respect for all people, always, in all places. She was a wonderful friend all my life, encouraging me, disciplining, criticizing in a constructive way that conveyed her love, never diminished by life's disappointments or some innocent misdeed on my part. From my mother, I learned to understand and value women, their wonderful sensitivity and ability to understand and lovingly share the problems of others. The bond we had was so strong and deep that it took me 25 years before I could reopen boxes of my parents' belongings to sort them out. I was extremely lucky, and I have known it for many years.

As pressing family urgencies waned, there was news that Kidder Peabody had limited program trading for its own account, and Merrill Lynch had stopped it, heeding complaints which had grown more vocal. This was fully two years after this new type of trading had been identified as a major cause of the Crash. The delay was unexplainable. As Wall Street was advising on the needs of its clients, it became apparent that it scarcely noticed its own weaknesses. Many firms were poorly managed and this sustained the skepticism of the investing public.

Kurt Rosenberg was a typewriter repair man without a future when we found each other. Bob Meli trained him to be a highly trusted messenger, giving Kurt and his family a comfortable living for many years. His 70th birthday was a reason for us all to share in his celebration.

Irwin had been successful in the Miami office, and in early December we moved to expanded offices at One Turnberry Place. At a time when many firms were contracting we were expanding our basic trading business. There was space there to develop a retail business, but we were careful, and stuck with our primary business.

Just before Christmas there was a tumult going on right outside our office at Bowling Green. Arturo DiModica, the sculptor of the now world famous "Charging Bull" had left his sculpture under the Christmas tree outside the Stock Exchange on Broad Street. This splendid gift was eschewed by the Exchange, and Arturo had to pay to remove it as soon as possible. It was in Queens for a couple of days, but then found a resting place at Bowling Green through the courtesy of Parks Commissioner Henry Stern and Mayor Ed Koch. The appearance of "Charging Bull" was exciting for everyone. Widely covered by the media, the bull attracted incessant crowds from all over the world and it has become a great favorite over the ensuing twenty-five years. In 2014, a film was made commemorating DiModica and one of the most famous icons in the world. The film, called "Lucky Balls," was shown at the Museum of American Finance for the first time to an enthusiastic invitation-only audience. And from our offices, we enjoyed the scene rain or shine, every single day.

As soon as 1990 was out of swaddling clothes, people began talking about the year 2000, and what a problem it might be for the entire securities industry. There were dire forecasts about how the century change would confound many systems, and that the changed millennial digit would necessitate new software. Experts said it would take a decade's preparation to be sure everything went through without a hitch. Then, like the end of winter and the spring thaw, these concerns dissolved for most of us, but a special team at the firm began to work silently on these long-term problems.

We benefitted from an article in the January "Personal Investor" in which bankruptcy securities were high-lighted. Mike Price, Peter Faulkner and Jim Malespina, an assistant vice president with the firm all commented on this fascinating area. Bankruptcy securities were of interest to me ever since I got a big check for F. L. Jacobs preferred after the company emerged from the shadows. We had become well known for railroad reorganizations with Max Heine and Hans Jacobson, two highly skilled and thoughtful traders of these securities, and it was a natural progression for the firm to become more involved in the bankruptcy field. We were once again fortunate in being noticed by the media, and especially so in a publication aimed at private clients, a part of the business we were hoping to expand beyond the 100,000 accounts on our books.

Interest rates are always being studied and their anticipated moves carefully conjectured. Now Hans Jacobson suggested Northern Pacific 3% bonds due 2047. The issue offered a good yield and a long maturity. His report was issued after Alan Greenspan gave testimony on the outlook for long term interest rates. He said that it was quite possible that rates would decline to 2.5%–3%, and in Jacobson's view this would mean that the Northern Pacific bonds would increase in value, providing the investor with a good short term income, over 8%, and long term capital gains. We were producing ideas such as this on a regular basis, and our retail business was growing.

The year had a dreadful event for me, and for the firm, as my father passed away on April 27th. Our founder was no longer with us, and many in the firm who had known him felt very sad. He was 89, and not at all well the last two years, when he no longer responded to me. I spoke at his funeral, and shared some anecdotal stories. When I was working on my Master's thesis, I found a check-book showing my father's weekly draw of $75; 40 years later, his draw was still $75. When I started trading, and would buy some stock, he would ask me, "Got a spot for those, sonny?" He was still going around the trading room asking traders the same question. He taught me how to take risks, and he taught me about people. Once, in the early days, he made a big trade and the day ended up with a $750 profit. He said to me proudly, "You should have 2 or 3 days like that each week." I loved his plain, straightforward ways. Losing him was a great emotional shock for me then, and for years afterwards, I would suddenly feel like picking up the telephone and calling him to relate some news I knew he would enjoy. His pride in what we had accomplished was like a warm blanket over all the firm, because he knew from vivid experience and from many personal sacrifices he had made, how important each person's contribution was. He loved a small number of people deeply. He was a quiet, determined and patient man. He would tell me "The mill of the gods grinds slowly." With difficulty, I emptied and closed their apartments, and as part of this process, I gave each stockholder in the firm an object from among my parents' belongings, each with my hand-written letter on his engraved stationery. I felt this would complete the transfer of the firm from the earlier generation to the present generation. The stockholders were deeply moved by these gifts, and I still get calls from some of them and they let me know they have the cuff links, or whatever, and think of my father and of me whenever they wear them.

Bob Meli's 70th birthday was a reason to celebrate. He started in the early days of low volume and handwritten records. He contributed to the growth and witnessed the great changes with pride, as volume and profits mounted. He endured a time of mandatory 10 percent salary reductions just so we could survive and keep trading. He had trained many of the clerks who then moved on to become important operations people. He had quietly gotten his degree in accounting because he knew he should have it, and never told me until he showed me his class ring and his diploma. We had a lovely party for him, and there were many complimentary words of appreciation for all he had given to so many different people. He was respected and close to many people he worked with long after he retired.

Experts continued to speculate on the conditions that produced the Crash. Walter Wriston, the chairman of Citicorp from 1967 until 1984, was critical of banking regulations, unchanged since the Roosevelt era. They prevented diversification of the asset base, and limited geographical diversification. He agreed with Paul Volcker that banks should earn interest on their reserve deposits with the Fed.

In the retail area, Harvey Wacht was creating new products and services, notably a Rule 144 Sales service which helped many founders and insiders reduce the holding time required to sell their unregistered shares. This was successful. In Miami, a twice-told tale was again recited as Bob Manghir joined the trading department there.

Finally, there were the inevitable comparisons between where we were as a firm in 1980, and where we had come by 1990. Here are some of the main numbers: Number of employees: 25 vs. 412; Stockholders Equity: $6.5 million vs. $34 million; office space: 7,000 square feet vs. 65,000.

The trading room did not accommodate new technology well or easily, and the 100 people who worked there coped with poor acoustics. We were in the Standard Oil Building, completed in 1928. It was well known as the one which burned oil on the top during the early days, and the legend that John D. Rockefeller "had money to burn." The interior construction was old and there were several pillars in the trading room obstructing the view. We needed unobstructed floor space. Our lease expired in September 1991, and we had already been thinking about alternatives, but we had no solution. We knew that 108 of our employees lived in New Jersey, and that taxes were lower there. We were now ranked first in the nation for the number of stocks we traded, and had just moved ahead of Merrill Lynch to number 2 in over-the-counter block trading volume. We were well known as the market maker in almost all new issues and secondary offerings, and frequently accounted for 60% of the first day's share volume in those stocks. We were also the leading broker for institutional order flow in over-the-counter stocks, thanks to Buzzy and the increasing appetite for these stocks due to Nasdaq. We had been at the right place at the right time, recognized the opportunities, and acted upon them. We had been very fortunate, and worked very hard. As the year ended, we began an analysis of the issues involved in moving once again to New Jersey. Early work on this project identified a ten-year savings of $19,781,000.

CHAPTER 20

The Early Nineties

We got 65th anniversary stickers and put them on everything. Another milestone approached and we were doing good business. We were confident. The stock market was strong and we had many interesting opportunities for growth.

Walter Raquet had been actively working on a few important issues, and had achieved a good measure of success. In a written summary, he explained his work, and told us exactly what had been happening. Walter led a cost-cutting effort. A committee was formed, and good results ensued. Then Walter had the idea to call our correspondent firms, and initiate a dialogue to deal with issues we were both facing. He did this on a personal basis with each firm, and what began modestly grew into a "Revenue Enhancement and Cost Cutting Survey" which was extremely successful. We showed our correspondents how we were making their interests a priority. The survey was shown to SIA management and they circulated it to their member firms and other important industry figures. In the end, some two hundred firms benefited from this work, and SIA began using the survey at CEO Roundtables. They offered to establish the survey as a continuing program under the auspices of our firm. This was a major contribution to the industry.

The anniversary dinner was held in the Pegasus Suite at the Rainbow Room in Radio City. I spoke and attempted to be witty, but the results were mixed. I admitted to being happy to be able to talk to the captive audience of 144, on an occasion marking a very special year for me. I dismissed the idea that the firm, having reached its retirement age, might be thinking about slowing down. Business had never been better. Our daughter Mary was there, and so was Jodi Geduld, Irwin's daughter, proxies for all the other children.

I recounted the story of General Economics Corp., a stock I was trading which collapsed unexpectedly while I was long instead of short. At the time, I was terribly discouraged, and went to Italy for a short break, answering an ad in the *International Herald Tribune* for a job as a broker in Paris. I got to Bache & Co, and the office of the managing partner was decorated with fine furniture and a big desk with a highly polished walnut top, unadorned, except for my letter. We chatted, and he offered me the job, which at 27, in Paris, sounded pretty good. But I stuck to my decision, and here we are. There were other obstacles on my way to our 65th. I had lunch with George Soros shortly afterward; he advised me to leave my father and get a real job. But I decided to stay, to keep going, and now my perseverance was being rewarded. I continued, speaking from the heart. I shared that for 32 years, my great pleasure, satisfaction and joy has come from hiring promising people, watching their development, and taking pride in their accomplishments. I wanted everyone to know that I could not have had that experience anywhere else.

Buzzy and Irwin said a few words, and then the stockholders posed for a photo, equally memorable for those present and absent. My mother and father and Abraham Geduld had passed in the interim, the gaps filled in a way by six female shareholders. We had matured, endured and succeeded far longer than most, with our principles intact.

The next big event had very little to do with our business, but was eagerly anticipated. It took place on June 11th, when there was a triumphant ticker tape parade up Broadway to celebrate the return of American troops from the Gulf War.

Our office windows provided the perfect vantage point for watching the parade. We let everyone get a peek at the Patriot Missile and Navy jet as they snaked down Broadway. A million people giving thanks to our service men returned from the Gulf War. A glorious, stirring and proud spectacle and we were front row, center. I stared out, grateful for those who kept us safe and free. If only my father could see this. It all felt wonderful to me. While I missed my parents terribly, our family had grown to be a source of great support. Unwavering in her devotion, Diana had always been my best adviser, and the girls were old enough to understand what we were about. They took pride in our accomplishments. My projects were progressing. Our reputation was secure. The firm was big, mature, important, respected. It was an institution, overshadowing any one of us. Midthought, and for the first time, I considered my age. I was the old timer, and that was as it should be.

With the firm at 65, Mount & Nadler had the idea to get an interview of Buzzy and me with an industry publication. *Traders Magazine* responded, and the interview appeared in the October issue. It was titled, "Herzog Heine Geduld at 65." It was a good session, and we covered all the high points. Daily volume of 14,000 trades, trading 4,000 other stocks, and $35 million in position risk each day. After just seven years, our institutional trading activities were highly ranked. We had 100 people involved in trading.

Buzzy elaborated on our growth. He identified several reasons: an explosive increase in trading volume, our well-trained personnel, the decision to enter the institutional trading business, and our investment in systems capable of handling the increased volume. He made it sound simple.

And it may have been simple. We watched, questioned and responded. We saw growing institutional interest in Nasdaq stocks, and adjusted to their needs. We constantly challenged ourselves with the simple question, "What business are we in?" When we found ourselves tempted to stray beyond our competence, we paused. Buzzy called that, "Watching our Ps and Qs." Our economy was increasingly driven by small businesses. Entrepreneurs created jobs. They disturbed, altered and changed the way we bought, sold, served and lived. They needed access to our market, as did the investors who wanted to participate. They both needed us.

The IPO market has always attracted interest, and it had been gaining vitality. Buzzy felt that the secret was "value." If new issues were properly priced, investors could feel comfortable participating, and there would be growth in that market. If there was greed overpricing and hype on the part of the issuers or underwriters, the market would suffer.

Buzzy joined me in singling out October 19, 1987, the day of the Crash, as the most memorable day in our careers. On that day my father's worst fears were realized, but even in the face of that terrible stress, we operated to plan, and our systems held up.

The October issue of *Equities* carried the survey results for "Who Are the Best Traders?" For the 5th year in a row, our firm was voted Number 1 among wholesale firms. Buzzy's leadership was being noticed.

The last week of August was the week of the coup attempt in Russia, and it was the end of a very big month for us with over $10 million in gross profit. We tried to imagine what the next weeks would bring. We sensed that trading activity was going to remain at increased levels. We were gaining prominence, and looking less like a boutique. We were poised to become a firm of influence, and couldn't wait for the next day's action. We had no desire to be complacent, and have opportunities dictate to us. With confidence and clarity of vision we put memories of 1987 aside and planned boldly for growth.

We needed more space. The firm expanded greatly since moving back to the city, and now we were ready to call Ted Moudis, our architect and office designer, once again. We knew we needed a different kind of space, not only larger, but suited to our technology requirements. We surveyed the real estate options, and again they pointed to Jersey City. The possibility of returning to Jersey City influenced our short-term decision making. We were emboldened by our largest one day gross ever — almost $900k on September 20.

Only two days later, a front-page story appeared in *The New York Times* titled "The Narcotic of Crime on Wall Street." The theme of the piece was how systemic abuse of regulations continued, despite ideal business conditions which were allowing most firms to thrive. I was motivated to write a letter which went to every one of our employees. In it I reminded them that every quarter I must sign a letter to our primary regulator, the Stock Exchange, in which I attested to the fact that "everything is as it should be." I wrote that I needed to rely on each employee before I signed my name to that statement. I encouraged people to think of the benefits of working in an atmosphere of integrity, in an interesting and well-paid position. I reminded them that abusing the rules endangered us all. I concluded with a disturbing observation. Despite favorable market conditions which allowed for plentiful honest earnings, there were some who skirted the law to try to "beat the system."

"Finally, I must also let you know that organizationally, we cannot rely on voluntary efforts. We are required to have compliance procedures in place for everyone's protection. While I earnestly hope there will not be compliance problems, should there be any evidence of problems, it will be pursued vigorously. Because management has been so upset by the revelations in the press, because the warning bells have sounded so clearly, because so many are hurt by the wrongdoing of so few, violations in the code of ethics in this firm will be fiercely resented and dealt with accordingly. Management knows its responsibility to each of you, and to the industry of which we are a part, and we will do our job."

Senior management took every opportunity to reinforce this message. Our weekly exception report which was closely watched, was one of the tools we used for detecting problems, and our Annual Compliance Review was another, both very effective.

We had much to do before year end, and our business purred like a well-tuned motor. As much as we embraced the challenge of a project, we savored those times when we could sit back and watch "business as usual," take stock of the small things, and address with precision the many little details that often were overlooked in the heat of a new initiative.

The stock market was favorable. January 1992 ended with $20,500,000 gross trading revenue, and anticipated excess net capital of $60,128,000, both numbers new highs. We followed up with our first ad in the *Financial Times* of London on February 3rd, with the headline: "Herzog Heine Geduld: At Home Abroad" with a London telephone number as well as one on the New York trading desk. We also mentioned correspondent firms in London, Paris, Milan, and the tag line: "Service — it's our stock in trade — Night and Day."

On March 23rd, we announced that David B. Bostian, Jr. had joined us as Chief Economist & Investment Strategist. David was also a futurist who had served on President Reagan's Economic Policy Advisory Board, and the White House Conference on Productivity. He gave me a photograph taken of him at one of these meetings, where he was proudly seated to the left of President Reagan. A year earlier he was working on "Imposing the Investment Decision Process — Better Use of Economic Inputs in Securities Analysis and Portfolio Management Conference," and now he was making the case for a strong recovery. We became good friends, and he would spend time with me explaining how his work as a futurist (of which I was skeptical at first) helped him with the issues of here and now.

David did a lot of work on his outlook for the next ten years or so, and predicted that the Dow Jones Average would reach 5,000 by 1995, and 10,000 by 2000, both of which happened. His astute and accurate observations of the economy led him to these predictions. I was sure that David's work would be valued by our clients.

Old problems persisted. In April, Irwin and I each made a subordinated loan to the firm for just under five years, as the need for additional capital in our expanding trading business was constant. Fortunately, we had options. For capital, we could look not only within the firm, but also to some of our retail customers. They were very happy to participate. We were doing well and they wanted to be part of the family. It was not unusual for a customer to drop in just to say hello and shake a few hands.

On May 17, 1992, the New York Stock Exchange celebrated its 200th anniversary. It was a splendid event, and Diana and I decided to buy expensive tickets to the formal dinner on the Exchange floor. After dinner, we were led outside, where magically we discovered that Broad Street had been converted into a dance floor. We had a great time. It was a once in a lifetime happening and we were privileged to be a part of it.

I had been in the habit of clipping Peter Drucker's articles from the *Wall Street Journal*, and his piece in July was titled "Planning for Uncertainty." In it, Drucker compared long term structural needs versus short term business needs, and concluded that the long term needs ought to be getting much more attention. His view echoed what David Bostian had been suggesting in our discussions about the future. I was impressed. Drucker urged us all to be more observant about details, something at which Buzzy and I excelled. Drucker also posited that we look past danger to find opportunity. There was danger in uncertainty, but there was also opportunity. Drucker was quoted in an AMA publication over the summer saying, "Managers had better assume that the skills, knowledges, and tools they will have to master and apply fifteen years hence are going to be different and new… And only they themselves can take responsibility for the necessary learning and relearning, and for directing themselves." I found this exciting thinking, and David Bostian was a good coach on this road. Duly inspired, we knew our retail clients wanted to invest in more than common stocks, so we opened a fixed income department. Starting with corporate bonds, we quickly added municipals, and the new department did well.

In August, we placed an ad in Japanese and we got a good response. At the same time, pioneer discount retail broker Quick & Reilly gave an interview in which it was mentioned they were looking for an acquisition of a sizable OTC operation, "of the scale of firms such as Herzog Heine Geduld or Troster Singer." It was nice to be mentioned in the press in this context.

The firm sent a large group to participate in the Wall Street Race in September, and shortly afterwards our softball team "does the seemingly impossible… The world of fantasy quickly became reality for Herzog Heine Geduld as they turned around completely an up and down roller-coaster regular season by reeling off successive playoff sweeps against the perennial giants to capture the 1992 Financial Community Softball League Championship. Never before has such an unlikely amassed the herculean achievements that Herzog Heine has…" as Captain Jerry Morano led the team in a sweep of MBF Clearing, DTC, Merrill Lynch and Swiss American with a 9-0 record. There certainly was joy in Mudville that day!

In many meetings and discussions during the year, there was heated debate about creating an ESOP for the firm. There were some important advantages in having every employee become an "owner" of the firm, but there was also a lot of complexity and regulation. We were educated and guided by our lawyers and accountants and following much debate, we agreed to go ahead. This was a difficult step, and we learned that these plans were not always successful. The ESOP remained controversial, even years later, as the number of "partners" grew. Many concluded it had been a mistake for us. Fortunately, the markets remained healthy, and the firm remained profitable, and that helped us live with the decision.

It was the time of year when the Stock Exchange auditors visited. They would make sure each of our positions was accurately marked to the market for balance sheet presentation. When warranted, we always marked positions down, and did so stringently, as we did not want to deceive ourselves about where we stood. But marking up positions was a completely different issue. First, doing so created an (unrealized) profit in the trading account. Though the auditors considered this treatment accurate, to me it was somewhat misleading since there was no way of knowing our ultimate profit until the stock was sold. There were other disadvantages. We would have to pay income tax on that phantom revenue, and the trader could draw down his participation in that unrealized gain whenever he wished. Both outcomes were undesirable. I said no to marking up, but year after year support grew in the firm for the auditor's position. I would not be moved. I asked them to drop the issue. And they did.

In October, the cover of *Equities Magazine* featured Buzzy's smiling face with the head of a ceramic tiger that was part of his office decor. This followed *Equities'* annual survey which declared us the best trading firm. Buzzy shined as a "trader's trader," tough and decisive. It was a great partnership, and everybody knew that. Buzzy had done a wonderful job teaching the others. We made our traders understand that their job was to serve their clients and anticipate their needs. Buzzy preached humility, making sure every trader remembered where they came from and that saving nickels and dimes adds up to a lot of dollars. Buzzy had skillfully moved us into institutional equity trading, and it was now our main business. With a nod to Drucker, Buzzy saw opportunity where others saw uncertainty. He said, "Principal market making is going to expand and we will take advantage of it."

And then the big news came! A long-awaited moment arrived came when Buzzy told us all that he was going to get married soon, to Victoria, a money manager and a beautiful woman. We were thrilled, and Diana and I were very pleased to be included in the small family wedding. I was told I could say a few words, and I took that opportunity in traditional firm style, advising Victoria about a few things she might always want to remember: "Keep your desk, your area, neat; keep your calls short; no calls after 9:15, no calls before 4:15; memorize a few phone numbers you think Buzzy will need; carry some matches at all times; and most important of all, get Sylvia's recipe for junket and mashed potatoes. That's all the help you'll ever need! Every good wish for happiness together…" And before long, there were three beautiful daughters in the family.

Executive Committee meetings were always on Monday mornings at 7:30. The first meeting of 1993 was on January 4th, and the primary issue was our capital adequacy. Projections indicated that with the expected increase in activity, our excess net capital would be diminishing. It was an outcome we did not want. After some discussion, we voted to raise an additional $5 million, and plans for that were put in motion at once. We knew there would be legal work, and that we would have to provide terms that would be attractive to our own retail client base. Having made that decision, we began the process.

We felt comfortable issuing a press release saying we saw continuing growth in the Nasdaq marketplace in 1993, following a record 1992. Here we had been advised by David Bostian, who believed small cap stocks would do well under a Democratic administration and our marketplace and firm would thrive. Buzzy added that the IPO market could continue to do well if quality companies were floated at sensible prices. "If the major issuers don't get greedy, everybody can enjoy another very good year." Finally, we announced that we had created a successful Employee Stock Ownership plan which held 30% of the firm stock. We went on record saying we believed there would be good growth in our markets for the next three to five years, and perhaps even longer. We reminded people of our trading specialties, IPOs and secondary offerings.

We were stunned at news that the World Trade Center had been bombed, on February 26, 1993, a date forgotten even before the events of September 2001. We knew several people who had been caught there and crawled to safety. It raised so many questions about our security, and those questions wouldn't get serious consideration for more than seven years. We just kept working right through it all, like everyone else.

David Bostian was getting frequent calls from the press for comments on various subjects. In *USA Today*, David colorfully replied to a question about fixed income, "The bond vigilantes are totally blind drunk with deficit reduction brew." Mortgage rates were then around 7.75% and a drop to 7.50% would reduce annual payments by $204 on a $100,000 mortgage. David also said he was looking for some inflation news, as he felt the economy was building strength. To exploit his increasing popularity, we scheduled a special press briefing and luncheon at the Intercontinental Hotel on January 12th. David addressed half a dozen current issues including his belief in 4% plus real GDP growth in 1993. It was a successful event, and the first of its kind for us.

Our Human Resources department had the idea to create a list of all employees ranked by the number of years they had been with the firm together with their anniversary dates. It allowed us to recognize those employees with big anniversaries, and to start regular celebrations of these milestones. We had established relations with Tiffany's, and their blue boxes were dispensed regularly to the surprise and delight of the troops. It was a great way to remind everyone how much we appreciated their work and dedication. We had very low turnover, and competent, hard workers, a valuable asset which never showed up on the balance sheet.

Our new promotional efforts included an ad titled "We've Earned Our Stripes" with the large face of our tiger whispering "Quietly" letting people know that Autex block data ratings placed the firm in the #1 spot once again for OTC securities. Publicizing our rankings had a genuinely positive effect on our call and on our income, and we never felt we were wasting money on print advertising.

Similarly, we issued another press release celebrating Hans Jacobson when he passed away at 88 while in a hospital in Cambridge, England where he was being treated for pancreatic cancer. Hans had come to America from Germany in 1929 to escape anti-Semitism. He found a position at A. G. Becker & Co. Enrolled at the New York Institute of Finance, he gained insights into the railroad industry and he was fascinated by an industry in decline which was being rejuvenated by the War effort. He saw the railroads' large real estate holdings as an asset overlooked by many analysts. As the years went by, the ideas Hans suggested proved correct as the lines made money developing their prime properties. These profits made it possible for railroads to pay off their defaulted bonds at rich premiums. When Hans joined our firm with the Heine Fishbein deal, his desk was near my office in what had been our old trading room at 26 Broadway. I could see him through my glass partition, and hear selected expletives as he harangued the comparison clerks over questioned trades coming up from the Exchange. He was a colorful and jovial person, and I enjoyed being in the office with him. He would be missed.

We took some erratic market days in stride, including a day when the market was down 85 points. We still ended the month of February with gross income of $13 million. We added eight new stockholders proudly with an announcement in the *Wall Street Journal*. In Philadelphia, Bill Leahy had been elected president of the Investment Traders Association and several of our New York traders went there to support Bill at the annual dinner.

In April, I was the subject of a front-page story about the fifth anniversary of the opening of the Museum of American Finance saying, "We're trying in the museum exhibits to show connections between history and the present. The same concepts espoused by Alexander Hamilton 200 years ago have tremendous pertinence in the world today."

Our Shareholders Meeting in April was back at India House. We reported some progress on the capital raising, in fact, some of the stockholders were planning to subscribe to the notes. We then had a brief discussion about an arbitration we were involved in because of a firm of "SOES bandits" objecting to our taking them off our Auto-Ex system. SOES bandits were retail traders who developed programs to manipulate weaknesses in the SOES system. They would profit from the lag in updating prices by some market-makers. They would also execute sequences of trades, the first smaller trade often at a loss, moving the market, enabling a much larger and profitable trade to follow. Many people in the industry were resentful of these traders who were gaming the system, but the NASD was slow to act. We announced another innovation that could be used with a touch-tone phone, called Maxi-Quote, and it was available all day, every day. This was a contribution of Max Ule, one of our retail brokers, who had introduced this system in 1982. He was the first to offer real-time stock and option quotes with a touch-tone telephone in 31 cities around the country. We loved innovation, and our computer department arranged for us to offer the service. It was also possible to enter an order over this system, and we picked up business.

In another new service, Vasiliy Sofiyskiy, our first Russian speaking registered representative, former Deputy Director of the Russian Exchange Center, convinced us to run an ad aimed at other Russian speakers. We did some business, and Vasiliy was persistent. He urged us to consider new deals to be done in Russia, but we backed off, preferring to stick with what we knew. He was an interesting man, and we became friendly.

Our analysts continued to get us great press. One standout was Charles Kaplan, an analyst of small stocks who had developed a following. In July, he was featured on the front page column, "Money Manager Interviews," of *The Wall Street Transcript*, an oft-quoted publication. His answers to questions went on for more than two full pages. Early in July, David Bostian was quoted in the *International Herald Tribune*, recommending to investors that they keep 40% of their money in cash (the highest figure he had suggested going back to 1987). For the balance, he suggested 20% in stocks, 25% in bonds, and 15% in gold, as a hedge against inflation. His gold call had been good earlier, and gold had risen to $379 that week. We consistently garnered more recognition than any of our direct competitors, and our clients appreciated that we were committed to keeping them informed.

Buzzy's new issue group circulated a list of IPO issues coming to market each day, and the first one on July 23rd was Amanda Phillips Eileen Geduld, his first child. The expected issue price was simply "Priceless" and there was much rejoicing.

This was also the beginning of the eight-year term of Arthur Levitt as Chairman of the Securities and Exchange Commission. The Street seemed to be pleased about his appointment. One of Levitt's first memos was about the value of continuing education. The program he established would require participation by all registered representatives.

Through the trading department, we received an introduction to Henry Krieger & Co., a unit of ABN Amro Bank. Krieger dealt in U.S. securities. The bank planned to dispose of the unit as part of a restructuring. I was invited to lunch by Allan Keene, the division's President. At the Union League Club, I learned that the business had been formed long ago in Poland by Allan's maternal grandfather. It had been a fine business, until one summer when war threatened Poland. The men running the business instructed their vacationing wives not to return, but to go to America, where they would meet as soon as they could. The men stayed in Warsaw to attend to the business. Their reunion did not occur until the end of the war, but the families all survived. Once resettled in New York, the business was started up again, providing the same thoughtful execution service in U. S. securities. Over the years, their connections to institutional clients in Europe had brought success to the firm, and along the way, they had acted on an attractive offer to join the 300-year-old Dutch bank. They were now looking for a new home. Allan provided their financials and we determined they would be accretive. We were able to reach a decision quickly, and brought them into our firm as the Henry Krieger & Co. division. In the remaining months of 1993, Allan and I worked out all the details, and in February 1994 they moved in to space we had constructed and equipped for them. We immediately benefitted from their excellent European institutional relationships. Their business was interesting and profitable. An added dividend was the personal relationship which developed between Allan and Margaret Keene and Diana and me, one which has endured long after we stopped doing business together. At the end of 1994, Allan compared their revenues for the previous year to the results of their first year with us. He confirmed that their business had almost doubled. Exactly what we had hoped.

Suddenly, there was some good fun on the horizon right outside our office. The iconic "Charging Bull" sculpture by Arturo DiModica had been resident at Bowling Green since its eviction from outside the Exchange. It was on loan from the sculptor and a destination greatly admired by tourists and native New Yorkers alike. Arturo was still the owner, and he was looking for ways to recover the $300,000 he had spent making the sculpture. He came up with a plan to sell it to a resort in Las Vegas, and when that became known, there was a bit of an uproar demanding that the Bull remain right where it was. As I had been there at the beginning, and knew it was an asset for the city, I raised my hand on behalf of the firm and we wrote a check for $3,000 to initiate a fund for its purchase. "Mr. Herzog says only 99 more investors are needed to come up with the $300,000 price tag to keep the Bull," I was quoted in *Crain's* in early August. We got some calls, and in a short time, the problem was solved and Charging Bull rests in his place as always, but we never got our $3,000 back.

We had another well-regarded authority, a market technician, whose reputation flourished in her time with us. This special lady was "Luv" Elaine Yager, who rose each morning at 4:30 to read everything, and then created her technical analyses using hand written charts - not a computer - as she said she liked to get a good feel for the numbers. She then interpreted what she had put together: first commodities news, then interest rate changes, and then melding these two elements, she applied her findings to equities. Small cap stocks were her specialty, and she observed they were particularly sensitive to interest rate changes. Her letter went out to less than a dozen institutional accounts, and to our traders, always signed: "Luv, Elaine." She advised our traders, and spent time in the trading room with them individually, and after the market closed she would explain and discuss what she had learned. "Elaine's work is just one more factor, one more piece of information we can use," said Buzzy. "If we're going to buy 100,000 shares of stock, we'd like to first know where it is going to bottom out," he told *Traders Magazine* in October. "We call Elaine to get a different perspective on the situation and to talk to someone who is not caught up in the emotion of the moment." Elaine's work was largely influenced by Edwards and McGee, whom she called the "godfathers of technical analysis." She loved her work and was eager to help when she could. "I find great satisfaction in contributing this piece to the puzzle," said Elaine.

It was also the fifteenth anniversary of John G. Ullman & Associates, Inc., of Corning, New York, and another opportunity to tell our story. Ullman had gone into business as our clearing account, and they prospered. We never held back our appreciation for their business, help and counsel. They did brokerage and investment management, and provided tax advice. They were trusted advisors. Their business grew, and we benefitted.

We saw value in every public relations opportunity, and we wanted to be sure we were doing everything we could. We scheduled a meeting with Mount & Nadler, for general discussion, particularly the best way to identify media contacts when one of the senior officers or research people was traveling. We were also concerned with consistency, and the best way to project the correct image of the firm. Our reputation had grown nationally, if not internationally. We knew that we would be recognized and asked questions whenever and wherever we appeared. To be beneficial, these opportunities needed to be handled correctly. With the help of Mount & Nadler, we crafted a message and decided who was best to say it. We were now getting exposure in the leading publications, and we wanted that to continue. We now had ninety different officers in the firm, but only certain senior officers were authorized to take calls from the press, and this was strictly enforced.

Unlike the old days, when someone left the firm, it was now newsworthy. Any termination could become a subject for fact-finding by the press. When Jeff Logan and Tom Premtaj left us late in the year, *Securities Week* wanted to know why. I got a call, and explained the situation. It wasn't that complicated. Both were good producers in the trading department, but as time went on they "heard the beat of a different drum," and decided on new directions for their careers. We thought it was all perfectly natural and not particularly newsworthy. But they were both stockholders, and with a developing 24-hour news cycle, the press sought a better story. We needed to learn how to manage the press, and tailor our comments accordingly, within the context of what the press was looking for.

Ever since my graduation from NYU Stern School, I made it a point to keep up my contacts there. I wanted to have a faculty member on the Board of the Museum. When Ed Altman was selected for the Heine Chair, I asked him about this, and he promptly agreed. This added credibility to the Museum, as it brought knowledge and respectability to the Board. Years later, when Ed decided to leave the board, he mentioned that a new professor of financial history had joined the faculty and offered to introduce him to me. That's how I met Professor Richard Sylla in 1990, and almost immediately we started working together on a couple of small projects, including a managerial review of the Museum and its opportunities for growth. Dick liked the Museum very much, and agreed to take the seat Ed Altman vacated.

Another year was ending, and the figures showed that the IPO market had been a little less profitable than in 1992. This was in part attributable to what Buzzy feared most about these markets. Early success attracted more investors and as demand grew pricing reflected the greed of sellers and the eagerness of market makers. Quality diminished, and when we look back we can see signs of a "bubble." The last investors are typically uninformed, and they suffer the largest losses. They also lack staying power, and when you have a rout, it is sudden and extreme. Our job was to maintain discipline.

David Bostian was asked for a comment by Financial World in December, and he appeared on the front cover saying, "The economy is trying to get over the hangover from the Eighties, and trying to become more globally competitive." At the end of December, the Stock Exchange sent out a letter of greetings and New Year wishes, with some highlights of the year then ending: Average daily volume above 260 million shares, total dollar volume topping $2 trillion, over 300 new listings, and more than twice as many foreign listings as compared to the prior year. These were new records by comfortable margins, indicating changes in our business and the global economy.

The New Year began with some very complimentary comments from Mark Lackritz, the president of SIA, about David Bostian's work on Productivity Economics and Democratic Capitalism, subjects he had been working on for years. David's economic model gives value to employee knowledge and motivation, subjects interesting to Washington at this time. David had been invited to discuss this model with Fed Chairman Alan Greenspan the previous fall. David had a request from President Clinton for an analysis. This reflected well on the firm. Our image rose, and our trading call improved along with the confidence of our clients. Our financials were evidence of that with a gross profit of $8.7 million in a choppy February.

The Stock Exchange announced the year just ended as its most successful ever, with record breaking volume and new listings. We used the Exchange's

SuperDot system for listed executions, and three quarters of our orders had been completed in less than 30 seconds, a tremendous improvement. It was another strong indication of the dramatic changes technology was bringing to the industry.

March 18th was my birthday, and 25 years earlier, Buzzy had joined the firm. I wrote to him on behalf of the firm, grateful as we all were for his leadership and achievements. He was one of the important people in the trading business, recognized widely and greatly respected. His integrity was admired, and customers knew that their business was safe in his hands. It was a success story in which we were all partners. To commemorate this anniversary, the entire firm gave Buzzy the dollar bill that had been on Harry Truman's desk at the White House, which he had autographed, "The buck stops here!" It had been consigned to one of the Smythe auctions. I knew Buzzy admired President Truman very much, so Diana and I bought it and had it framed and authenticated by the White House. The gift was made from the entire firm. It was the perfect piece, and complementing the newspaper bearing the headline, "Dewey Beats Truman," which we had given him years before. Buzzy was pleased, and it still hangs in his office at Cougar Capital LLC.

More change was coming as Nasdaq decided to publish quotations in increments of 1/64 of a point, hardly good news for traders who make made their living on the spread. It was viewed by some as a trivial irritant. Nasdaq felt the change was beneficial to investors, as it made for better markets, and was consistent with the need for increased disclosure and transparency. We contemplated how this change would impact us. At first, it didn't. April was proof, as we came in with a gross profit of $12,863,000. We continued to hire new traders, and one of those was Irwin's daughter Jodi who began working in the Miami office in April.

May 25th was a busy day for us, with an Executive Committee meeting at lunch time, and the Annual Shareholders Meeting in the late afternoon. The first discussion at the Executive Committee concerned plans for the move back to Jersey City to Newport Tower, where Ted Moudis and his team had been working. There were great expectations as we anticipated modern new offices across the Hudson River. Changes would then be made to the 26 Broadway office where retail would stay along with the listed order room. Vilas & Hickey would be expanding, as they were growing and the municipal bond department would become larger as well. We discussed disaster recovery facilities, upgrades to COLT, the Krieger business, and growth plans for the trading department. One sad development was the decision of Mike Price and the Mutual Shares group to leave our firm and restructure their business as an investment management organization. They would no longer directly execute orders for clients. We discussed the millennium which still seemed distant, but we wanted to be prepared.

We felt confident about our franchise. After all, it was a business we virtually built from scratch. But the markets were changing, and we would hear ideas floated which challenged our existence. Discount brokerage spread to Europe, and through Krieger we were introduced to a Basel-based discount brokerage that wanted to partner with us. We considered a business that would enable us to execute trades in listed options. Some speculated about the possibility of creating an organization to do what we were doing, but it would be funded by selling stock to our correspondent firm customers who were sending us order flow. We listened, but we decided against it.

At the Shareholders Meeting my remarks began the drill. We introduced eleven new shareholders, three of them women. I commented on the last several incredible years, sharing my hope that good business would not enshrine bad habits. I urged that we not let bigger bonuses become a right rather than a reward. There were many other things to report. We added the new firm E-Trade, as a clearing account, the appointment of new accountants Goldstein, Golub & Kessler, the move to Jersey City at a cost of $13 million, and the disaster recovery facility now operational costing $1 million annually. As important were those with significant anniversaries with the firm, Buzzy 25 years, me 35 years, and Donna 20 years. I never grew tired reminding everyone of the pride we took in our shareholders and in their knowledge, experience and enthusiasm. It was the same old incredibly optimistic story in which we all believed, with fingers crossed.

In June, the firm became one of the initial participants in the Fixed Income Pricing System ("FIPS"), another Nasdaq innovation that so dramatically changed corporate, convertible and preferred stock trading. We had acquired the well-known bond trading firm, Vilas & Hickey, and we wanted to be at the forefront of the technology developments in this area, as we had been in stocks.

By July, we were ready to announce our move back to New Jersey, to Newport Tower, a very modern building where we would join other well-known tenants. This was a big project and Ted Moudis had been working on the designs and construction issues for months. Several of us would go over to monitor the progress from time to time, and it looked very promising. At

1976   Mickey Weinberg, Buzzy Geduld, Tony Geraci at Irwin's goodbye party

(and on the occasion of its 50th anniversary), Herzog & Co. crossed the river on April 5th.

All hands arrived safely. Not a man or woman lost.
Our new WATS line is 800 631-3095.
In New York, however, call 962-0300 as usual.
In New Jersey, call (201) 332-7700.
For options and commodities, call (212) 349-8010.
For a description of the New York skyline
from across the river, call us first. **Herzog &Co.**
30 MONTGOMERY STREET, JERSEY CITY, N.J. 07303
ESTABLISHED 1926

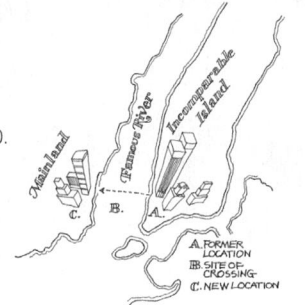

A. FORMER LOCATION
B. SITE OF CROSSING
C. NEW LOCATION

1976   "In the Spirit of '76"

PARMER, HERZOG & CHADWICK Phones
                                HANOVER
25 Broad Street   INVESTMENT SECURITIES   7898
NEW YORK CITY   7899

1926 First company postcard

1927 George Busch and his yellow Nash

HERZOG & CO.

UNLISTED BONDS

FOREIGN INDUSTRIAL UTILITY
MUNICIPAL   FEDERAL LAND BANKS

Specialists in
German Dollar Bonds

60 BROAD STREET   NEW YORK
HANOVER 2-1226

1932 First advertisement, *Security Dealers of North America*

1933 The trading room at 30 Broad Street

As we were saying...

We were saying that we make markets in over 1500 OTC stocks. And that things are looking up. (As usual.)

We're members of the New York Stock Exchange, the American and Boston Exchanges, and the CBOE.

We've added two new branch offices recently: Philadelphia and Dayton. And we have a very fine network of correspondents across the country—as follows, alphabetically:

Birr, Wilson & Co., Inc.; Blair Kerr & Bell, Inc.; J.C. Bradford & Co.; Alan Bush Brokerage Co.; Coburn & Meridith, Inc.; Continental American Securities; R.G. Dickinson & Company.

Equity Securities Trading Co.; First Financial Securities; Freehling & Co.; Hill & Company; Hinkle Northwest, Inc.; Investment Corp. of Virginia; Manley, Bennett, McDonald & Co.; A.E. Masten & Co.

McDonald & Co.; Schneider, Bernet & Hickman, Inc.; Smith, Moore & Co.; Southwest Securities, Inc.; Stern Brothers & Co.; Sutro & Co., Inc.; Tennessee Capital Corp.; Vercoe & Company.

Did we tell you we were established in 1926—55 years ago?

Call us about those 1500 stocks. Our WATS line is 800 631-3095. In New York, call (212) 962-0300. For new issues: (212) 962-0122. Ask for E.E. Geduld.

HerzogHeineGeduld

Established 1926. Offices in New York, Jersey City, Miami, Philadelphia, Dayton. SIPC

1981 Tiger ad, two new offices

We're back.

And we're delighted to be home again.

Herzog, Heine, Geduld, Inc. has moved all its financial services to one new location. At 26 Broadway.

Here's what has happened in the meantime: In 1976, we left the city with 40 employees; we're returning with 260. In 1976, our net worth was $1,000,000; at our last fiscal year-end, it was up to $11,500,000. Back then, we made markets in 800 stocks. Today, we make markets in 1800.

Call us. Over-the-Counter Market Making—(212) 962-0300. WATS line—800 221-3600. Retail and Exchange Services—(212) 908-4000. We mean business.

And how does it feel to be back? Just great.

Herzog Heine Geduld
26 Broadway   New York, N.Y. 10004. Established 1926
Members: New York Stock Exchange,
American and Boston Exchanges, CBOE.

1981 "We're Back"

1950 Robert Herzog and Herb Singer of Singer, Bean & Mackie, Inc

1951 25th anniversary dinner. *From left:* Murray Gilbert, Hugo Weinberger, Al Kennedy, Robert I. Herzog, Leonard Berlinger, Louis Weingarten, Ben Grody.

When the Empire State Building was completed in 1931, we hardly noticed. We were too busy celebrating our 5th birthday. We have continued to grow, and we're making markets right now in 3500 over-the-counter stocks.

Call us. We mean business.

Herzog Heine Geduld
60th Anniversary 1926~1986
Members: New York Stock Exchange.
26 Broadway, New York, N.Y. 10004. (212) 962-0300.
WATS: 800 221-3600. Institutional Traders: (212) 908-4132.

1986 60th Anniversary Tiger Ad

1986 Mary, Sarah, John, Diana Herzog

1991 65th anniversary party: Irwin and Buzzy Geduld

In a world of Bulls and Bears, it's good to know that there's still room for Reindeer.

During this Holiday Season, it gives us a lot of pleasure to recall the many good friends we've made throughout the past forty years, and to wish you, as one of them,

A Very Merry Christmas

We sincerely hope that 1966 will bring us Peace, and will strike a new high for you in Prosperity and Happiness.

HERZOG & CO., INC.

1926 • Our Fortieth Anniversary • 1966

1966 Herzog & Co., Inc. 40th anniversary Christmas card

1969   Christmas party, in 170 Broadway office

1969   Leonard Berlinger

1994 DuPasquier & Co., Paris office. Dorothy Moran, second from right.

1994 John, Buzzy and Irwin

A dialogue with Herzog Heine Geduld

"What's the best position to take with initial public offerings or secondaries?"

"Our best position is *no* position."

But that never happens!

We have to satisfy our customers' trading needs. In our business, this means being willing to commit substantial capital every day, to satisfy the constant demands of our growing roster of client banks, insurance companies, brokerage firms, money managers, mutual funds and pension accounts.

So we make a market in every IPO and secondary that comes to market on NASDAQ. It's been one of our areas of specialization for years.

**The needs of our clients come first.
That's our stock in trade.**

Herzog Heine Geduld

Established 1926. Members of the New York Stock Exchange/SIPC.
26 Broadway, New York, NY 10004. (212) 962-0300; (800) 221-3600.
Institutional Trading: (212) 908-4132; (800) 843-4845,
International Trading: (212) 908-4151.
NEW YORK / MIAMI / PHILADELPHIA / BOSTON / RHINEBECK

1994 Our Best Position ad

1971 45th Anniversary party

1971 STANY Party: Buzzy, Tom Poston, Irwin Geduld

1972 Christmas party. Norma Herzog, fifth from left.

Herzog & Co. (HRZG) makes markets in 300 active stocks and new issues, and has direct lines to L.A., Chicago, St. Louis, Dallas, Richmond and Minneapolis. Herzog & Co 170 Broadway, New York, N.Y. 962-0300. WATS line: 800 221-7143.

1972 Herzog & Co. new logo ad

Merrill Lynch

is proud to announce the closing
of our merger agreement with

Herzog Heine Geduld

and to welcome Herzog and its
employees into our firm.

This combination creates one of the three largest
Nasdaq market makers, and the number one trader of
Internet stocks globally.

Herzog Heine Geduld will retain its name and its long
tradition of outstanding client service.

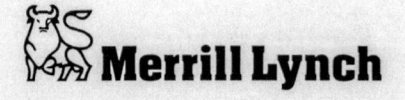

Merrill Lynch

HERZOG HEINE GEDULD

2000 Merrill Lynch merger ad

this point, we did not have a move-in date, but it would certainly be within the year. Things were going well for us, and we were once again Number 1 on Autex ratings for block trading, ahead of Merrill Lynch, not surprising since we traded four times the number of stocks they did.

Bill Donaldson decided not to run for re-election as Chairman of the Stock Exchange in May 1995. He was very well liked, and it was sad to think of his leaving the post. Mike Price had restructured Heine Securities Corporation, and applied for NASD membership as Clearwater Securities. He would be leaving our firm after a run of twenty years. We had also developed the capability to access to our customer's records from a CD-ROM. We were all thrilled with the opportunities software development offered us.

Irwin's 25th anniversary was a good excuse to look back. In a letter, I reminded him of our long walks together, reciting, sharing our dreams and Irwin's wonderful sense of humor punctuating the discussion. A lot of time had passed, and we had come a lot farther than either of us had dared to imagine. There was no Nasdaq then, and my idea of marketing was sending a post card to out of town dealers indicating a bid or offer for an inactive stock.

The government was investigating price fixing on Nasdaq. This is a hazard for all markets, as greed, and disregard of the rules go hand in hand. Whether it's human nature or ambition unrestrained, rules will always be abused. We tried to stay ahead of these issues. We had our human resources department publish a comprehensive revision of our personnel manual which clearly stated our position on all the sensitive topics.

David Bostian took a position on fixed income in writing "The Bear Market in Bonds is History," which he published in early November. It brought more positive comment about the firm and its skilled talented people. Now, ten of our stockholders were women, and they were also officers. Soon we would be moving to state of the art offices in a modern new building. We had great things to look forward to as we closed the old year out and headed home to celebrate.

CHAPTER 21

New Office and New Challenge
1995

The new year had hardly dawned when commentators were reminding us that David Bostian had predicted in 1992 that the Dow Jones Average would hit 5,000 during 1995. Would it come to pass? There were plenty of skeptics, but David's futurist training combined with his skill at economic analysis was rarely inaccurate. Traders, who were compensated on incentives alone, were wondering how their incomes would shape up in the months ahead. Activity was good, and by this time, we were writing 15,000 to 20,000 tickets each day. And volume almost always meant profits. The Stock Exchange once again summarized its performance for the year just ended. It was another record year with average daily volume of 291.3 million shares, and much of this volume was processed on the SuperDot trading platform which routed orders directly to the specialist. The system received 63 million orders for executions on 44 billion shares. This volume meant a lower cost per trade for each member firm.

There are always surprises in business, especially in trading. We were shaken by the news that Barings, the outstanding London firm, was having serious difficulties. This was a splendid name in the industry, an old-time merchant bank with which Robert Morris had done business in the 18th century. It was the Queen's bank, and deeply respected everywhere. How could this have happened? How could there be a question about them? The trouble came from Singapore, where a trader, Nick Leeson, had been doing well for a while, a star. He was also in charge of operations for the Singapore branch of the firm. When some of the trades he made turned out badly, he placed them in an error account, rather than leaving them in his trading account, where much more attention was focused. Errors built up, and Leeson attempted to erase his losses with increasingly larger positions. His bad luck continued. The final problem came from his bet that the Japanese Stock Exchange would not move significantly the night of January 16, 1995. Alas, the Kobe earthquake struck early in the morning of January 17th, and prices moved dramatically lower as people heard the news and panicked. Leeson lost his bet. His combined losses reached $1.4 billion, causing Barings to become insolvent by February 26th. This story again shows why a trader cannot also oversee operations, a cardinal rule. I was stunned and saddened, as I had followed Barings for some time, had visited their archives in London, and knew much about their important activities in the earliest days of American finance.

The year's first issue of *Financial Trader* featured a six-page center spread story about our firm with a "Then and Now" theme. Buzzy was asked to comment on how the firm had changed since he joined 25 years ago. He said traders were now far better educated, and candidates for positions would need at least a Bachelor's degree. He also observed that new traders were better informed, a byproduct of improved information channels and the proliferation of computers. He opined that tremendous increases in volume and a rising stock market had made a great difference in the trading room. He talked about pressure and how it was different for each individual, and the difficulties traders encountered in meeting management expectations. Despite pressures Buzzy confessed that he still loved the daily experience. I added some historical comparisons. It was nothing short of stunning that we went from 4 to 15–25,000 trades a day. The trades we used to make a living on were now a nuisance. It made me think about how diverse our traders were when it came to background and temperament.

Some traders had come to the firm because they knew the business from their summer jobs while in college, and they loved the excitement. Others relished the competitive nature of trading, comparing it to athletic efforts, and they wanted to compete vigorously. Others saw trading as a people business, so they pursued a career that rewarded their interpersonal skills. We had introverts who made money and extroverts who were consistently profitable, and it seemed that the markets were big enough to accommodate all personality types. All it took was the ability to make a quick decision and a willingness to admit it when wrong. The market is large and complex enough to accommodate everyone who wanted to participate. Auction market compared to negotiated Nasdaq trading got a lot of attention, with negotiated markets being far better for the customer. Mistakes need to be corrected as quickly as possible, and the old Wall Street saw that "your first loss is your best loss" is still in fashion.

We benefitted from the important market movers of 1995. Buzzy was in the forefront of new issue trading, making a market in just about every new issue, and some weeks we welcomed as many as 50 new names to public ownership. This was great exposure for the firm, and we could see the action and volume roaring back as the calls kept improving. E*TRADE, our customer, was advertising a $19.95 commission for any OTC stock in any quantity. This was a genuine cost savings for the active trader, and it contributed to ever increasing levels of volume.

For months, we worked on a plan to expose David Bostian's work to Allan Keene's European clients. Allan was sure that the Krieger clients would take to David's bold predictions and research. Allan suggested we visit Europe with David and make a series of presentations. Buzzy and I thought this was a good idea, and we were always happy to promote the firm in Europe. The entourage consisted of Allan and Margaret Keene, Diana and me, and David. The plan was for me to open meetings with our outlook for the Nasdaq market. David would then talk about his view of the markets, and his thoughts about the medium-term future. We rehearsed, and in mid-February, we found ourselves in Brussels ready for the challenge. Our first event was a phenomenal dinner in Brussels with the Chairman of Bank DeGroof. Then it was on to the Banque de Luxembourg where we got a warm welcome from a sizeable audience.

After these presentations and some sightseeing, Diana left us to go to London, and the rest of us traveled on to UBS in Zurich, where we addressed a large and enthusiastic audience. Apparently, groups like ours were not common, so fittingly our hosts made these lunches and dinners grand events. We had a good story to tell. By this time, our firm accounted for about 8% of daily Nasdaq volume. We were trading 5,400 stocks, and Nasdaq volume was then a bit more than half of the NYSE daily volume. We told our European customers to expect an explosion in volume, far more automation, much greater transparency, and more automated access, reducing the time required to confirm an executed order. We talked about everything we did, including our bond brokers. It was a worthwhile trip, even more rewarding because it was the first time we had ever attempted such an effort. Krieger gladly paid for all of David's expenses, and there were many orders to follow. Moreover, it was great fun.

Louis Keene, Allan's father, knew my father. I wrote to Louis on my father's letterhead:

March 28, 1996

Dear Louis,

I think you must be aware how proud I am to have your sons in our firm. They enjoy the rich heritage of your experience and accomplishment. Now they have become stockholders, bringing them closer to the heart of the firm, risking their hard-earned capital with the rest of us. For success in these endeavors prayers and luck are enduring companions. This coin was among my father's things, and I ask that you keep it warm and safe, that we may enjoy in the future the benefits which you and my father have provided in the past.

With many thanks, and fond regards,
John

Before our trip, David was interviewed and took that opportunity to call the beginning of a new bull market. "We have seen the last of the Fed's tightening," David said, adding enthusiastic comments for at least the next two quarters. Chairman Greenspan confirmed this view during a Congressional hearing shortly afterward. While we were in Europe, the Dow Jones had passed the record 4,000 level, responding to the Chairman's remarks. This was a good sign, and we were well on the way to David's prediction of 5000 during 1995. He also felt the undervalued U.S. dollar would gain strength, bringing capital into the U.S. markets. Advances in technology would help drive the markets, and the high-tech companies would be considered growth stocks very soon. To accommodate the steady increase in volume, Depositary Trust Company moved the settlement cycle to trade date plus 3 days, to reduce risk in the system.

We had 25 clearing firm accounts, and they were very pleased with our service. Grodsky Associates, one of our accounts, wrote a letter praising our staff, and I took pleasure in sharing it with the home team. Buzzy was also featured in the Relationship Spotlight of Donaldson & Co., another clearing account. He was asked why we were a good trading firm. "Three reasons: hard work, hard work, and more hard work. You're only as good as your last trade...and trading is a business where medium term planning can cover a period as short as 5 or 10 minutes. Keeping clients happy means handling important phone calls promptly and effectively, and that's why I haven't been to lunch in 15 years."

By now, COLT was a mature system with high user satisfaction, but it wasn't perfect. We discussed the need for a next generation version which we'd develop while running and enhancing the original. We summarized management's consensus: "Herzog must look to technology to meet new regulatory requirements, lower operational costs, control risk, maintain liquidity, and provide expanded client services." We then began to formulate a strategic plan for accomplishing these objectives.

In June, "Luv" Elaine Yager spoke to the Bloomberg Forum, saying it was "likely the Fed would cut rates for the first time in three years to rejuvenate the economy" so that "its carefully planned 'soft landing' would not suddenly crash and burn." She characterized the market as a combination of moderate growth without inflation "a successful designer-type landing remains to be seen, but I do believe the Fed will be there over the summer, ready to cut rates if necessary." She also felt that tech stocks were overvalued at this point, and that "A pullback of 5%–7% would not be out of line, when a stock like Intel had doubled so far this year." Elaine believed her work was highly interpretive. David Bostian was still bullish on the bond market, despite some declines to what he called a "more sustainable level." He also stuck to his prediction of a 5,000 Dow before year end.

Preparations for our move to Jersey City had been going on for months, and the time had come. Our last day at 26 Broadway was July 7th, and on Monday July 10th, we were in business in the Newport Tower building. Everything went smoothly and the new office was a big hit. I got the job of hanging the pictures. The entire result was state of the art. Ted Moudis Associates had done a splendid job. Other firms wanted to see what we did, and I was the tour guide. Our facilities manager, Tom Ackerman, had outdone himself making sure everything was in order, and he rapidly became the best liked person in the firm. He anticipated problems, and addressed them early on, pleasing everyone.

Opening our new office door revealed a beautiful entry foyer and a large desk for the receptionist. The traders and their assistants sat in unobstructed luxury. A special sound absorbent ceiling diminished ambient noise. Buzzy's desk was at the center of the room, on the highest of the three levels. He could be seen and he could see all. Dow Jones machines and Bloomberg terminals were visible to everyone, along with Nasdaq and COLT monitors. Visitors were impressed. My office was luxurious and spacious, with views on both sides. Buzzy had a private office off the trading room, with great views and beautiful appointments. It was exactly right, deserved and earned. It was all very advanced, and people wanted to see it even if they didn't do business with us. It was a pleasure to get to work — though the PATH trains were sometimes a problem.

The "Staying Committee" was now hard at work making plans to transform the old office. Work was about to begin in earnest, with a plan to finish by the end of December or early January. I preached optimism, and was hopeful. We began a short series of "Town Meetings" to let everyone voice their concerns and offer solutions. We realized the big move had been traumatic, as it resulted in the reduction of various support services at the old office. Everyone had a big backlog, and projects were put on hold. I took responsibility for all that was wrong, and worked hard to fix things. Frayed nerves calmed as things began to settle down to general satisfaction.

October market uncertainty prompted David Bostian to suggest that investors raise some cash in case falling prices prevailed. On September 29th, the Dow was 4,784, and while David stuck to his 5,000 prediction, he also was cautious. Our business remained good, with days of 30,000 trades and respectable profits. Pope Paul II came to New York, and his ticker tape parade up Broadway was a memorable event. When his Holiness was celebrated in Central Park on October 9th, Buzwin Donut Corp., pride of the firm, was asked to supply 325 dozen of its finest for the attendees.

In early November, I got a letter from Marconi's International Register. They sent tear sheets from their current edition with the listing of our firm, making me very proud. This was the primary source for listings of financial firms doing business outside the country. It ended our long absence from the directory dating back to a very brief period in the 1930s when we were active in European bonds. This may have contributed to our all-time record, a single day's profit of $1,766,762, and 37,736 trades on December 15th. This was a week after the Dow Jones Average hit 5156.86, just as David predicted. But anxiety about the upcoming Fed meeting manifested itself in a sell-off on December 18th, and David Bostian was quoted saying, "This is premature selling ahead of the Fed meeting. Once the meeting is over with, they won't have anything to worry about." We appointed David to Vice President on December 22nd. It was a well-deserved recognition of his importance and he appreciated our confidence in him. The month ended on a high note with a profit of $15,675,530 and a monthly total of 837, 718 trades, excellent figures. On the last business day of 1995, we wrote 45,339 trades, another record.

As the year dissolved into the next, the focus of our activities changed somewhat. We were no longer preoccupied with the structure of the firm, or where to find capital, or the businesses we should be in. We began to have more time to analyze what we each could do to promote the firm's success. We became preoccupied with ideas which would directly or indirectly benefit our core trading business. Logically, discussions started with an assessment of our strengths. Individually we were capable of starting and sustaining relationships with major global firms at levels above their trading departments, to the benefit of our trading business. We could identify and consolidate attractive businesses that would bring additional order flow to the trading room and allow us to make deeper markets in more issues. We disseminated David Bostian's insights throughout Europe, boosting order flow, which allowed us to make better markets for all our customers and gain a meaningful share of big blocks and million share orders. It all progressed well, a logical progression from the earliest days, and none of us ever forgot that. We humbly confessed to being in the right place at the right time, lucky perhaps, but it was not chance that led us to assemble an extraordinary group of talented, principled and devoted people.

CHAPTER 22

The Home Stretch

Despite economic headwinds, our eagerly anticipated 70th anniversary year arrived in good form. We were pleased with coverage David Bostian received in the *Wall Street Journal* of January 2nd, but his message pointed to some end of year weakness. Christmas sales had not gone well, and he felt that would carry over into the New Year, prompting him to reduce his growth forecast from 1.6 to 1.2%. The feeling among experts was that the Fed had not lowered interest rates soon enough.

A story in the January issue of *Financial Planning* began with the familiar words: "Past performance is no guarantee of future results." It was an appropriate title for a piece on charting and technical analysis which of late had come back into favor. There were some new studies which examined whether charting revealed what its enthusiasts said it could. Technical analysts believed they could forecast future performance by looking for patterns in past performance on a variety of charts. For proponents of technical analysis, the results were positive. A back test of the Dow Jones Industrial Average for its 90-year history indicated that returns would have been meaningfully enhanced if charting theories had been used consistently. Our technician, Elaine Yager, had been interviewed, and one of her charts was referenced in the story to illustrate "left shoulder, head, and right shoulder" formations. Her picture was included and it was great publicity for us and it generated some business.

The New York office was operating smoothly. We had 60 people there including all the retail activities of Vilas & Hickey and Henry Krieger & Co. At the SIA New York Area Firms Meeting, members decided on the year's projects and prepared for presentations to be given at the Securities Institute at

Wharton. It was ironic that as a leader of a firm which moved deliberately and carefully, where the possible outcome and consequence of every decision was debated, that I was asked to lead a panel called, "Betting the Ranch." It was well attended and contrary to the title, I talked about the need for planning and modelling and staying ahead of the scrutiny of the regulators. I shared a series of experiences at the firm.

To attract attention to our anniversary, we prepared a new edition of the firm brochure. I had done a lot of the writing for the first one, working with Mount & Nadler, and it was well received. But the new one had a different approach. It was shorter, more pointed, and included more photographs of our people. This was consistent with our focus on the talents of our individuals. We wanted to give our customers a more intimate glimpse into who we all were.

I had always been very strict about our written communications. I encouraged others to contribute written work to our publications, but no one was permitted to send anything out, or print any marketing materials, without my approval. I insisted on reading every piece, editing with my famous red pen. You did not pass "quality control" until I affixed my initials with an "OK."

We also created new advertisements for the anniversary, and one of the first was called, "The Evolution of the Markets...Has Required the Evolution of the Market Maker." We had evolved as a firm, and it was important for us to have others recognize these changes. With trading volume outstripping our most optimistic forecasts, the focus on finding new business receded, and we aimed at improving how we handled the business we had. There was less focus on the risks of each trade and more attention paid to how we could help our customers with their needs. Anxiety about the structure of the firm receded, as our organizational confidence strengthened. These were milestones worthy of celebration.

The Stock Exchange surpassed its previous records with average daily volume levels of 346.1 million shares, a 19% increase over the 1994 figures. There were 175 new listings, bringing the total to a record 2,675 companies with a market value of more than $6 trillion. Of these, a record 234 were from other countries. The Exchange saw international companies whose stock traded as ADRs, (American Depositary Receipts) as a big growth area. Our results were in line. We executed trades of 36,676,440 shares on the Exchange, a figure not dreamed of years before. These results validated our important decisions.

David Bostian was the keynote speaker at the annual dinner of the North Carolina Society in New York and he had invited Diana and me to attend.

As we moved along the receiving line to meet one of the state senators, I was asked where in North Carolina I was from, and I answered proudly, "Brooklyn, North Carolina." I earned a good laugh. David again said he thought interest rates would be lower later in the year, and that there might be a sharp decline in stock prices in the second or third quarter. He was considered "brilliant" by some because his projections had been very accurate, particularly his prophetic call that the Dow Jones Average would be at 5,000 in 1995. He was talented, charming, and with his new title and stock, a big asset and valued partner. He had also become a good friend.

In my remarks at the stockholders meeting in May, I summarized some major items, notably the move and the re-modeled space in New York. This had been a $20 million project. I asked my partners to recognize personal sacrifices on the part of the facilities managers who were in attendance, and they were enthusiastically applauded. Right after the move, volume obligingly increased, and we were now doing 35–45,000 trades daily. Our regulatory inspections indicated that we had operated well under intense scrutiny. I was gratified. Senior management had been strengthened with Steve Nelson, Vice President – Special Projects, now with the firm a year, and Arthur Feder, in house counsel, formerly with law firm Fried Frank now with us. Donna Connolly was now serving in an advisory capacity as Ken Bradley became CFO and Joe Frazzitta, Treasurer. I also announced our participation in a Nasdaq look alike for Europe called Easdaq.

My last topic was unexpected. I announced that I needed to reduce my common stock position in the firm, and had agreed to a 10-year plan for that purpose. It was important for my partners to understand that my confidence in the firm was undiminished. While selling stock might appear counterintuitive given our results and outlook, I explained why it would promote the long-term health of the firm. I wanted to create opportunity for others while I addressed the longer-term needs of my family. This was well received, and we all felt comfortable. I gave the floor to Donna, who gave the financial report.

And then it was time to celebrate. The anniversary party was once again at the Pegasus Suite in the Rainbow Room at Rockefeller Center. It was June 13th and spirits were high. The menu featured baked Alaska flambé. We had pins made for the anniversary, an upright rectangle with the firm name, the years 1926-1996 and a tiger's face. Unlike the roaring tiger pin we did for the 60th with the tiger roaring, the tiger was now the strong silent type, a creature of experience, successful, sophisticated and self-assured. I echoed those attributes when I spoke, comparing our current numbers to those of only five years earlier. Gross revenue was $178 million, up from $70 million, daily trades 50,000, up from 10-15,000, and net worth $126 million, then $46 million, all splendid accomplishments. There were new hires and a few retires. We celebrated all.

Buzzy then said some words about his pride in the way the firm was going and growing, and offered a sincere thank you to all assembled. It was a good moment, with 135 people in the audience, stock-holders, some spouses, and outside professionals very close to the firm. There was standing and clapping, and everyone was very happy. Ten years ago, we celebrated a transition to the people now in the trenches. The older generation bequeathed their problems to new, young faces eager to find solutions and add challenges of their own.

As time went on, all sorts of new issues and trends came to the surface. The Stock Exchange was puzzling over the continuing loss of volume to Nasdaq. Elements of the market were being questioned, like short selling, protection of customer limit orders, and Blue Sky requirements. Compliance was growing more onerous and complex and new rules and procedures for Nasdaq trading were imminent. We participated in several committees and were always interested, but we always looked at our own situation first and foremost to see where we could improve operations, reduce expenses and increase activity and profits.

The 70th Anniversary managers' luncheon was held at the new office with new members attending for the first time. There were gifts for all to commemorate the occasion. These events were great for bonding and team building. We let everyone know that as the firm matured, we intended to be concerned and responsible corporate citizens by offering support to charitable organizations we were personally involved in. Among the early beneficiaries were the Holocaust Memorial Museum in Washington, the Ellis Island Ethnic Coalition (on the occasion of my receiving the 1996 Medal of Honor), Long Island College Hospital, Resources for Children with Special Needs, and the Museum of American Finance. Our employees were proud of these commitments.

David Bostian remained active, but we were concerned and saddened to learn about some health challenges. He gave an interview on Reuters Financial TV about Steve Forbes and the Republican convention. He had been working from home increasingly, and we were all concerned about him.

Buzzy was profiled in *The New York Post* in September, where he was referred to as "the over the counter stocks king." The article concerned the SEC and Justice Department inquiry into allegations of collusion among Nasdaq dealers to set prices and trading spreads. It was impossible for us to know what was going on at other firms, but Buzzy was quoted powerfully in the article saying, "I beat my brains out every day trying to compete against 50 different market makers. It's really the most dog-eat-dog thing you've ever seen. Collusion? I want to bury my competitors."

Our reach went beyond the U.S. markets, and the U.S. markets were no longer independent of the balance of the major global markets. The changes we were seeing at home were occurring everywhere at the same time. We were host to a group from the Japan Securities Dealers Association who were gathering information for policy changes they were thinking about for their home markets. I always looked forward to these visits, and encouraged them as much as I could. During these visits, we learned as much as our guests. We wanted to know about the concerns our visitors had about the U.S. markets.

We were thinking globally. We finished all the filings required to create our new London branch office, called Herzog Heine Geduld International, and we had agreed to join the new Easdaq Exchange. We had filed an application to join the London Stock Exchange, as well as another innovative initiative, the Alternative Investment Market, a market for smaller startups and growth companies. "We believe we can make a major impact on the Easdaq market, helping it fulfill its promise as a strong force for capital formation and wealth creation in Europe," Buzzy commented. Our office was to be managed by Steven Burnham in trading, and Malcolm Stevenson in operations. Both had good experience managing Cresvale International for 12 years before. I looked forward to more trips to London.

We declared a five-for-one stock split of the firm stock and clarified some rules we had about transferring or selling stock to people outside the firm. The stock was getting more and more valuable, and people needed to deal with this value in their estate plans. We wanted to avoid the adverse outcomes we would occasionally read about because of unusual estate plans. I was addressing my own estate issues and the firm agreed to acquire my holdings in small increments over ten years.

Ethel Williams decided to retire, and we lost one of the most interesting and entertaining people in the firm. She would be hard to replace.

David Bostian joined commentators from Merrill Lynch and Morgan Stanley to share his outlook for 1997 with *The New York Times*. His Macro-Economic Index was forecasting a recession for the year. David called attention to the larger issues: peace among the superpowers, the triumph of democratic free enterprise over communism, and the growing progress of international cooperation and free trade. He emphasized that the recession would be mild, and that the economy would be growing again by the fourth quarter. David called attention to the multifaceted character of U. S. capitalism and predicted the success of medium and smaller sized firms, which comprised the growing base of Nasdaq listings. He counseled that this would be very beneficial for our firm. He felt the dynamic quality of these smaller firms would withstand the recession, and the "growth recession" would be mild. Outwardly courageous, David was seriously weakened by cancer and worked from home.

This was the time that new Nasdaq rules went into effect, and Buzzy was interviewed by *The Washington Post*. The rules addressed concerns about publicly displaying customer limit orders and private trading networks, and the size of dealer bids and offers, which dropped from 1,000 shares to 100 shares. Buzzy had objected to the new rules, which initially applied to the 50 biggest, most heavily traded stocks. The list was to expand over a seven-month period. Our business, he said, was to commit capital to help our customers complete their business. To the extent that these new rules reduced our opportunity to profit, this would logically reduce our willingness to commit capital. These changes were a direct result of the Justice Department's price fixing charges which were settled the previous last year, despite our objections. The new rules would have the effect of altering the Nasdaq market from a dealer market to a more exchange-like specialist market. This was frustrating because there was irrefutable evidence that investors and traders were comfortable with Nasdaq's current structure. There was proof. Nasdaq volume was increasing while exchange volume was decreasing. The initial days of trading under the new rules were problem free, but the real test would come later, with the addition of less actively traded stocks, where dealers supplied capital to complete orders. Our first trading day under the new rules worked out well enough, with trading profits of $1,657,000 and 52,000 trades. Our January figures were good, despite our concerns. "It remains to be seen if investors will truly benefit," Buzzy said in *The Washington Post* where he commented on the new rules.

The official opening of the seven employee office of Herzog Heine Geduld International was February 17th. In a letter Buzzy and I wrote to all employees about the new London office we said, "We believe the firm's experience building a trading firm from relatively small beginnings can be usefully applied to HHG International's efforts to build a stock trading business in the European

Markets." Our intergenerational training by way of my father's experience of "slow and steady" was once again there when we needed it.

Technology changed the way trading rooms looked and operated. In March, British Telecom announced its "Trading Desk of the Future," which used infrared signals to link communications from a variety of systems. Space on the trading desk became a big problem, as each new bulky machine became indispensable, requiring space, challenging the creativity of our architect, Ted Moudis. Data and telephone systems were integrated, both backed by powerful computers. Our new trading room was cited as an exemplary accomplishment.

When Congress became aware of underworld involvement in "penny stocks," the NASD was pressed to investigate. Our firm had been named as one of the market makers in one of these stocks. We had not realized that trading in this company had come under mob influence. We immediately stopped trading the stock. Our public relations firm learned of this, and an article was published in *The New York Post* with my picture as the "hero" of this very small action. Laudatory calls followed, even one from the owners of Herzog Wine, who were no relation, but they were pleased I had cleared the good name we shared. They invited me to lunch. It was mainly a great laugh for us all, and I was given a sampling of their wines for my strong stand against shady dealing.

In May, Wilma Mooney announced she was leaving for an exciting opportunity at Charles Schwab & Co. She had been with the firm since 1981 and made important contributions to the institutional trading area. We had learned to handle these events, and took them in stride. Our loyalty and best wishes remained, even as a key contributor departed. We accepted the fact that each individual defined success in their own way. When someone did leave, we wanted them to leave knowing that their departure didn't change our opinion of them. We hoped they left with positive feelings about the firm and we wished them luck.

The Internet was still very new, and two of our employees took the initiative to create what we might call a blog. It would seem primitive today, but they cobbled together an internal memo called "Tiger Online News," an effort to try to bring useful ideas to everyone. It's interesting to note how quickly general understanding and use of these innovations moved ahead. Hi-tech was newborn and it was the start of Web fascination, with "page hits" and "eye-balls," the new metrics.

On June 6, 1997, Buzzy and I wrote to all our employees about the settlement of the Nasdaq class action brought against our firm and 34 others firms three years before. This involved our writing a check for $30.6 million, a bitter pill. As I signed the check, I recalled the pain I felt during the negotiation. I had been to several meetings during which we discussed possible responses to this alleged behavior, but they were not productive. There were too many firms involved, an excess of opinions, and while I felt we had nothing to fear, others were not so confident. I concluded that this adverse outcome was more about our having become a leading trading firm and a convenient target. It was the price of success and the downside of playing in the big leagues. When the government knocked at your door, you pretty much had to do what they said. In this case, the NASD was acting upon Justice Department assertions, and the whole thing became a costly, dreadful nuisance which simply had to be put behind us. Our letter to the staff said:

"We did nothing wrong. Our decision to settle was based on a realistic assessment of the situation facing the firm and the negative impact and frustration of protracted litigation, which would have continued to drain managerial and financial resources. The long-term integrity of our firm and our ability to meet the needs of our clients were best served by moving forward and settling the case."

I was stung deeply by this, as the check I signed was written without a single word of deposition. We were simply doing what we were advised to do to get rid of this situation. I was very pleased my father was not around to experience this, as I don't know how I would have explained it to him.

I couldn't make sense of it. It was a turning point. I became filled with doubt. After 38 years at my desk, I realized I must give serious thought to relinquishing my position, and leaving my tasks to others. It was more than the settlement, more than the dollars. So much had moved beyond my grasp. The systems I knew so well had been replaced or modified beyond my recognition. The manner of trading itself had changed so greatly that I was no longer in command, or confident as to how it should be managed. The industry had changed dramatically, and my success and standing in the firm was more and more about my past than about my ability to meaningfully influence the future.

We welcomed 14 new stockholders in July, and one of them was Steven Geduld, Irwin's son. I thought this was wonderful. Steven was doing well in the trading department with great training supplementing his great lineage. Another new stockholder was Elaine Yager, whose title, Chief Technical Analyst, attracted media attention to her work and opinions.

Following release of the news of our settlement of the legal issues, we thought it would be a good time to have what we called a "Town Meeting." We stressed that the settlement was a money problem, not one of compliance, respect or integrity. We knew we had been named because we were leaders, confirming in an awkward way that the firm had arrived and was now in the company of the big boys. We all knew there was a lot of opportunity in the marketplace, and we were confident we could earn back the settlement money and then some.

We were doing well, but not quite as profitable as the year before. London emerged with a $10,000 profit in their first week in business, which was applauded, and they planned to add markets in 25 more stocks each week up to 250 in all. Anticipating the year 2000, Richard Grasso, President of the Stock Exchange, suggested we start planning now. We studied the years just after 1900 to better understand what we might encounter after the millennium. A hundred years earlier, the markets adopted several new technologies and prices responded favorably. Everybody hoped for a repeat, but the real focus and fear was how systems would cope with the looming change in the first digit of the next thousand years.

Increased volume and various regulatory issues prompted Buzzy and me to focus more carefully on compliance and internal audit. These departments had become larger, with inevitable turf wars periodically erupting between managers unable to stifle competing egos. Our managers were highly skilled in the technical aspects of their specialties but were often lacking in people skills. Tears and resentment sometimes replaced collegiality. Other times these differences boiled beneath the surface, undetected by senior management. My calm spirit was sometimes the right antidote, but as often it proved frustrating to people, as I seldom gave the desired answers, particularly when the issue was money or authority. We managed to keep the peace and defused rivalries.

Options had become a major investing area since the Chicago Board Options Exchange (CBOE) came into existence, expanding access to options dramatically. They provided a marketplace that was transparent, offering investors much needed information, as compared to the former over-the-counter variety. We had tried trading options on some of our stocks, but it was more difficult than we had anticipated. It added risks instead of hedging them. We terminated our options activity quickly. Although we exited the business we knew that exchange traded options would be a success. There were consistent educational efforts to teach more individual investors about options, programs provided by the Options Industry Council.

We had become members of the SIA Webmaster Roundtable, and interest in the Internet was growing rapidly. I remember talking to one of our traders who came in one day thrilled with his online discoveries of the night before. I told him I wanted to explore, too, and I asked him if he had any pointers. He advised that I should be sure to do anything that I needed to do first, before getting involved with the Internet, because it would be hard to leave the fun once I started. I took this advice to heart, and it was certainly true. SIA was having a conference about these subjects, and there was some competition about who would be going to it. This came up in the Executive Committee, and Buzzy gave some guidance to relieve the anxiety. Investors, analysts and meeting attendees were preoccupied with eyeballs, not earnings, and this would come back to haunt us all.

On October 27th, the market caved, falling 554.26 points, a 7.2% decline. Despite this big drop, the market was still up 18% for the year. This gave everyone a jolt. A reassuring fax had been prepared by the SIA called, "Talking Points in Light of Market Drop, October 27, 1997." The text called attention to the more than $11 billion invested by the securities industry in information technology in 1996, and how effective this investment had been during the October 27th trading day, when 1.64 billion shares had changed hands. With soothing words, the fax reminded readers about the industry's success in recent years and the planning that went into the orderly handling of the day's activity. We were then reminded that "smart money" was in stocks for the long term and that $100 invested in the S & P 500 in 1990 was worth $248.16 on the close. "The industry upheld its principle of putting the investors' interest first" was the closing line. While it sounded like industry bravado, to me it was a tepid response to uncertainty. It lacked conviction and confidence. October figures for our firm were good: $14,579,000 trading profit, with 1,496,687 tickets. We were working hard to earn back that big check. We ended our year with very satisfactory performance. We had also raised capital in the form of subordinated loans of $32 million, a very healthy figure. Our financial statement was strong, and we felt confident.

Our New Year's present was news that we had placed $10 million in Senior Subordinated Debt with insurer ReliaStar. The debt was due in seven years, with interest at 7.95%. This was once again done with Jim Tobin, who remembered that I was the only person among all his debtors that called to let him know how we were doing after the Crash of 1987. This emphasizes once again the importance of relationships, and the necessity of initiating them and maintaining them on the right terms, always with thoughtful consideration of the other person's needs.

The New Year was the time when conversations began about workloads, relative contributions, effectiveness and compensation. The order room personnel let us know how hard they worked all year. In fairness, volume had been rising and there were added pressures. Increases were justified. It was a ritual. We could see it coming as soon as we let everybody know how good the figures were. These conversations were a good exercise, but as managers, we would at times voice observations or criticisms which the staff did not like. When I was in charge, I'd initiate the discussion. I would go to the employee first and offer a raise, or an increased bonus. This was disarming and it usually worked to our advantage, and I could reach agreement without acrimony. There were rare exceptions when employees harbored exaggerated ideas as to their value or unique talents. Bolstered by the continuous stream of calls and resumes I'd get from people in the job market, it was rare for me to concede to unreasonable demands. The calls I got from prospective hires were always answered and unsolicited resumes were reviewed. I made some excellent hires that way, and these new employees were doubly happy, not only with a job at a good firm, but because they initiated the search and the boss responded. I interviewed many people over the years and I learned what to look for, and which questions to ask, and they weren't always the obvious ones. I tried to get people to talk less guardedly, to open up, so I could observe what they were really like.

We had expanded our retail capabilities. This pleased Harvey Wacht as he had an over-ride incentive on that part of our business. We thought about ways to drive retail revenue. It was a time of increasing concern about retirement assets, and we wanted to address that concern with something unique. We talked with a public relations firm, and the result was a re-formatting of some work they had previously done. Titled, "Will the Money Last?" we developed a 56-page wire bound book which contained a lot of information about retirement planning, aging, health, legal concerns and estate planning. The book attempted to summarize all the latest thinking on retirement planning in readable, workbook style pages. We covered the new elder law issues, and the importance of having up to date wills and health proxies. We sent out many hundreds of these books. The Philadelphia office further developed this idea in an ad to "Join a Creative Private Client Investment Team." The marketing worked and we could identify new revenue, proving the success of the effort. We also allowed retail brokers to solicit their clients for Subordinated

Loans to the firm, and as a group they raised $4,775,000. We continued to innovate.

Discount brokers were growing rapidly, and these firms did their business through the Internet. Using advanced technology, they brought speed and dynamic record keeping to retail customers. Schwab & Co. was the leading firm in this business. It was founded in 1971, and it offered the first discounted brokerage trades on May 1, 1975, the day negotiated commissions became legal. Growing rapidly, Schwab introduced the first 24-hour quotation service in 1980, by which time it had 147,000 accounts. In 1982 it offered the first 24/7 order entry service, and the firm continued to demonstrate strong growth with offices across the country, and millions of clients. E*TRADE, another discount broker, was founded in 1991. It had revenues of $850,000 in 1992, and by 1994 revenues had grown to $11 million. All the discount brokers became clients of ours, each needing a somewhat different computer interface which kept our technology people busy.

The Annual Stockholders Meeting was held on April 14th at the Down Town Association. The first order of business was a moment of silence for Al Galetti, our excellent margin manager who had recently died. This was followed by a moment of prayer for David Bostian, struggling at home with cancer.

The firm was in sound financial shape with a conservative capital ratio. I had my time at the podium. I reported on London, where we were now operating profitably. I announced I was stepping down as CEO, something I had been considering for some time. Diana and I agreed on this move and after so many years I knew the time was right. Senior management was experienced, and I had little to worry about. Buzzy would be assuming the title and responsibilities, but he would remain in the trading room to continue his excellent work there. Buzzy spoke last, the highlight for everyone, and he began by saying he had never been more optimistic. "We have reinvented ourselves in the trading room, learned the new rules and adapted to the new environment. There have been some meetings with our regulators, and these were going well. We will renegotiate our contract with ADP, and the managers in the trading room have assumed a lot of responsibility, and will assume more." Buzzy assured everyone he will be at his post for the duration, and then thanked everyone for all their efforts. Another milestone, another transition.

Cost cutting initiatives were implemented, and in June the committee presented a two-page report of accomplishments. The report also discussed new areas to be investigated and new objectives. Lots of minor abuses came to light, and the sum of all these amounted to meaningful relief in expense accounts. Managers meetings resumed in June. Managers discussed the impact of new rules in trading, and the fact that our customers had become very price conscious, and our business more competitive and very fast moving. We had demonstrated ten years of incredible performance, with annual records almost every year, but we vowed not to become complacent. More than ever, we needed to work together cooperatively. It was a good meeting, and we planned to meet again at the end of the month. Suggestions were solicited, and people responded. Other agenda items were the final version of the plan to purchase my stock and planning for my smooth transition to a position on the sidelines. I remained convinced that this was the best move for me and the firm.

Annual bonuses were once again generous, and the fiscal year ended with solid results. We were now writing about 100,000 trades each day, the greatest percentage of which were completed by our computers, which in some cases were connected to systems maintained by others.

Bob Meli's wife Esther passed away. She and Bob had a wonderful long marriage which gave Bob the support he needed as he enthusiastically devoted his efforts to the firm. It was a very moving experience to go to their Sephardic synagogue in Queens and join in a dinner of condolence with Bob and his many friends. I was honored to be there. Diana and I had been very close to Bob and Esther, and we visited them in their home to enjoy Esther's wonderful meals. These relationships were born in the firm and they flourished and it made the firm feel like a very large family.

In October, Chris Gerbehy retired and sent me the following letter:

Dear Mr. Herzog,

I feel very fortunate to have been a member of your company for the past twenty years. I am deeply grateful for the opportunity given me by yourself, Buzzy and Tony. I have made many friends all of whom I will miss very much. In a time where many people move frequently from one company to another, I feel very privileged to have spent my whole career at Herzog. Finally, on behalf of myself and my family, Thank you,

Sincerely yours,
Chris.

One of our important traders, Gus DeVito, retired and he wrote:

To Buzzy and John —

The party came as a surprise to me, completely unexpected. I just wanted to let everyone know it was a joy for me to see them there. The clock is a handsome piece, typical of a class firm that you are. I'm glad to be associated with Herzog all these years. In closing I just want to say thanks, the party was a happy ending to a memorable career.

Best wishes to all,
Gus

These sentiments validated all the things we tried to do.

In recent years, the industry made it advisable, and at times necessary, to correspond by e-mail, and to use other Internet tools. This helped expedite business, but there were also abuses as people used these tools for personal purposes. This was expected once terminals were placed on every desk, but we wanted to cut down on the abuse. Buzzy and Tony conveyed that in a letter to all employees late in the year.

The new order-handling rules caused a loss of trading profits throughout the Street. *Traders Magazine* of December had a feature article about a way to address the problem. The suggestion was to replace lost spreads with a commission. Several traders interviewed believed that charging a commission would bring more liquidity into the market, especially for stocks that were not heavily traded. Buzzy was asked to comment for the article, and his view was that Nasdaq would "evolve into an agency business. It's going to look like a listed market three to five years down the road. And market makers will do what a listed block desk does. You commit capital; it's one price. You trade without risk; that's another price. It's a transition from a negotiated market to a quasi-auction market. The regulators have said that's what their preference is. Agency business on Nasdaq will generate full disclosure, or more clarity over pricing. The mechanics will all be worked out by the regulators and the market itself."

The year ended well in the trading department. However, the bad news was the passing of David Bostian, who succumbed to cancer after a long and very uncomfortable illness, having tried several experimental drugs. This was a great loss to the firm, and to me personally.

The New Year 1999 arrived, and the market continued to be strong and profitable. January 6th was a record day for us, with trading profit of $1,792,000 and 110,000 trades. These figures felt a bit like a fantasy to me, but they were real. No sooner had we established an all-time record than it was exceeded by another record. A week later we achieved $3,523,559 profit with 145,000 tickets. Our advanced computer capabilities were bearing fruit.

My agreement with the firm to sell a portion of my stock each year was now signed, effective January 1st. The execution date was the first business day in July in advance of the July-end closing of our fiscal year. This was a milestone for me, as I passed the firm on to others, younger and better versed in the changed ways business was being done. I was no longer conversant with all the new systems, and these were sure to continue changing. It was now forty years into my time with the firm, and I wanted to do whatever was required to promote the firm's vitality, even if that meant stepping aside. This was exactly how I thought it ought to be. When that day arrives many feel that it has come all too soon, but I was ready. I knew I needed to be thinking about my next steps. I felt very lucky that I had other interests, and I was not fearful of giving up the regular routine, but those days were still a ways off. I understood my role as the senior statesman.

Dramatic change continued, and one of those eager to see it was Frank Zarb, Chairman of the NASD. He was talking about prospects for the first global stock exchange, as trading volume moved closer to overwhelming the execution capacity of the industry. The industry struggled to keep up with the growing volume as well as rapidly changing regulations. Computer capabilities were prepped for a flawless Y2K, investing millions to achieve a non-event. As reported in the *Institutional Investor*, Zarb traveled to several cities around the world, hoping to form partnerships with organizations willing to participate in his idea for a global stock exchange. A year before he suggested merging Nasdaq with the American Stock Exchange, and those talks were ongoing. This was happening against the background of a strong up market with increasing volume.

Our audit firm was now Grant Thornton LLP. Their exit conference was held on January 12th, and this deserves a few comments. Overall their assessment was very positive and complimentary. These were the comments we wanted and we worked hard to deserve them. Then there were the deficiencies, specifically budgeting. Buzzy and I had similar views about this. We knew what the numbers ought to look like, but how could we make meaningful projections and accurate budgets when the business was moving so quickly? We always did our best, we were mindful of expenses, and we let everyone know our objectives. The auditors felt differently, as they were unimpressed with our efforts. At their insistence, we adopted a rigid budgeting process and we did our best to adhere. We remained skeptical.

Exchange Chairman Dick Grasso advised member firms a few years earlier that we were supposed to have a Y2K plan in place, but ours had not been completed. We were advised to have system security measures in writing, in place, and adhered to, as if we wouldn't be able to operate properly without formal preparation. We were innovators, but we functioned informally, and that had always worked for us. With our group of talented people, we could complete projects that were little more than dreams in a few short days or a week. We were successful because we anticipated changes and executed. We handled increases in volume that were beyond imagination, but the accountants were critical. They urged a more formal "IT" planning process that reflected overall foreseeable firm requirements, not short term needs. As managers of a business that outran projections before they could be put on paper, we were stumped. But we had been innovators in technology, and we had developed a wonderful group of people who did beautiful work. Still the suggestion was for a more formal IT planning process, the object of which was to ensure that the overall goals of the company and our customers would be met. But we were discovering that new requirements emerged by the time formal plans were completed. Disaster recovery received a good deal of attention, and rightly so, though our approach was to do what we could to make sure we would never need it.

The market continued to be kind to us, and London began to make larger profits. On February 11th, London provided trading profit of $299,000. Harvey Wacht was working hard to develop our retail business, and in March, the firm was featured in a story in *Registered Representative*. Our book *Will the Money Last?* was a big help in finding prospective sales people for our growing retail division.

Technology provided another surprise as the electronic trading network (ECN) came into full view. *The Wall Street Journal* covered this subject in its March 1st issue, reporting that in January, an ECN known as Island, owned by Datek Online Holdings, had accounted for 17% of the total trading volume in Amazon for the month, 55.6 million shares. These networks had been around since 1969 when Instinet was created, long before the term ECN was in use. Now the successful ECNs were talking about connecting to the Stock Exchange and Nasdaq. Where would that leave us? We participated in Instinet, but how many more networks would there be? And why was the SEC allowing all these networks to exist? They lacked security and the established reputation of the exchanges and Nasdaq. This was all happening around us, but increasing volume levels made it possible for our profits to grow despite of all these new participants.

During the intersession break at the Wharton School each year, the SIA organized a Securities Industry Institute. This was very popular, and it usually had a sellout crowd. I had helped to plan this, and I arranged for Buzzy to give the market-maker point of view. The agenda included thinning markets, disappearance of spreads, quality of execution, decimalization and T+1 settlement. Tom Joyce, head of Merrill Lynch Equities, was to be the moderator.

The Zicklin School of Business at Baruch College was also having a conference, organized by Professor Robert A. Schwartz, about "a broad spectrum of issues pertaining to regulation's contribution to the efficiency of the U. S. equity markets." Keynote speakers included representatives from Nasdaq, the NYSE, the American Stock Exchange, and the SEC. This was one in a series and they had always been useful and well attended. There were so many questions unanswered, and so few certainties about what would happen next.

In light of the continuing market strength, we issued a press release in early April saying that our average daily volume exceeded 101,000 trades per day, a 100% increase over the same period a year earlier. Our on-line order flow had increased, and accounted for 89.5% of our trades, up from about 67% a year earlier. Buzzy was quoted saying that on-line order flow was "an overwhelming force in the market" that had created tremendous challenges for the industry, but that we had "the necessary systems, people and expertise in place to handle the volume and provide quality executions to support the on-line investors who are the customers of our brokerage firm clients." He continued, "While I can't predict whether the Internet stocks will continue to trade at their current incredible price multiples...two things are clear: individual investors will continue to dominate the market, and electronic trading is here to stay. Knowing this, we are determined to increase our system capacity as needed to remain on the leading edge of this market." We were then trading 5,500 Nasdaq issues and we accounted for about 8–10% of daily Nasdaq trading volume.

We were rewarded: an all-time record on April 13th, with trading profit of $3,820,000 and daily trades totaling 186,810. Before the ink had dried, we topped those figures on April 14th when we netted $3,918,836, on 196,661 trades. We had created a wonderful dream machine, hard work for the traders but they loved it. On May 4th, Buzzy commented once more: "There is no sign of a let-up in demand for Internet stocks, especially for IPOs. And much of that demand appears to be coming from individual investors trading through the Internet. Regardless of how the overall market—and even technology stocks in general—perform, online investors are not blinking." Nasdaq announced that it intended to extend trading hours over the summer, creating a lot of adverse sentiment in the trading community. Buzzy said: "At Herzog, we are prepared to handle our customer's orders in any environment, but this is an extremely difficult time for the industry to confront this issue. We have all had to deal with Year 2000 issues—we just finished eight weekends of industry-wide testing. All of us have stretched our systems and staffs thin, and we still must accomplish decimalization. With the explosion in volume, traders are exhausted at 4 P.M. It is unreasonable to ask our people to stand in for another shift." Geduld asked, "Why is it necessary to do this all at once? Wouldn't it be better to phase in after-hours trading, say a half-hour at a time?"

All this became background for our annual stockholders meeting on May 5th. Our guest at this meeting was Cono Fusco, the partner in charge of our firm at Grant Thornton. We welcomed 17 new stockholders, and two of these were former stockholders who had left the firm and had returned. We now had 181 people in the trading room, and the new offices had been expanded, causing us to sacrifice a conference room. The Board of Directors was re-elected, and then I made some remarks. It was a challenge to put the firm's accomplishments in perspective. I was, however, glad to report that in the eight months following the July end of the 1998 fiscal year, we had generated $44.4 million in pre-tax net income, an increase of $32.4 million from the previous year. I thanked everyone for their help accomplishing this, and once again for their attention to me after my heart operation in August of last year.

Joe Frazzitta, the new chief administrative officer of the firm, spoke next about his focus on the millennium, and he commented a bit early on the new vocabulary we were all learning—no more companies, only enterprises. No more employees, only human resource capital. Ahead of the media, he mentioned the need to use warm and fuzzy words to describe unpleasant things. We committed to a new trading system, and he informed that the new accounting system would be live on August 1st, giving us an infrastructure for continued growth. He also mentioned that our medical plan was first rate, and other benefits were good. Joe introduced Cono Fusco, partner in charge at Grant Thornton, now the 6th largest accounting firm in the United States with 18,000 employees worldwide. They were very proud of their relationship with our firm.

Ken Bradley gave the financial report and elaborated appropriately. Then Andy DaPonte spoke about marketing, and our efforts to add one new clearing broker each month, and that the Order Execution Business on the stock exchange floors was finally contributing to profit. Harvey Wacht gave the continuing good results of the pension and profit sharing plan investments.

Buzzy took the floor last. He was happy about the year's results and compared them to the more subdued results of the last few years. He was pleased with our reduced costs. He stated confidently that we would remain a strong competitor. He disclosed that we were speaking to investment bankers. There was applause, refreshments, and we put another stockholders' meeting to bed.

Walter Raquet let us know about a new competitor. Knight/Trimark Group would be executing customer orders received before the opening at the mid-point of the NBBO (National Best Bid/Offer) quotation, "reinforcing the Company's unwavering dedication to 'Best Execution'" commented CEO Kenneth Pasternak. More competition with apparently no room for profit on the part of the dealer. We were puzzled. Our London office was now trading every stock on Easdaq, and the people in our office believed that innovation in European market making would follow along the lines of what we saw at home. London had just been admitted to Xetra, the electronic system for the Deutsche Bourse, and their growing business necessitated plans to find larger space. June started with more than 136,163 trades.

In July Frank Zarb at the NASD reported on meetings with the SEC about extending trading hours. Traders were hopeful when he stated that the meetings "...surfaced many issues which must be faced prior to lengthening the trading day." Four committees had been established to study the issues, and there was agreement that there would be no longer trading hours. That was a relief in trading rooms. By November 1st, however, Operations Management newsletter reported that First Clearing Corp. planned to offer its clients after-hours trading on the Chicago Stock Exchange, and they thought others would follow their lead. Requests for this service had come from the West Coast firms, in order to lengthen their trading day.

On July 15th, Buzzy was quoted on the PR Newswire about the slowdown in online trading in the second quarter, saying: "The public has found a new way to invest in stocks, and it is not going away. This is just the beginning, and we have a long way to go before the transition is complete. We've barely scratched the surface so far." He said our firm was rapidly preparing for the increase in volume we expected. In September, our ranking for Nasdaq volume dropped to 4th, behind Knight Securities, Mayer & Schweitzer and The Island ECN. We still did 4% of total Nasdaq volume, a big number.

I was quite pleased to learn that Gmul Sahar Securities in Tel Aviv had decided to become our correspondent in Israel. Diana and I had visited them when we were there and I thought the firm would be a good connection for us. We were going to make markets in Israeli company shares and Gmul would provide research on them. Several Israeli companies were planning to go public in the coming months, and we felt very constructive about this arrangement.

November was a good month, with gross trading profit of $37,266,475 and ticket volume of more than 250,000 on several days. These were exciting numbers, but challenging as well. On the first day of the December trading month, we wrote 272,000 tickets. The month ended with gross profit of $49 million, and on a few days we did more than 300,000 trades.

It was during the last days of 1999 that Buzzy got a call from Goldman Sachs, who had been our investment banker in the negotiation to sell the company to Smith New Court in 1986. We had kept in touch with Goldman, asking periodically if they had any other ideas. Now they were calling us to say that they didn't want to represent us, they wanted to speak to us as principal to principal. This was big news, and we agreed to talk after the New Year. We weren't sure what would happen. There was plenty to think about over the holidays.

CHAPTER 23

A New Century

We went to sleep in the 1900s on a fateful Friday night, and woke the next morning on the first day of 2000, and it felt genuinely different. We got a bit of that feeling as we watched the ball drop in Times Square. The morning felt strangely new. The big news for the securities industry was that none of the dreadful possibilities occurred. Everyone had paid attention, and millions had been spent to be sure things would work without a hitch. Monday morning, disaster-free, felt good, and there was a whole new world to conquer. The feared Y2K had been contained, and the sigh of relief was audible. There were changes in attitude, and some new words like "millennials," the generation we'd call Generation Y, people who were joining the working world now.

Our firm was highly respected, our people became authorities in their specialties, and the senior managers were often approached for interviews. Journalists wanted their opinions on the issues of the day. Buzzy was increasingly sought after, as the new issue market was hot and he was the acknowledged leader in that specialty. January turned out to be a spectacular month with $69,757,000 in trading profits and 5,479,000 trades, including several days with 300,000 trades.

Early in February, we opened a dual-purpose office in Jericho, on Long Island. Outfitted with redundant hardware and systems, it would serve as our operations center in the event of a disaster. The office would also house some new producers from the area who joined knowing that they could avoid long commutes into the city. Buzzy expected to attract 30 to 40 people to that office.

The market continued strong, and the trading month of February was again outstanding, ending with profit of $68,660,000 with many days when we did more than 300,000 trades. These were truly spectacular figures. We were carried along on this magic carpet of a market feeling very confident and self-assured. Buzzy was moved by this activity, and he knew better than anyone how much effort was required to accomplish such results. On March 20th, he wrote to our employees about the "unprecedented," historic level of business in the Nasdaq market. "As you well know, Herzog has more than participated in its share of this volume. The enormous strains put upon you, as well as the tremendous effort put forth by all of you to help us get through these exciting times has not gone unnoticed or unappreciated." Attached to each letter was a check for an extra week's pay, a token of the appreciation of management. Buzzy was generous and considerate, and this was an important gesture for a mature manager not known for his writing.

March ended with gross profit of $90,290,300, and ticket volume of 8,456,382, astounding results. There were many days of more than 350,000 tickets, and several days with 400,000 trades plus, with one day at 457,000 trades. On March 1st, our firm transacted 14% of Nasdaq volume. We were all in a state of excited exhaustion, unprepared for upside activity of this magnitude, not wanting it to end.

I attended the March SIA conference at Wharton. I sat in on a class taught by finance professor Jeremy Siegel during which he commented on the Nasdaq market. It was a Friday, and he referred to large charts of market movements displayed in the front of the room. He thought the numbers were very high, and the market would have difficulty going farther up. I remember being in the class hearing that, and thinking I should leave the class and call my broker with sell instructions, but I didn't do that. On the following Monday I was back in the office, and that was in fact the high point of the Nasdaq market. The "eyeballs" the analysts were promoting to the investing public, were about to become fewer in number, revenues and profits remained distant and the market began a decline. Ignoring Siegel, many viewed the dip as a buying opportunity.

Goldman Sachs' call to us late in 1999 was followed up with further conversation and a meeting. No longer our adviser, they were indeed interested in purchasing the firm, and they asked us if we would consider a proposal. Stunned, we recovered our breath, and said we would supply them with the information they requested. Only a few of our senior people were aware of this, and we continued our regular business as these talks progressed. This was a magnificent and weighty secret to be carrying around, and for the few of us who knew about it, we struggled to contain our excitement with poker faces. With Easter and Passover upon us, we took the opportunity to publicly share our good fortune, or perhaps garner guidance from the divine, with gifts to One Great Hour of Sharing, Catholic Charities, and UJA-Federation. It felt exactly right.

A few senior officers were negotiating the sale of the company. Buzzy and I were talking about things, and he told me it would be great if there could be some competition for a deal. Could we find another prospective acquiring firm? I suggested calling the Smith New Court people, thinking they might still have some interest. Since that time, Smith New Court had been acquired by Merrill Lynch, and one of the people involved in the 1986 conversations was now on the Merrill Lynch Board. Buzzy called him, and got a constructive response. Buzzy was to expect a call from David Komansky, the CEO of Merrill. The call came in, and Buzzy had an opportunity to explain what was happening on our end. He asked if there was likely to be any interest on Merrill's part. The answer was yes! Buzzy let them know that we were well advanced in our talks with another firm and that we would need them to move quickly. Komansky assured Buzzy that he would be back with something firm very soon. Whether it was luck, or the influence of the divine, our timing was inspired.

The Merrill Lynch bid was substantially higher than Goldman's. I remember the moment. Buzzy returned to the conference room where several of us were waiting for another meeting to begin. He asked us to guess what the Merrill bid was, but none of us responded. He told us with a grin that made him look like the cat that had just eaten the canary. We were all staggered. We began at once to think through how we would get organized to make the deal work. We had decided to hire our own investment bankers, Wasserstein Perella. They assigned the deal a code name, "Project Lightyear," and soon there were meetings, phone calls, and preparation for Merrill's due diligence efforts.

Merrill Lynch's team was headed by Tom Joyce, the mediator Buzzy met on the panel at the Wharton School. Buzzy was managing everything on our side, and he knew exactly what he wanted to accomplish. He managed the process with precision and discipline, making sure that the tasks leading to a deal were being done accurately and quickly. There were dozens of calls to make, especially with our law firm, Fried Frank, Arthur Feder's former firm, where Arthur Fleischer was the leader of the group working on our deal. Each day brought new urgencies. This was all going on while our business pressed ahead with high octane activity. The trading month of April ended with trading profit of $58,362,000 and many days of 450,000 tickets. April 17th had been a great day with $7,945,000 in trading profit. These were great numbers to have during a deal to be acquired.

The annual shareholders' meeting was on May 2nd. Seven new shareholders were admitted to the firm, and the Board was re-elected, as usual. I spoke first, with updates since the meeting a year ago. I remember saying "Hosannas of Thanksgiving" for our good fortune. Last year had been a record year, and this year was far better. Less than three years ago, I signed a check for $30 million to settle allegations against the firm, and that had been a very discouraging moment. A month ago, we had trading profit of more than twice that amount, quite a turnaround. London had become consistently profitable. Y2K had gone away without a problem. We had a new Jericho office with disaster recovery capability, accomplished in house by our own technical and communications group. We had worked hard, and we had been extremely lucky, and we had not exhausted the opportunities.

There were financial reports by Ken Bradley and Joe Frazzitta. For the eight months since the end of the 1999 fiscal year last July 31st, we had generated $165 million in pre-tax net operating income, an increase of $121 million, or 270%. During these eight months, we had processed 38 million tickets. All the numbers were unimaginable, astoundingly higher, but they were real. All divisions of the firm were highly profitable. Stockholders' equity was now $267,626,000, compared with $40,000 in 1959. Yes, the numbers were real.

Work on the deal proceeded. Merrill announced their planned acquisition of our firm on June 6th. The purchase price was 8.5 million shares of Merrill Lynch stock, for all our stock, and that valued our firm at $914 million. "In 32 years, I've never been more excited about the business than I am today," said Buzzy to CNN.com. "Their internal trading flow, their ability to open institutional flow for us throughout the states and their business in Europe and Asia made this a marriage made in heaven for us."

We were all elated by the news, and our telephones brought wonderful congratulations from all over. It was extremely exciting, as each employee began to calculate what this might mean to them. No longer a secret, we wanted to help spread the news. Soon there was a closing date July 14th, only weeks away. Merrill told us that of all the deals they had done, ours was the first without due diligence problems. For me, this was one of the most rewarding parts of the deal and a splendid compliment for the end of my brokerage career. I was greatly relieved.

We did not pause. Our regular business moved ahead, and our public relations firm announced our latest innovation, "E-Tiger" an Internet based on-line trading capability for institutional investors. Users did not have to buy or install anything, just reach us by way of a link on the Internet. All communications were encrypted to ensure confidentiality. This was a big step ahead, and was well received. On May 17th, Gmul Sahar, our new correspondent from Israel, came to the office for a conference, and to meet and greet many of our people who would be handling their business. There was good give and take, and everyone was pleased with the new relationship. Profits for the trading month of June were very good, though down from the previous months, at $31,175,000. The Finance Department furnished its report for the month of June, with comparisons, and they were quite extraordinary. Stockholders Equity had grown to $318 million from $171 million the year before, and total capital and subordinations were $318 million, up from $204 million, a gain of 56%. Excess net capital was $217 million, a very conservative figure. Pre-tax net income at June month end was $202 million, an increase of 143% from the year earlier figure of $83 million.

As July 14th drew near, there was the normal anxiety about the closing going smoothly. Much had changed in our business, but worrying never went out of style. I had difficulty sleeping the night before the closing. I decided to write Buzzy with some thoughts I wanted to share. I have included that letter here:

July 13, 2000

Dear Buzzy,

It's a little after three in the morning, and once again, like so many other moments in darkness when I know I ought to be asleep, I'm wide awake. So, instead of tossing around on a hot pillow, I decided to write a while. Who knows, maybe this will make me sleepy.

I have been thinking about this letter for some time, knowing there were things to say but aware as always of how little time there is to speak them, and feeling strongly that the event we are hoping will occur tomorrow morning should be commemorated by more than a breakfast and some handshakes and hugs. The old reliable medium for me, and even the composition time is quite familiar.

There are so many things to say, so many things to remember, so many to forget. How deep is that reservoir, after all our years together, passing through those many crises, exceeding the milestones with increasing speed and confidence as the years went by. With this deal in my thoughts so fully, memories long dormant have been racing past like photos in an old family album, all at once, not in order, some difficult to identify with certainty. The overall effect is tremendous, reviewing so many years at fast forward.

We have run an incredible marathon, with most of the training along the way. And the relationship we have enjoyed has become the defining element in two long and wonderfully successful business lives. We have so much to be thankful for, and so much to look back on with satisfaction and a genuine spirit of accomplishment. I know this cherished relationship will be changing, as indeed it has been, and perhaps selfishly, I wanted to say some things now. The new season will require changes in style as well as substance.

For me, one of the great hallmarks of our years managing the firm is the time we didn't spend together. I've always marveled at that, and while we often made attempts to change that, we never succeeded. I remember once in the old office we had a visit from a reporter, and you were called to go back to the desk just after he came. So, we talked to him in turns, instead of the usual routine. As he was leaving, he told me how surprised he was that we had both said exactly the same things, and I remember thinking that while we never rehearsed those interviews, we just knew how we were thinking.

And I know how often we disagreed about issues when they first appeared, but we managed to accept each other's divergent views and meld our thoughts into meaningful policies which worked. Often the good cop, bad cop routine was just the right thing, though looking back, I don't think we realized what a good tool that was until we were pretty far along. Lately, people in the firm have been coming to me with thoughts similar to these, and there is a universal appreciation of our techniques - not to say anyone fully understood them as they were unfolding any more than we did - but they liked what they experienced and are extremely complimentary. That's nice, especially for a couple of kids from the neighborhood whose real training for the job came from thoughtful and devoted parents.

I want you to know how very much I have always appreciated your respect and consideration, and the deferential way you have always treated me. I know that I must have been terrifically irritating to you on lots of occasions, and while the reverse is also true, you never let me feel diminished in any way; I was always your partner. I have always been grateful for that, and it has led us to that special kind of teammate love I feel so strongly.

It is good and perfectly natural that things should change, and that this change should be nurtured and encouraged, that it may be the agent of many new developments and opportunities more grand and exciting than those of yesterday. Tomorrow always holds more promise and enhanced possibilities since our imaginations participate so fully, while yesterday encourages our regrets and recriminations. As I get older, it is more and more clear to me that these regrets must be forced into their proper small dimensions, in preparation for being forgotten as a regular spring cleaning activity. I think increasingly that we must rely on our experience, the "gut" you mentioned to me recently, retaining the distilled version and forgetting many of the details.

Because of my strong sense of history and my overriding optimism about what we are about to see in the industry, I am deeply interested in your success in the new days. I know first-hand how rich is your reservoir of experience, and I can only encourage you to rely on it, and to lead with a strong, tempered hand. You have few peers and the road ahead is rife with opportunity. I will always be there to support you. You will be carrying forward the many hopes and dreams everyone has always had, a heavy responsibility, but one which you are well able to bear. This is not to be confused with the fact of the deal: there we hope to exchange assets of one kind for another. The yearning for success in our endeavors, the striving for better solutions to the old problems, the consistent attempts to achieve higher levels of service, the tedious struggle for improvements in the administrative formula all are enduring issues, never exchanged for different kinds of assets because they are the core values which have defined the firm over many years. They are the values our parents taught us, and the values which have attracted the right people to the firm, and held them in place. They are the values I know you will be carrying forward, and the reason why I am so confident and optimistic about your success in the future.

At times like this, I wish I was twenty years younger. At least I would be sleeping better! But time marches on, and certainly I must fall into step. I never thought during my business career how I could make more money, a surprising reality which I realized lately. I only thought about how I could do the things I was supposed to be doing a little bit better each day, and fortunately that seems to have worked out all right. Now that my active years at the firm are rapidly drawing to a close, I am not sure how

I will be able to help in the days ahead, but you know I will be thinking about that, and that I will be eager and happy to participate.

I must say that this most recent kafuffle over the ESOP really spooked me, and briefly I actually did think the deal might not materialize. I was almost afraid to return your call, but by the time I did, I realized it would be unthinkable for the deal to abort at this point. Now I am hoping that there just won't be time for any more of these ghosts to be stalking the landscape, and that things will go as scheduled. And, once again, I have said my prayers as well, in Trinity Church, not our well-remembered St. Paul's. It satisfied for me an objective of all my years with the firm that every employee should benefit from our success in ways different from the salary and bonus: in some special way that expressed the years of service and loyalty in a cumulative manner.

Now at last this long night has turned into daylight, and I see the early sunlight on the tall buildings across the river, and the beginning of the stream of cars going downtown on the drive to start a new day. I feel my emotion welling up, strongly acknowledging the tremendous joy of this wonderful relationship we have shared, and as the tears make it difficult for me to see the keys on my computer, I am hoping that we will go on to new forms of old glories, and be able to enjoy each other's friendship and respect for many years to come. These are good thoughts for a brand new day.

Thank you, Buzzy, for everything that you have given me.

John

With the announcement of the deal, we each heard from many people, some we hadn't spoken to in years. Congratulations came in from all over. The most gratifying ones were from our own employees, grateful for the opportunity we had given them, and excited about their terrific payday. This year, something was added to the consolidated balance sheet we always published. Below our logo and tiger, underneath it read "A Merrill Lynch Company." More than anyone else, I knew we had come a long, long way.

Appendix

*Herzog, Heine, Geduld, Inc.
Income and Expense History*

INCOME STATEMENTS

	7 Mo. Ended Jul. 31 1929	10 Mo. Ended Oct. 31 1929	10 Mo. Ended Oct. 31 1933	4 Mo. Ended Jul. 31 1934	3 Mo. Ended Mar. 31 1946
Income					
OTC Trading Profits					
Bond Trading Profits					
Trading Profits	28,870.27	53,994.28	4,336.60	1,081.22	34,245.39
Retail Commission			17,732.57	9,957.35	2,946.31
Stock Loans					
Interest					
Clearance					
Corporate Finance					
Other	—	118.52	(500.37)	7.12	2,776.56
Total	*28,870.27*	*54,112.80*	*21,568.80*	*11,045.69*	*39,968.26*
Expenses					
Salaries and Employee Benefits	7,590.50	11,537.35	2,862.50	2,021.91	8,736.98
Commissions	1,843.43	2,902.67	2,636.75	3,069.08	
Pension/Profit Sharing/Bonus					
Floor Brokerage and Clearing Charges	2,699.15	5,302.10			
Communications	2,513.28	4,430.14	1,937.15	1,166.20	1,636.42
Quotation Service			435.00	245.18	481.26
Occupancy Costs	808.77	1,273.59	300.00	404.00	480.27
Interest	641.41	1,624.12	73.90	126.18	160.03
Data Processing					
Correspondents' Fees					
Professional Fees					
Corporate Franchise, Transfer, NYS and NYC Taxes	75.08	97.84			
Other	1,764.70	2,661.98	5,234.66	1,042.10	7,267.29
Total	*17,936.32*	*29,829.79*	*13,479.96*	*8,074.65*	*18,762.25*
Adjusted Net Income [Loss] Before Fed. Inc. Taxes	**10,933.95**	**24,283.01**	**8,088.84**	**2,971.04**	**21,206.01**
Less: Provision for Federal Inc. Taxes					
Net Income [Loss]	**10,933.95**	**24,283.01**	**8,088.84**	**2,971.04**	**21,206.01**
Less: Preferred Dividends					
Net Income Attributable to Common Stock					

6 Mo. Ended Jun. 31 1946	FYE Jul. 31 1947	FYE Jul. 31 1948	FYE Jul. 31 1949	FYE Jul. 31 1950	FYE Jul. 31 1951	FYE Jul. 31 1952	FYE Jul. 31 1953
53,193.97	31,100.90	32,238.65	19,029.06	23,116.44	29,110.03	23,302.18	17,384.36
5,861.26	3,851.79	5,619.24	4,356.40	11,210.87	9,609.26	7,962.27	8,315.28
	31.21						
4,482.64	3,194.99	4,649.87	2,289.05	2,262.03	7,130.80	2,367.65	2,075.55
63,537.87	*38,178.89*	*42,507.76*	*25,674.51*	*36,589.34*	*45,850.09*	*33,632.10*	*27,775.19*
14,333.92	16,493.00	14,362.00	8,725.00	13,528.00	15,128.00	14,127.91	7,630.00
3,195.16	5,974.38	5,716.10	4,547.46	3,914.21	4,332.34	3,483.70	3,362.57
879.18	1,553.91	1,678.31	1,573.10	1,215.70	1,264.86	1,214.04	1,113.00
956.15	1,907.93	2,014.94	2,223.68	2,155.58	2,160.81	2,149.00	2,015.96
371.92	843.21	990.44	874.67	856.44	956.88	1,126.53	1,176.28
	1,092.07	650.94	272.31	413.82	717.62	253.35	249.98
14,741.84	14,508.20	12,028.39	9,626.90	13,649.67	17,356.19	13,143.03	14,261.23
34,478.17	*42,372.70*	*37,441.12*	*27,843.12*	*35,733.42*	*41,916.70*	*35,497.56*	*29,809.02*
29,059.70	(4,193.81)	5,066.64	(2,168.61)	855.92	3,933.39	(1,865.46)	(2,033.83)
29,059.70	(4,193.81)	5,066.64	(2,168.61)	855.92	3,933.39	(1,865.46)	(2,033.83)

Continued on next page

	3 mos Apr. 30 1973	FYE Aug. 28 1980	FYE Aug. 28 1981	FYE Aug. 28 1982	FYE Sep. 30 1985
Income					
OTC Trading Profits					15,510,000
Bond Trading Profits					1,319,000
Trading Profits	131,197	18,693,649	18,130,117	8,735,493	16,829,000
Retail Commission	39,404	3,067,919	4,032,644	3,047,670	10,620,000
Stock Loans					1,083,000
Interest	5,668	3,410,875	4,698,647	3,554,336	4,143,000
Clearance		1,201,477			1,302,000
Corporate Finance					138,000
Other	5,666	857,344	2,253,338	1,451,483	1,388,000
Total	*181,935*	*27,231,264*	*29,114,746*	*16,788,982*	*35,503,000*
Expenses					
Salaries and Employee Benefits	86,719	12,976,915	9,411,715	5,478,687	11,307,000
Commissions	215				
Pension/Profit Sharing/Bonus	750				1,678,000
Floor Brokerage and Clearing Charges	14,810	1,512,267	1,986,738	1,402,469	2,669,000
Communications	28,887	2,190,540	1,915,205	1,027,081	2,238,000
Quotation Service	21,193				
Occupancy Costs	9,335	399,868	910,832	1,483,310	2,165,000
Interest		2,413,801	5,007,367	3,351,968	4,257,000
Data Processing		578,464	709,853	514,346	1,307,000
Correspondents' Fees					2,131,000
Professional Fees	1,000				1,549,000
Corporate Franchise, Transfer, NYS and NYC Taxes	15,911				576,000
Other	74,477	1,895,167	3,956,275	3,321,001	3,292,000
Total	*253,297*	*21,967,022*	*23,897,985*	*16,578,862*	*33,169,000*
Adjusted Net Income [Loss] Before Fed. Inc. Taxes	(71,362)	5,264,242	5,216,761	210,120	2,334,000
Less: Provision for Federal Inc. Taxes		2,637,000	1,995,433	(769,281)	843,000
Net Income [Loss]	(71,362)	2,627,242	3,221,328	979,401	1,491,000
Less: Preferred Dividends	8,195	18,000	18,000	18,000	
Net Income Attributable to Common Stock	(79,557)	2,609,242	3,203,328	961,401	

Appendix

	$000's	$000's	$000's	$000's	$000's	$000's	$000's
FYE	FYE	FYE	FYE	FYE	FYE	FYE	FYE
Sep. 30	Sep. 30	Sep. 30	Sep. 30	Sep. 30	Sep. 30	Sep. 30	Sep. 24
1986	1987	1988	1989	1990	1991	1993	
24,759,000	35,002	31,912	30,915	34,477	50,480		
1,219,000	1,233	1,061	1,492	1,011	2,219		
25,978,000	36,235	32,973	32,407	35,488	52,699	85,359	
14,067,000	15,019	10,011	10,859	8,277	10,014	11,557	
972,000	838	753	1,047	1,152	1,639		
5,485,000	7,364	8,858	12,239	15,319	13,772	13,017	
3,008,000	3,939	2,304	2,883	3,738	3,516	2,603	
214,000	264	170	(124)	—	—	—	
1,002,000	1,020	1,319	985	483	1,244	2,974	
50,726,000	*64,679*	*56,388*	*60,296*	*64,457*	*82,884*	*115,510*	
13,109,000	15,531	15,349	13,664	17,563	17,818	35,832	
4,900,000	6,628	5,659	5,593	3,875	6,875		
3,638,000	3,792	3,700	3,810	3,919	4,014	7,498	
2,670,000	3,191	3,372	3,750	3,812	4,498	5,046	
2,250,000	2,776	4,080	4,781	4,679	2,789	4,361	
4,904,000	6,553	8,539	11,933	13,990	13,490	9,177	
1,925,000	2,647	2,748	2,332	2,941	2,917	5,463	
3,609,000	4,379	4,957	5,404	3,542	1,506		
1,388,000	1,777	1,657	1,290	1,163	1,481	940	
1,446,000	2,135	269	101	632	4,853		
2,787,000	2,070	3,040	3,912	4,044	5,996	5,059	
42,626,000	*51,479*	*53,370*	*56,570*	*60,160*	*66,237*	*73,376*	
8,100,000	*13,200*	*3,018*	*3,726*	*4,297*	*16,647*	*42,134*	
3,861,000	5,399	1,056	1,666	1,553	6,113	18,888	
4,239,000	*7,801*	*1,962*	*2,060*	*2,744*	*10,534*	*23,246*	

BALANCE SHEETS

	7 Mo. Ended Jul. 31 1929	10 Mo. Ended Oct. 31 1929	10 Mo. Ended Oct. 31 1933	4 Mo. Ended Jul. 31 1934	FYE Dec. 31 1942
Assets					
Cash in Banks and On Hand	5,930.43	9,210.31	4,458.86	3,079.64	7,080.70
Cash & Securities Seg'd/On Deposit w/Clearing Org'ns					
Securities Borrowed					
Due from Brokers and Dealers/Clearing Organizations	288,085.20	287,463.70	4,962.84	6,226.38	16,822.18
Due from Clients	1,027.76	240.58	20,976.63		902.00
Securities Owned	34,598.25	21,281.25	255.12	532.23	17,108.76
Due from Clearing Organizations					
Loans/Secured/Demand/Notes Receiveable				80.00	3,530.96
Exchange Memberships Owned — Cost					
Exchange Memberships Contrib'd for Company Use					
Investment in Herzog Commodities, Inc. at equity					
Furniture, Fixtures, Leasehold Improvements — Net of A/D	673.51	673.51	414.50	461.25	441.64
Other	23.80	—	—	—	61.50
Total	*330,338.95*	*318,869.35*	*31,067.95*	*10,379.50*	*45,947.74*
Liabilities and Shareholders Equity					
Liabilities					
Securities Loaned					
Money Borrowed from Banks	49,000.00	19,000.00			10,181.20
Due to Brokers and Dealers/Clearing Organizations	265,723.44	262,148.00	600.00		20,025.85
Due to Customers					1,083.14
Securities Sold but Not Yet Purchased		2,575.00			31.37
Cash Securing Secured Demand Note					
Payable to Employees					
Deferred/Income Taxes Payable					
Due to Officers/Directors					
Other Liabilities and Accrued Expenses	1,065.20	1,356.12	500.00	66.74	737.72
Total Liabilities	*315,788.64*	*285,079.12*	*1,100.00*	*66.74*	*32,059.28*
Subordinated Liabilities					
Subordinated Debenture					
Pursuant to Secured Demand Note Collateral					
Exchange Membership					
Total Subordinated Liabilities	—	—	—	—	—
Shareholders' EquityLiabilities					
Capital - Net of Drawing Account — or — Class A/B par value	14,550.31	33,790.23	29,967.95	10,312.76	13,888.46
Preferred Stock + Capital in Excess of Par [Class A & B]					
Common Stock — $.01 par value + Capital in Excess of Par					
Retained Earnings					
Less: ESOP Contra Equity					
Less: Common Stock Held in Treasury					
Total Shareholders' Equity	*14,550.31*	*33,790.23*	*29,967.95*	*10,312.76*	*13,888.46*
Mark to Market Adjustment					
Total Liabilities and Shareholders' Equity	*330,338.95*	*318,869.35*	*31,067.95*	*10,379.50*	*45,947.74*
CPAs	SPK & C	SPK & C	SPK & C	SPK & C	G & B

Appendix

FYE Dec. 31 1943	FYE Dec. 31 1944	FYE Dec. 31 1945	3 Mo. Ended Mar. 31 1946	6 Mo. Ended Jun. 31 1946	FYE Jul. 31 1947	FYE Jul. 31 1948	FYE Jul. 31 1949	FYE Jul. 31 1950
11,218.30	18,560.86	49,332.00	38,455.92	25,364.19	22,487.14	28,293.25	22,607.47	19,586.18
28,239.04	53,179.87	70,952.62	64,135.17	83,388.24	9,630.00	39,691.19	15,014.00	13,826.50
2,091.15	3,093.75		2,225.00	601.40		54.50		
27,478.39	40,202.06	46,978.05	47,282.67	71,086.82	48,512.02	20,601.27	21,167.50	23,917.65
621.80	621.80	621.80						
527.00	338.15	458.15	458.15	458.15	1,039.00	2,975.01	2,245.44	1,810.31
274.00	149.82	25.00	25.00	25.00	100.00	1,203.80	1,533.00	417.42
70,449.68	*116,146.31*	*168,367.62*	*152,581.91*	*180,923.80*	*81,768.16*	*92,819.02*	*62,567.41*	*59,558.06*
15,090.16	15,070.84		5,006.98	17,198.95	12,245.74			
23,293.27	54,343.97	85,694.72	58,750.19	72,675.98	7,266.75	39,159.97	19,502.98	13,847.70
5,507.68	6,622.40	28,547.45	26,532.01	30,697.69	9,220.28	6,182.45	6,996.51	4,613.96
487.63	220.50	281.25	5,863.88	2,527.63	2,108.75	59.00		746.15
					33,971.40	24,772.59	16,230.21	17,633.41
1,203.18	13,577.61	14,746.61	10,827.16	12,826.06	1,149.05	1,772.18	901.47	2,422.01
45,581.92	*89,835.32*	*129,270.03*	*106,980.22*	*135,926.31*	*65,961.97*	*71,946.19*	*43,631.17*	*39,263.23*
—	—	—	—	—	—	—	—	—
24,867.76	26,310.99	39,097.59	45,601.69	44,997.49				
					20,000.00	20,000.00	20,000.00	20,000.00
					(4,193.81)	872.83	(1,063.76)	294.83
24,867.76	*26,310.99*	*39,097.59*	*45,601.69*	*44,997.49*	*15,806.19*	*20,872.83*	*18,936.24*	*20,294.83*
70,449.68	*116,146.31*	*168,367.62*	*152,581.91*	*180,923.80*	*81,768.16*	*92,819.02*	*62,567.41*	*59,558.06*
G & B	G & B	G & B	SPK & C	SPK & C	SPK & C	SPK & C	SPK & C	SPK & C

Continued on next page

Appendix

	FYE Jul. 31 1951	FYE Jul. 31 1952	FYE Jul. 31 1953	? Feb. 28 1954	? Dec. 31 1954
Assets					
Cash in Banks and On Hand	30,423.98	24,141.66	23,125.09	22,233.34	19,889.27
Cash & Securities Seg'd/On Deposit w/Clearing Org'ns	1,672.50				
Securities Borrowed					
Due from Brokers and Dealers/Clearing Organizations	11,655.58	9,892.75	11,047.42	29,419.04	45,094.46
Due from Clients					2,814.73
Securities Owned	17,407.59	19,958.63	16,996.86	20,963.65	35,778.29
Due from Clearing Organizations					
Loans/Secured/Demand/Notes Receiveable			2,500.00	2,626.89	
Exchange Memberships Owned — Cost					
Exchange Memberships Contrib'd for Company Use					
Investment in Herzog Commodities, Inc. at equity					
Furniture, Fixtures, Leasehold Improvements — Net of A/D	872.51	4,167.24	3,015.55	2,535.69	1,298.18
Other	420.20	182.66	425.36	453.35	341.67
Total	**62,452.36**	**58,342.94**	**57,110.28**	**78,231.96**	**105,216.60**
Liabilities and Shareholders Equity					
Liabilities					
Securities Loaned					
Money Borrowed from Banks					
Due to Brokers and Dealers/Clearing Organizations	9,978.64	6,099.33	10,622.87	27,468.37	48,446.46
Due to Customers	6,323.19	5,248.33		10,167.77	1,189.65
Securities Sold but Not Yet Purchased	—	4,055.80	1,110.95	112.50	
Cash Securing Secured Demand Note					
Payable to Employees					
Deferred/Income Taxes Payable					
Due to Officers/Directors	20,026.97	18,774.47	23,983.35	21,980.84	27,849.67
Other Liabilities and Accrued Expenses	1,898.79	1,825.60	1,087.53	344.90	809.18
Total Liabilities	**38,227.59**	**36,003.53**	**36,804.70**	**60,074.38**	**78,294.96**
Subordinated Liabilities					
Subordinated Debenture					
Pursuant to Secured Demand Note Collateral					
Exchange Membership					
Total Subordinated Liabilities	—	—	—	—	—
Shareholders' EquityLiabilities					
Capital - Net of Drawing Account — or — Class A/B par value				18,157.58	26,921.64
Preferred Stock + Capital in Excess of Par [Class A & B]					
Common Stock — $.01 par value + Capital in Excess of Par	20,000.00	20,000.00	20,000.00		
Retained Earnings	4,224.77	2,339.41	305.58		
Less: ESOP Contra Equity					
Less: Common Stock Held in Treasury					
Total Shareholders' Equity	**24,224.77**	**22,339.41**	**20,305.58**	**18,157.58**	**26,921.64**
Mark to Market Adjustment					
Total Liabilities and Shareholders' Equity	**62,452.36**	**58,342.94**	**57,110.28**	**78,231.96**	**105,216.60**
CPAs	SPK & C	SPK & C	SPK & C	D & R	D & R

Appendix

FYE	?	?	?	?	?	?	?	?
Jul. 31	Aug. 31	Aug. 31	Jul. 31	Aug. 31	Aug. 31	31-May	Oct. 31	Oct. 31
1956	1957	1958	1959	1960	1961	1962	1968	1972
17,365.55	10,204.79	17,308.59	53,544.15	46,296.44	149,659.56	78,293.32	576,114.73	340,162.81
24,992.50	28,092.01	50,156.74	33,363.39	335,706.04	72,722.59	33,462.89	1,322,115.14	1,143,909.67
2,611.87			765.23	102,765.00	3,301.52	873.66	6,575.95	205,346.96
41,432.42	41,969.50	33,130.35	38,403.38	68,844.63	-	32,593.48	433,010.53	792,724.60
								65,000.00
								11,500.00
92.20			3,049.50	2,247.00	1,994.40	951.08		9,863.98
416.57	83.70	66.54	998.00	664.32	5,265.76	1,137.88	6,471.46	19,150.88
86,911.11	*80,350.00*	*100,662.22*	*130,123.65*	*556,523.43*	*232,943.83*	*147,312.31*	*2,344,287.81*	*2,587,658.90*
				99,240.55				
25,441.58	20,817.96	36,768.96	30,764.76	314,888.01	85,851.28	28,917.62	1,145,340.97	932,846.18
5,154.55	3,449.05	44,725.90	25,992.56	11,158.73	20,376.99	4,509.25	28,690.29	161,150.94
1,745.00	2,575.00		9,083.38	16,588.25	5,360.67	43,174.75	146,348.87	203,203.08
							254,050.26	179,495.58
							133,000.00	31,000.00
28,557.23	25,465.73						135,162.16	165,161.72
122.98	532.37	330.44	791.40	8,322.80	14,911.67	23,920.83	77,589.88	20,553.71
61,021.34	*52,840.11*	*81,825.30*	*66,632.10*	*450,198.34*	*126,500.61*	*100,522.45*	*1,920,182.43*	*1,693,411.21*
—	—	—	—	—	—	—	—	—
25,889.77	27,509.89	18,836.92	63,491.55	106,325.09	106,443.22			
								450,000.00
						50,000.00	50,000.00	238,353.00
						(3,210.14)	211,198.82	205,894.69
25,889.77	*27,509.89*	*18,836.92*	*63,491.55*	*106,325.09*	*106,443.22*	*46,789.76*	*261,198.82*	*894,247.69*
							162,906.81	
86,911.11	*80,350.00*	*100,662.22*	*130,123.65*	*556,523.43*	*232,943.83*	*147,312.31*	*2,344,287.86*	*2,587,658.90*
D & R	D & R	D & R	D & R	D & T	D & T	D & T		

Continued on next page

Appendix

	? Apr. 30 1973	? Jul. 31 1973	? Jan. 31 1974	? Jul. 31 1974	? Oct. 31 1974
Assets					
Cash in Banks and On Hand	280,831	71,910	202,680	127,555	228,991
Cash & Securities Seg'd/On Deposit w/Clearing Org'ns		144,000		366,234	
Securities Borrowed					
Due from Brokers and Dealers/Clearing Organizations	833,139	1,036,502	875,161	561,073	781,400
Due from Clients	115,987	244,368	199,256	121,679	275,118
Securities Owned	868,429	738,995	816,118	862,095	868,601
Due from Clearing Organizations	65,000	15,000	65,000	152,369	34,307
Loans/Secured/Demand/Notes Receiveable					
Exchange Memberships Owned — Cost	11,500	11,500			
Exchange Memberships Contrib'd for Company Use					
Investment in Herzog Commodities, Inc. at equity					
Furniture, Fixtures, Leasehold Improvements — Net of A/D	7,665		2,401		2,149
Other	188,851	128,550	310,486	84,762	77,725
Total	**2,371,402**	**2,390,825**	**2,471,102**	**2,275,767**	**2,268,291**
Liabilities and Shareholders Equity					
Liabilities					
Securities Loaned					
Money Borrowed from Banks		60,000	23,000		100,000
Due to Brokers and Dealers/Clearing Organizations	677,173	468,915	615,860	152,532	462,448
Due to Customers	186,720	388,357	205,162	711,128	400,709
Securities Sold but Not Yet Purchased	311,102	410,661	554,911	298,158	326,057
Cash Securing Secured Demand Note					
Payable to Employees	116,133	171,192	234,831	176,946	201,716
Deferred/Income Taxes Payable	7,747		22,894		7,556
Due to Officers/Directors	116,621				
Other Liabilities and Accrued Expenses	54,698	99,353	10,560	176,736	21,452
Total Liabilities	**1,470,194**	**1,598,478**	**1,667,218**	**1,515,500**	**1,519,938**
Subordinated Liabilities					
Subordinated Debenture	100,000	100,000	75,000	75,000	75,000
Pursuant to Secured Demand Note Collateral					
Exchange Membership					
Total Subordinated Liabilities	**100,000**	**100,000**	**75,000**	**75,000**	**75,000**
Shareholders' EquityLiabilities					
Capital - Net of Drawing Account — or — Class A/B par value	801,208	692,347	728,884	685,267	673,353
Preferred Stock + Capital in Excess of Par [Class A & B]					
Common Stock — $.01 par value + Capital in Excess of Par					
Retained Earnings					
Less: ESOP Contra Equity					
Less: Common Stock Held in Treasury					
Total Shareholders' Equity	**801,208**	**692,347**	**728,884**	**685,267**	**673,353**
Mark to Market Adjustment					
Total Liabilities and Shareholders' Equity	**2,371,402**	**2,390,825**	**2,471,102**	**2,275,767**	**2,268,291**
CPAs	R.W.Taylor & Co.	OA & D		OA & D	

Appendix

? Apr. 30 1975	? Jul. 31 1975	FYE Jul. 31 1975	? Jul. 31 1976	5 Mos. Jan. 28 1977	? Jul. 31 1977	5 Mos. Jan. 27 1978	? Jul. 31 1978	5 Mos. Jan. 26 1979
357,488	125,352.27	120,692	56,930	265,430	358,390	502,017	338,558	331,000
	13,000.00	426,028	72,310	165,013				
1,140,798	586,440.80	788,256	3,787,403	6,699,841	3,419,750	5,035,601	8,795,791	12,259,000
491,682	446,312.88	454,519	1,038,738	8,792,636	7,647,776	11,266,487	16,623,123	14,170,000
952,738	1,699,139.89	1,150,218	2,108,523	2,725,071	2,850,722	3,622,756	3,866,366	5,473,000
32,449	231,726.73	451,568						
				400,000	400,000	400,000	575,000	575,000
	750.00			200,050	99,300	134,390	130,000	130,000
		63,000	88,800		85,000	30,000	40,000	50,000
		15,794						
6,469	8,851.98		91,070	77,846	130,221	107,186	209,768	178,000
30,100	55,632.98	40,348	124,136	264,632	317,007	168,548	277,837	223,000
3,011,724	**3,167,207.53**	**3,510,423**	**7,367,910**	**19,590,519**	**15,308,166**	**21,266,985**	**30,856,443**	**33,389,000**
	214,700.00	214,700	876,667	8,793,266	7,291,667	11,632,144	16,821,833	12,227,000
811,180	460,871.13	460,871	864,913	3,785,734	2,483,240	4,689,086	6,128,737	11,327,000
657,691	1,208,087.36	1,208,427	3,149,716	2,829,994	1,980,763	904,549	2,493,489	2,576,000
326,403		275,818	302,531	548,150	433,348	675,530	850,038	794,000
				400,000	400,000	400,000	234,894	
275,483		371,258	631,273	733,228	435,621	372,905	681,133	—
			206,200		—		42,000	—
42,971	464,312.87	92,715	172,925	619,285	298,533	391,692	468,195	2,626,000
2,113,728	**2,347,971.36**	**2,623,789**	**6,204,225**	**17,709,657**	**13,323,172**	**19,065,906**	**27,720,319**	**29,550,000**
75,000	75,000.00	75,000	75,000	85,000	110,000	264,000	193,000	246,000
				400,000	400,000	400,000	575,000	575,000
		63,000	88,800	120,000	85,000	30,000	40,000	50,000
75,000	**75,000**	**138,000**	**163,800**	**605,000**	**595,000**	**694,000**	**808,000**	**871,000**
822,996								
	714,559.00	450,000	450,000	450,000	450,000	450,000	450,000	450,000
	20.36	264,579	264,579	408,159	443,277	521,478	521,178	521,000
	32,876.75	37,275	288,526	417,703	496,717	535,601	1,356,946	1,997,000
	(3,219.94)	(3,220)	(3,220)	—	—	—	—	—
822,996	**744,236.17**	**748,634**	**999,885**	**1,275,862**	**1,389,994**	**1,507,079**	**2,328,124**	**2,968,000**
3,011,724	**3,167,207.53**	**3,510,423**	**7,367,910**	**19,590,519**	**15,308,166**	**21,266,985**	**30,856,443**	**33,389,000**
	OA & D	OA & D	OA & D					

Continued on next page

Appendix

	? Jul. 31 1979	? Aug. 31 1979	5 Mos. Feb. 29 1980	12 Mos. Jul. 31 1980	? Aug. 29 1980
Assets					
Cash in Banks and On Hand	188,572	1,300,000	271,000	41,697	848,000
Cash & Securities Seg'd/On Deposit w/Clearing Org'ns					
Securities Borrowed					
Due from Brokers and Dealers/Clearing Organizations	16,157,580	7,629,000	21,601,000	25,802,211	26,036,000
Due from Clients	16,518,095	16,488,000	23,130,000	23,456,853	27,044,000
Securities Owned	6,612,967	7,168,000	8,849,000	10,346,914	12,102,000
Due from Clearing Organizations					
Loans/Secured/Demand/Notes Receiveable	575,000	495,000	420,000	420,000	420,000
Exchange Memberships Owned — Cost	130,300	130,000	138,000	140,300	140,000
Exchange Memberships Contrib'd for Company Use	60,000	85,000	120,000	120,000	160,000
Investment in Herzog Commodities, Inc. at equity					
Furniture, Fixtures, Leasehold Improvements — Net of A/D	152,655	147,000	122,000	106,970	108,000
Other	322,679	1,089,000	539,000	761,569	1,505,000
Total	*40,717,848*	*34,531,000*	*55,190,000*	*61,196,514*	*68,363,000*
Liabilities and Shareholders Equity					
Liabilities					
Securities Loaned					
Money Borrowed from Banks	16,382,333	13,891,000	15,553,000	19,516,485	23,380,000
Due to Brokers and Dealers/Clearing Organizations	12,995,589	6,820,000	17,163,000	16,409,332	14,988,000
Due to Customers	2,855,585	3,666,000	7,341,000	9,509,010	11,149,000
Securities Sold but Not Yet Purchased	2,005,936	1,859,000	1,795,000	4,893,705	4,328,000
Cash Securing Secured Demand Note	80,000			20,000	
Payable to Employees	997,235	—	—	1,975,274	—
Deferred/Income Taxes Payable	520,000	1,270,000	2,750,000	887,000	2,137,000
Due to Officers/Directors					
Other Liabilities and Accrued Expenses	808,677	2,372,000	3,368,000	1,461,759	4,939,000
Total Liabilities	*36,645,355*	*29,878,000*	*47,970,000*	*54,672,565*	*60,921,000*
Subordinated Liabilities					
Subordinated Debenture	246,000	246,000	246,000	289,000	351,000
Pursuant to Secured Demand Note Collateral	575,000	495,000	420,000	420,000	420,000
Exchange Membership	60,000	85,000	120,000	120,000	160,000
Total Subordinated Liabilities	*881,000*	*826,000*	*786,000*	*829,000*	*931,000*
Shareholders' EquityLiabilities					
Capital - Net of Drawing Account — or — Class A/B par value					
Preferred Stock + Capital in Excess of Par [Class A & B]	450,000	450,000	450,000	450,000	450,000
Common Stock — $.01 par value + Capital in Excess of Par	521,178	521,000	596,000	595,949	596,000
Retained Earnings	2,220,315	2,856,000	5,388,000	4,649,000	5,465,000
Less: ESOP Contra Equity					
Less: Common Stock Held in Treasury	—	—	—	—	—
Total Shareholders' Equity	*3,191,493*	*3,827,000*	*6,434,000*	*5,694,949*	*6,511,000*
Mark to Market Adjustment					
Total Liabilities and Shareholders' Equity	*40,717,848*	*34,531,000*	*55,190,000*	*61,196,514*	*68,363,000*

CPAs   FST

Appendix

5 Mos. Feb. 27 1981	12 Mos. Jul. 31 1981	12 Mos. Aug. 28 1981	5 Mos. Feb. 26 1982	? Feb. 25 1983	5 Mos. Feb. 25 1983	6 Mos. Mar. 30 1984	6 Mos. Mar. 29 1985	FYE Sep. 30 1985
672,000	518,004	1,897,707	243,000	923,000	425,000	996,000	1,526,600	3,811,000
								—
40,273,000	29,210,276	18,052,697	15,716,000	17,971,000	69,111,000	28,813,000	31,739,400	54,250,000
27,303,000	30,556,483	30,207,386	23,435,000	24,477,000	31,376,000	39,065,300	45,849,200	53,951,000
11,110,000	12,192,767	17,480,212	10,900,000	9,475,000	26,557,000	35,659,000	30,605,600	32,220,000
420,000	314,000	314,000	314,000	207,000	207,000	100,000	100,000	2,600,000
140,000	140,300	140,300	141,000	141,000	141,000	141,000	141,000	141,000
190,000	190,000	265,000		180,000				
121,000	725,868	899,659	1,740,000	1,902,000	1,886,000	2,478,000	2,540,700	2,836,000
9,820,000	2,240,193	1,195,607	4,954,000	3,799,000	5,413,000	2,331,200	3,295,700	4,918,000
90,049,000	**76,087,891**	**70,452,568**	**57,443,000**	**59,075,000**	**135,116,000**	**109,583,500**	**115,798,200**	**154,727,000**
26,443,000	24,528,333	23,612,910	15,576,000	18,956,000	24,823,000	20,260,000	2,554,500	6,266,000
17,061,000	16,191,143	11,306,757	9,446,000	8,633,000	44,364,000	17,501,000	12,789,300	42,741,000
12,687,000	11,485,747	9,458,688	8,392,000	10,643,000	25,486,000	23,492,000	45,697,500	48,104,000
4,086,000	8,231,573	6,484,322	2,951,000	5,865,000	13,682,000	12,837,000	13,871,900	16,261,000
	15,000	80,938						
—	2,428,158	3,413,263	—	971,000	—	8,527,000	9,873,000	10,018,000
5,288,000	1,840,000	2,613,000	2,950,000		5,146,000	5,472,000	6,616,800	4,676,000
13,398,000	796,662	2,365,215	6,721,000	2,085,000	6,458,000	2,177,000	4,924,200	5,253,000
78,963,000	**65,516,616**	**59,335,093**	**46,036,000**	**47,153,000**	**119,959,000**	**90,266,000**	**96,327,200**	**133,319,000**
640,000	715,000	715,000	715,000	725,000	745,000	1,127,000	1,009,900	1,045,000
420,000	314,000	314,000	314,000	207,000	207,000	100,000	100,000	2,600,000
190,000	190,000	265,000		180,000				
1,250,000	**1,219,000**	**1,294,000**	**1,029,000**	**1,112,000**	**952,000**	**1,227,000**	**1,109,900**	**3,645,000**
450,000	450,000	450,000	450,000	450,000	450,000	337,500	337,500	338,000
705,000	705,235	705,236	685,000	730,000	790,000	1,214,000	1,219,000	1,296,000
8,681,000	8,197,040	8,668,339	9,243,000	9,630,000	12,965,000	17,874,000	18,794,800	18,170,000
—	—	—	—	—	—	(1,335,000)	(1,990,200)	(2,041,000)
9,836,000	**9,352,275**	**9,823,475**	**10,378,000**	**10,810,000**	**14,205,000**	**18,090,500**	**18,361,100**	**17,763,000**
90,049,000	**76,087,891**	**70,452,568**	**57,443,000**	**59,075,000**	**135,116,000**	**109,583,500**	**115,798,200**	**154,727,000**
	FST	FST		FST				

Continued on next page

Appendix

	6 Mos. Mar. 27 1986	FYE Sep. 30 1986	6 Mos. Mar. 27 1987	FYE Sep. 30 1987	6 Mos. Mar. 25 1988
Assets					
Cash in Banks and On Hand	2,325,600	4,179,000	7,874,500	12,603,000	21,810,600
Cash & Securities Seg'd/On Deposit w/Clearing Org'ns		6,668,000	37,054,300	25,473,000	34,272,800
Securities Borrowed					
Due from Brokers and Dealers/Clearing Organizations	91,222,400	96,005,000	299,654,000	195,393,000	132,152,500
Due from Clients	67,957,400	72,989,000	68,499,800	82,731,000	68,638,900
Securities Owned	32,266,400	37,551,000	39,823,600	44,768,000	49,459,700
Due from Clearing Organizations					
Loans/Secured/Demand/Notes Receiveable	2,670,000	6,635,000	7,135,000	5,660,000	2,260,000
Exchange Memberships Owned — Cost	177,600	182,000	181,700	218,000	218,300
Exchange Memberships Contrib'd for Company Use					
Investment in Herzog Commodities, Inc. at equity					
Furniture, Fixtures, Leasehold Improvements — Net of A/D	3,355,100	3,510,000	3,365,100	3,138,000	3,548,500
Other	4,982,400	4,777,000	3,436,000	5,243,000	5,236,900
Total	**204,956,900**	**232,496,000**	**467,024,000**	**375,227,000**	**317,598,200**
Liabilities and Shareholders Equity					
Liabilities					
Securities Loaned					
Money Borrowed from Banks	12,710,500	13,099,000	12,589,800	1,517,000	5,066,100
Due to Brokers and Dealers/Clearing Organizations	55,733,800	83,385,000	265,999,000	170,987,000	124,999,700
Due to Customers	67,471,600	68,629,000	97,222,400	101,819,000	101,453,100
Securities Sold but Not Yet Purchased	24,033,400	15,315,000	21,146,600	22,439,000	9,831,900
Cash Securing Secured Demand Note					
Payable to Employees	10,568,000	10,651,000	12,851,100	3,299,000	6,569,400
Deferred/Income Taxes Payable	4,446,500	4,897,000	6,805,900	4,841,000	5,223,900
Due to Officers/Directors					
Other Liabilities and Accrued Expenses	6,328,800	7,332,000	16,827,400	16,160,000	10,668,300
Total Liabilities	**181,292,600**	**203,308,000**	**433,442,200**	**321,062,000**	**263,812,400**
Subordinated Liabilities					
Subordinated Debenture	1,099,900	1,090,000	1,289,900	19,389,000	19,427,900
Pursuant to Secured Demand Note Collateral	2,670,000	6,635,000	7,135,000	5,660,000	2,260,000
Exchange Membership					
Total Subordinated Liabilities	**3,769,900**	**7,725,000**	**8,424,900**	**25,049,000**	**21,687,900**
Shareholders' EquityLiabilities					
Capital - Net of Drawing Account — or — Class A/B par value					
Preferred Stock + Capital in Excess of Par [Class A & B]	337,500	338,000	337,500	338,000	337,500
Common Stock — $.01 par value + Capital in Excess of Par	1,296,100	1,323,000	1,350,000	1,425,000	1,425,300
Retained Earnings	20,354,200	21,902,000	25,584,100	29,477,000	32,459,000
Less: ESOP Contra Equity					
Less: Common Stock Held in Treasury	(2,093,400)	(2,100,000)	(2,114,700)	(2,124,000)	(2,123,900)
Total Shareholders' Equity	**19,894,400**	**21,463,000**	**25,156,900**	**29,116,000**	**32,097,900**
Mark to Market Adjustment					
Total Liabilities and Shareholders' Equity	**204,956,900**	**232,496,000**	**467,024,000**	**375,227,000**	**317,598,200**

CPAs

Appendix

FYE Sep. 30 1988	6 Mos. Mar. 31 1989	FYE Sep. 30 1989	6 Mos. Mar. 30 1990	FYE Sep. 30 1990	6 Mos. Mar. 28 1991	FYE Sep. 30 1991	6 Mos. Mar. 27 1992	6 Mos. Mar. 26 1993
10,780,000	12,271,500	12,740,000	3,779,800	24,559,000	14,498,669	17,824,000	18,074,190	20,634,000
33,701,000	33,540,000	49,124,000	76,557,400	87,124,000	124,168,013	117,589,000	94,710,736	66,261,000
			146,052,600		91,141,721		141,687,161	231,342,000
127,844,000	104,285,900	201,796,000	30,617,300	98,186,000	27,520,706	143,720,000	51,507,612	91,329,000
77,859,000	81,836,300	87,259,000	84,395,100	77,585,000	78,774,402	78,563,000	102,683,679	159,343,000
44,406,000	46,102,400	42,836,000	42,478,800	27,098,000	39,230,945	21,723,000	93,958,270	92,944,000
					inc. above		inc. above	inc. above
2,260,000	2,260,000	1,610,000	1,610,000	540,000	540,000	1,590,000	1,590,000	1,240,000
218,000	218,300	218,000	218,300	218,000	208,250	208,000	208,250	208,000
3,561,000	3,527,400	3,135,000	2,680,900	1,184,000	856,740	491,000	565,534	1,056,000
5,779,000	7,000,300	5,842,000	6,164,100	4,934,000	4,858,811	4,335,000	10,137,559	6,913,000
306,408,000	***291,042,100***	***404,560,000***	***394,554,300***	***321,428,000***	***381,798,257***	***386,043,000***	***515,122,991***	***671,270,000***
			136,950,300		65,438,700		108,772,608	207,274,000
977,000	756,100	541,000	3,056,200	230,000	143215	109,000	86,379	71,000
123,059,000	106,621,400	187,838,000	5,532,400	82,443,000	4,413,688	88,061,000	6,754,517	35,512,000
95,336,000	95,106,000	129,755,000	148,639,500	144,569,000	192,560,080	177,769,000	*	208,676,000
12,895,000	13,818,800	13,732,000	19,662,200	19,529,000	28,502,807	14,719,000	71,304,199	85,982,000
2,632,000	2,844,800	2,707,000	5,586,900	2,639,000	8,878,469	7,430,000	11,067,677	4,856,000
2,593,000	2,725,500	2,694,000	2,606,700	3,233,000	3,791,752	8,167,000	15,142,086	14,853,000
10,898,000	11,811,400	9,550,000	12,350,000	7,436,000	15,437,567	14,697,000	16,996,171	22,852,000
248,390,000	***233,684,000***	***346,817,000***	***334,384,200***	***260,079,000***	***319,166,278***	***310,952,000***	***230,123,637***	***580,076,000***
24,543,000	22,593,000	22,754,000	24,862,900	25,035,000	23,081,903	24,173,000	26,757,833	31,500,000
2,260,000	2,260,000	1,610,000	1,610,000	540,000	540,000	1,590,000	1,590,000	1,240,000
26,803,000	***24,853,000***	***24,364,000***	***26,472,900***	***25,575,000***	***23,621,903***	***25,763,000***	***28,347,833***	***32,740,000***
							37	
338,000	337,500	338,000	337,500	—	—	—	—	—
1,644,000	1,594,400	1,770,000	1,769,500	2,053,000	2,064,107	2,352,000	2,415,545	288,000
31,425,000	32,764,700	33,474,000	33,853,900	35,985,000	39,286,222	49,369,000	60,635,947	73,166,000
								(15,000,000)
(2,192,000)	(2,191,500)	(2,203,000)	(2,263,700)	(2,264,000)	(2,340,253)	(2,393,000)	(2,393,687)	
31,215,000	***32,505,100***	***33,379,000***	***33,697,200***	***35,774,000***	***39,010,076***	***49,328,000***	***60,657,842***	***58,454,000***
306,408,000	***291,042,100***	***404,560,000***	***394,554,300***	***321,428,000***	***381,798,257***	***386,043,000***	***319,129,312***	***671,270,000***

Continued on next page

Appendix

	12 Mos. Sep. 24 1993	6 Mos. Mar. 31 1994	6 Mos. Mar. 31 1995	6 Mos. Mar. 29 1996
Assets				
Cash in Banks and On Hand	7,752,750	17,200,000	26,612,000	24,782,000
Cash & Securities Seg'd/On Deposit w/Clearing Org'ns	58,669,155	53,802,000	40,820,000	85,580,000
Securities Borrowed	291,597,984	260,994,000	326,471,000	292,424,000
Due from Brokers and Dealers/Clearing Organizations	45,640,252	70,752,000	35,605,000	35,314,000
Due from Clients	190,118,650	222,372,000	198,259,000	275,718,000
Securities Owned	107,091,942	106,886,000	119,874,000	122,453,000
Due from Clearing Organizations	inc. above	inc. above	inc. above	inc. above
Loans/Secured/Demand/Notes Receiveable	1,240,000	1,240,000	1,240,000	1,190,000
Exchange Memberships Owned — Cost	208,250	208,000	208,000	208,000
Exchange Memberships Contrib'd for Company Use				
Investment in Herzog Commodities, Inc. at equity				
Furniture, Fixtures, Leasehold Improvements — Net of A/D	807,057	670,000	3,143,000	4,960,000
Other	6,500,547	8,085,000	10,100,000	5,355,000
Total	**709,626,587**	**742,209,000**	**762,332,000**	**847,984,000**
Liabilities and Shareholders Equity				
Liabilities				
Securities Loaned	278,258,250	245,718,000	315,977,000	258,159,000
Money Borrowed from Banks	71,000	71,000		
Due to Brokers and Dealers/Clearing Organizations	7,819,437	9,092,000	4,950,000	5,523,000
Due to Customers	214,879,103	234,864,000	202,805,000	308,728,000
Securities Sold but Not Yet Purchased	66,026,947	83,112,000	61,295,000	61,404,000
Cash Securing Secured Demand Note				
Payable to Employees	7,280,375	10,889,000	9,629,000	19,570,000
Deferred/Income Taxes Payable	16,241,708	18,855,000	11,338,000	16,122,000
Due to Officers/Directors				
Other Liabilities and Accrued Expenses	11,913,826	20,534,000	22,199,000	31,077,000
Total Liabilities	**602,490,646**	**623,135,000**	**628,193,000**	**700,583,000**
Subordinated Liabilities				
Subordinated Debenture	32,452,000	30,512,000	30,707,000	29,724,000
Pursuant to Secured Demand Note Collateral	1,240,000	1,240,000	1,240,000	
Exchange Membership				
Total Subordinated Liabilities	**33,692,000**	**31,752,000**	**31,947,000**	**29,724,000**
Shareholders' EquityLiabilities				
Capital - Net of Drawing Account — or — Class A/B par value	46			
Preferred Stock + Capital in Excess of Par [Class A & B]	25,000,000	25,000,000	25,000,000	—
Common Stock — $.01 par value + Capital in Excess of Par	797,323	810,000	2,137,000	3,174,000
Retained Earnings	59,082,955	72,952,000	84,477,000	124,578,000
Less: ESOP Contra Equity	(11,258,370)	(11,258,000)	(9,146,000)	(8,676,000)
Less: Common Stock Held in Treasury	(178,013)	(182,000)	(276,000)	(1,399,000)
Total Shareholders' Equity	**73,443,941**	**87,322,000**	**102,192,000**	**117,677,000**
Mark to Market Adjustment				
Total Liabilities and Shareholders' Equity	**709,626,587**	**742,209,000**	**762,332,000**	**847,984,000**

CPAs   FST

Appendix

	6 Mos. Mar. 27 1997	6 Mos. Mar. 27 1998	6 Mos. Mar. 31 1999	6 Mos. Mar. 31 2000	
	5,213,000	101,255,000	139,602,000	287,266,000	
	134,050,000	89,005,000	174,477,000	229,397,000	
	591,492,000	520,228,000	703,286,000	1,339,982,000	
	42,330,000	51,049,000	77,053,000	214,691,000	
	157,435,000	197,464,000	126,714,000	243,768,000	
	144,913,000	79,259,000	58,774,000	77,678,000	
	inc. above	inc. above	inc. above	inc. above	
	1,190,000	840,000	615,000	615,000	
	208,000	208,000	208,000	208,000	
	9,400,000	12,308,000	14,077,000	23,551,000	
	11,354,000	7,643,000	12,829,000	24,863,000	
	1,097,585,000	**1,059,259,000**	**1,307,635,000**	**2,442,019,000**	
	546,491,000	487,560,000	667,847,000	1,163,558,000	
	5,069,000	21,362,000	47,111,000	78,164,000	
	267,575,000	289,714,000	303,431,000	670,029,000	
	55,117,000	37,446,000	16,812,000	34,670,000	
	17,534,000	15,515,000	27,610,000	63,807,000	
	8,067,000	789,000	12,971,000	40,988,000	
	29,312,000	37,121,000	49,381,000	92,924,000	
	929,165,000	**889,507,000**	**1,125,163,000**	**2,144,140,000**	
	31,344,000	43,326,000	33,439,000	32,288,000	
	31,344,000	**43,326,000**	**33,439,000**	**32,288,000**	
		1000			
	—	—	—	—	
	3,761,000	4,855,000			
	147,212,000	136,269,000			
	(8,412,000)	(8,054,000)			
	(5,485,000)	(6,645,000)			
	137,076,000	**126,426,000**	**149,033,000**	**265,591,000**	
	1,097,585,000	**1,059,259,000**	**1,307,635,000**	**2,442,019,000**	

CPAs:

SPK & C
Stern Porter Kingston & Coleman
551 Fifth Avenue

G & B
Graenum & Berger
One Madison Avenue

D & R
Dunn and Rollins
40 Exchange Place

D & T
Dunn & Taylor
40 Exchange Place

RWT
Robert W. Taylor & Co.
160 Broadway

OA & D
Oppenheim Appel & Dixon
One New York Plaza

FST
Frederick S. Todman & Co.
111 Broadway

Index

Ackerman, Tom, 167
acquisitions, business. *See* mergers and acquisitions
Adelsberger, Paul, 42
advertising activity
   for 60th anniversary, 120
   for 70th anniversary, 172
   in *Financial Times* of London, 149
   firm brochure, 117, 172
   introducing tiger logo in, 99–101
   New York move, 105–106
   retirement planning, 181
   See also tiger (logo)
after hours trading, 188, 189
Albright, Bob, 58
Alternative Investment Market, 175
Altman, Edward I., 136, 157–158
American Founders, 11
American Stock Exchange, 4, 123–124
Amott, Baker & Co., 43, 65
Amro Bank, 17
Anderson, Bill, 49
Annual Compliance Review, 123, 148
annual shareholders meeting, 111, 137–138, 159–160, 194
antique certificates, 49
A.P. Montgomery & Co., 63
Arkansas Louisiana Gas, 35–36
Armistice Day, 2

Arthur D. Little & Co., 136–137
artificial silk shares, 17
Asher, Norman, 32, 41
Asher, Tom, 69
ask price, definition of, 9
AT&T stock certificates puzzle, 120
Auto-Ex, 126, 127
Automatic Data Processing (ADP), 83

Baldwin, G. Tyler, 17
Ball, Douglas, 50
Bank of Manhattan, 16
Bank Stock Dealers Association, 19
bankruptcy securities, 109, 136, 140–141
Banks, Charlie, 29
Barings, 163–164
Barysh, Burt, 36
"The Bear Market in Bonds is History" (Bostian), 161
Berlinger, Leonard, 23–24, 28, 38, 53, 59
bid price, definition of, 9
"Big Bang," 113, 124
Bishop, Bob, 126
Bleibtreu, Fred, 47
Bligh, Godfrey, 47
block trading activity, 125
"blotter," 61
Boesky, Ivan, 123
Bond Richman & Co., 104
bookkeeping system, 61, 62

Bostian, David B., Jr.
   as chief economist & investment strategist, 149
   death of, 184
   Dow Jones Average prediction, 163
   economic model, 158
   in Europe, 165
   on fixed income, 152–153, 161
   forecasting a recession, 175–176
   health challenges, 174, 182
   investor recommendations, 155
   as keynote speaker at North Carolina Society, 172–173
   Macro-Economic Index and, 175–176
   on new bull market prediction, 166
   quoted in *Financial World*, 158
   as vice president, 163
Boston Stock Exchange, 80
Boynton, Elwood, 36
Bradley, Ken, 173, 189, 194
Brady, Nicholas F., 133
The Brady Commission, 133
British Type Investors, 11
Broker's Bank, 16–17
Bromson, Bill, 61–62
Brotherhood Synagogue, 44
Brown, Walter, 47
Burnham, Steven, 175
Burton, Martha, 103

217

Index

Busch, George L., 9, 13
Buzwin Donut Corp., 168

Campbell, John W., 7
Campbell, Princess, 7
Carrol, McEntee & McGinley, 58
Central Mercantile Bank, 2
Chadwick, Nat, 3
The Changing World of Financial Services conference, 118
"Charging Bull" sculpture, 140, 156
Chasin, Phil, 10
Chatham and Phenix Bank, 2
Chemical Bank, 17, 65, 77
Chicago Board Options Exchange (CBOE), 179
Chicago Mid-Winter Dinner, 66
Chicago Stock Exchange, 189
Christofilis, Charles "Chris," 134, 137
Cincinnati Stock Exchange, 97
Clark and Clark, 72
clearing firm accounts, 166
Clinton Corners, 79–80
Cohen, Mrs., 47
Cohen, Simonson & Co., 10, 13, 29
COLT (Continuous On Line Trading) system, 110–113, 115, 136–137, 167
common stocks, 150
"Competing in High Activity Markets" paper, 112
compliance
focus on, 103, 179
letter to staff on, 148
computerized batch system, 57
Computers in the City conference, 111–113, 118
Computing and Tabulating Company, 10
Cone, Don, 62
Connolly, Donna, 119, 136, 137, 173
Constitution Realty Corp., 103
consumer market, 23
Conti, Craig, 110, 112

Continental Bank & Trust Company, 16–17
contra-broker risk, 78, 86, 96
Cornell Business School, 115
corporate finance, 11
correspondent firms, 71–72, 117
Crain's, 127
Crash of 1987, 10–12, 128–130
crisis planning committee, 126
Custom House, 130

D'Amato, Alphonse, 104
DaPonte, Andy, 189
data processing system, 62, 83–84
Datek Online Holdings, 186
"A Dealer's Experience of Automated Trading" talk, 118
Delaware Fund, 35
delisted issues, 71
Dempsey Tegeler & Co., 64
dePasquier & Co., 136
DeVito, Gus, 184
Dillon Read & Co., 124
DiModica, Arturo, 140, 156
disaster recovery, 160, 186
discount brokerage, 160, 182
Donald, Harry, 81
Donald & Co., 81
Donaldson, Bill, 161
Dorosh, Ed, 42, 43
double indemnity stocks, 11–12
Dow Jones Average prediction, 163, 168
Druckman, Gil, 58, 65

E. D. Boynton & Co., 36
Easdaq, 173, 189
Eastern European immigration, 1
Eastman Dillon, 29
electronic trading, 187–188
electronic trading network (ECN), 186–187
Employee Stock Ownership Plan (ESOP), 151, 152
Engel, Nathan, 62
Englander, Bill, 13–14
Englander, Jacob, 16, 22

Englander, Mary, 16
Englander, Norma. *See* Herzog, Norma
Equities, "Who Are the Best Traders" survey, 147
Ernst, Howard, 36
Ernst & Co., 36
E-Tiger, 194–195
E-Trade, 160, 165, 182
expense committee, 135

Faulkner, Peter, 140
Feather, Bill, 100
Feder, Arthur, 173
Federal Reserve, 19
Femcon Associates, 110
Femino, Paul, 110
Ferguson, Mark, 112
Ferris, Jim, 38, 47, 55
Finance Magazine, feature story on Godfrey and John, 49
"Financial Analysts Journal," 24
Financial Community Softball League Championship, 150
Financial Planning, 171
Financial Trader, 164
firm brochure, 117, 172
First Boston Corp., 29
First Clearing Corp., 189
fixed commissions, 80–81, 113, 124
fixed income, 150, 152–153, 161
Fixed Income Pricing System (FIPS), 160
Flaherty, Robert J., 109
Fleischer, Arthur, 193
FOCUS report (Financial and Operational Combined Uniform Single Report), 93
Forbes, over-the-counter market article, 127
foreign bonds, 5, 23
foreign transactions, 17
Fortune, "Hitting it Big Over the Counter" article, 116
Frazzitta, Joe, 173, 188–189, 194
Fried Frank, 193

Index

Friedman, Richard, 89
Friedman Rosner Inc., 78
Fusco, Cono, 188–189

G. & A. Seligman, 3
Galetti, Al, 182
Geduld, Abraham, 65, 73, 122
Geduld, Amanda Phillips Eileen, 155
Geduld, Buzzy
  on Crash of 1987, 131–132
  featured in Relationship Spotlight of Donaldson & Co., 166
  in *Fortune* magazine, 116
  interested in new issues, 63–64
  Irwin teaching trade to, 53
  loyalty of, 123
  managing institutional business, 105
  marriage of, 151–152
  Merrill Lynch and, 76
  on Nasdaq new rules, 176
  as over-the-counter stocks king, 174–175
  as partner, 67
  as president and CEO, 123
  as president of Securities Traders Association, 125–126
  profiled in *The New York Post*, 174–175
  as secretary, 66–67
  speaking at annual shareholders meeting, 137–138, 182
  as STANY president, 126–127
  suggests firm name change, 94
  as "trader's trader," 151
  25th anniversary with firm, 159
  on various boards, 137
Geduld, Irwin
  as integral part of market making, 59
  joining Greenman & Co., 63
  leaving Herzog & Co., 63
  managing Miami branch, 93
  on Planning Committee, 58
  returning to Herzog & Co., 56, 64
  starting own business, 63
  25th anniversary with firm, 161
  as vice president, 65
  at V.S. Wickett & Co., 52–53
Geduld, Jodi, 145, 159
Geduld, Steven, 178
Geduld, Sylvia, 65, 122
Geduld, Victoria, 151–152
General Economics Corporation (GEC), 38
General Electric, 124
Geoscience, 44
Geraci, Tony, 84, 86, 96–97, 99, 120
Gerbehy, Chris, 183
Gilbert, Murray, 24
global stock exchange, 184
globalization, 127
Gmul Sahar Securities, 190
Goldman Sachs, 110, 122, 126, 190, 192
Goldsmith, Stephen, 50
Goldstein, Golub & Kessler, 160
Graham, Benjamin, 18
Grant Thornton LLP, 184–185
Grasso, Dick, 186
Grasso, Richard, 179
Green, John, 79
Greenman, Brian, 63
Greenman & Co., 63
Greenspan, Alan, 141, 158, 166
Gregory & Sons, 64
Grodsky Associates, 166
Grody, Benjamin, 8, 24
Gulf War, 146
Gutfreund, John, 112, 124

H. J. Weinberger & Co., 43
Hamilton Brothers, 67
Hanson & Hanson, 74–75
Hebrew Immigrant Aid Society (HIAS), 55
Heine, Fishbein & Co., 80, 84–85, 92

Heine, Lotte, 86
Heine, Max, 85, 123, 134, 140
Henry Krieger & Co., 155–156, 171
Herzeg, Armin, 1, 2
Herzog, Diana, 41–42, 50, 51, 54
Herzog, Elizabeth, 1, 4
Herzog, Heine & Co., Inc.
  creation of, 85
  profit-sharing plan, 94–95
  tax-induced exodus to New Jersey, 93–94
Herzog, John
  birthday poem for, 102
  as board chairman, 123
  as board member of National Securities Clearing Corporation, 96
  company transition to, 45
  compliance, focus on, 103
  developing firm Procedures Manual, 59
  at Eastman Dillon, 29
  on father's passing, 141
  first days at father's firm, 31–33
  focusing on compliance, 37
  founding Museum of American Finance, 31
  at graduate school, 24, 52
  home purchase in Clinton Corners, 70
  joining father's firm, 29
  joining Philadelphia office, 25
  joining Smythe, 50
  marriage of, 41
  meetings with behavioral psychologist, 92–93
  Mexico trip, 41
  mother's effect on, 30–31
  on mother's passing, 139
  moving to Brooklyn Heights, 69
  on NASD Options Committee, 91–92
  at NYU, 44
  optimism of, 103
  organic gardening, 90
  on passing firm to others, 184

Index

as president and CEO, 75
reflecting on memories of
  the firm, 195–198
speaking at Computers in
  the City conference, 118
speaking at The Knox
  School, 128
stock certificate collection,
  31
as stock delivery clerk,
  24–25
supervising regulatory
  requirements, 91–92
at Union Securities & Co.,
  24–25
Herzog, John, letters
  to Arthur Svenson, 87–91
  to Buzzy, 195–198
  from Chris Gerbehy, 183
  to father, 76–77
  to Louis Keene, 166
  from mother, 29–30
Herzog, Kahn, Peck & Co., 75
Herzog, Lily, 1, 4
Herzog, Mary, 145
Herzog, Norma
  Bob begins dating, 13–14
  death of, 139
  effect on John, 30–31
  at first Board of Directors
    meeting, 51
  letter to John, 29–30
  marriage of, 16
  meeting Robert, 7
Herzog, Robert Imre
  as air raid warden, 23
  approach to risk, 28–29
  arriving in America, 1
  attitude influencing
    employee experience, 53
  belief in fairness, 17
  Chadwick and, 3
  company transition to
    son, 45
  as currency trader, 2, 3
  death of, 141
  expense allowance for, 51
  growing resentment of
    John's business decisions,
    53
  letter to Louis Weingarten,
    21–22
  on management, 21–22

marriage of, 16
as member of New York
  Society of Security
  Analysts, 23–24
Noram Englander and, 7
respect for all people, 5
in Richmond, Virginia, 8
on risk, 22
studying photography, 7
as teller and ledger clerk, 2
on trader's position, 21–22
Herzog, Rose, 16
Herzog & Chadwick, 4
Herzog & Co.
  25 year anniversary dinner,
    24
  clearing at Trust Company
    of North America, 9–10
  clearing with Cohen,
    Simonson & Co., 10
  expanding the business into
    trading, 33
  firm photo, 42
  first Board of Directors
    meeting, 51–52
  foreign transactions of, 17
  founding of, 4–5
  hiring outside counsel, 37
  inactive securities
    department, 49
  incorporating, 24
  joining National Stock
    Exchange, 62
  office expansion, 8, 54, 67
  Officers Meeting, 66–67
  Planning Committee, 58
  succession planning, 52
  surviving the Crash, 12
  trading activity, 9
  trading American
    Founders, 11
Herzog Commodities
  Corporation, 84
Herzog Heine Geduld, Inc.
  60th anniversary
    celebration, 119–122
  65th anniversary
    celebration, 145–146
  70th anniversary
    celebration, 173–174
  annual compliance review,
    123, 148
  audit firm for, 184–185

Boston office, 100
budgeting process, 184–185
creation of, 94
crisis planning committee,
  126
cutting costs, 135–136
Dayton office, 100
employee milestone
  celebrations, 153
expense committee, 135
firm brochure, 117, 172
firm members serving the
  industry, 137
fixed income department,
  150
human resources
  department, 153
identifying media contacts,
  157
Jericho office, 191
major competitors to, 102
Merrill Lynch bid for,
  193–195
as a Merrill Lynch
  Company, 198
on Nasdaq class action, 178
New Jersey office, 159,
  160–161, 167
New York office, 103,
  104–105
Philadelphia office, 100
potential buyer for, 116, 122,
  190, 192–193
retail division, 138–139, 181
retaining public relations
  firm, 111
Specialists List, 116
"Staying Committee," 168
stockholders photo, 146
sustaining loyalty at, 101
trading Canadian issues,
  100
Herzog Heine Geduld
  International, 175,
  176–177
"Hitting it Big Over the
  Counter" article, 116
Hoit Rose & Co., 62
Hollander, Marvin, 108

IBM, 10, 54
immigration, Eastern
  European, 1

Index

inactive securities, 31, 42–43, 49, 56, 61–62, 161
index arbitrage, 124
individual investors, 187–188
insider trading, 125
Instinet, 186–187
institutional business, 104, 105, 117, 127
intergenerational mentoring, 8, 57, 74, 177
Internet, 177, 180
Internet stocks, 187–188
Inventory Average Cost Report (IAC), 63
investment banking, 11
investment grade securities, 11
"Investor Attitudes in the spring of 1988" survey, 135
IPO market, 117, 147, 158
Island (electronic trading network), 186

Jacobson, Hans, 85, 140–141, 153
January-effect, 66
Japan Securities Dealers Association, 175
John G. Ullman & Associates, Inc., 157
John J. Meyers & Co., 43
Josephthal & Co., 3
Joyce, Tom, 187, 193

Kahn, Arthur, 75
Kahn, Peck & Co., 73, 75
Kaplan, Charles, 154–155
Kassel, Bud, 33, 35
Keene, Allan, 155–156, 165
Keene, Louis, 165–166
Keuffel and Esser, 2
Key Color Laboratories, 36–37, 121
Keynes, John M., 18
Kidder Peabody & Co., 124, 126, 139
Klarman, Seth, 94
Kleinman, Suzie, 58
Kletz, Michael, 2
Knauthe, Nachod & Kuhne, 2–3
Knight, Hugo, 42, 53
Knight, Townsend J., 37

Knight/Trimark Group, 189
Koch, Ed, 140
Komansky, David, 193

Lackritz, Mark, 158
Laing & Cruickshank, 113, 117
LaMantia, Sam, 58
Lasher, Mary Margaret, 28
Leahy, Bill, 154
Lee, Warren, 78, 95, 101
Leeson, Nick, 163–164
Levine, Michael, 58, 59, 72, 90, 91
Levitt, Arthur, 155
Lipper, Michael, 94
loan accommodation, 77
Logan, Jeff, 157
logo. *See* tiger (logo)
Lombard Securities Co., 78
Lombard Street, 73
London Stock Exchange, 111, 175
Lord, Abbett & Co., 108
"Lucky Balls" film, 140

Mackie, Robert A., 99
Macro-Economic Index, 175–176
Malespina, Jim, 140
Manghir, Bob, 42, 58–59, 72, 142
Manufacturers Hanover, 2
The Manuscript Society, 50
markdowns, 72
market making
  banking relationships and, 86
  challenging financial integrity, 72
  European, 189
  new phase for, 76
  short side of, 53, 59
Max L. Heine Professor of Finance, 136
Maxi-Quote, 154
McCarthy, John, 108
Meli, Esther, 183
Meli, Robert
  10th anniversary with firm, 94
  70th birthday, 142
  joining firm, 55
  performance at the firm, 62

on Planning Committee, 58
  retirement plans, 111
  signature privileges of, 65
  training Kurt Rosenberg, 139
mergers and acquisitions.
  Amott, Baker & Co., 65
  Hanson & Hanson, 74–75
  Heine, Fishbein & Co., 80, 85
  Henry Krieger & Co., 155–156
  Kahn, Peck & Co., 75
  R. M. Smythe & Co., 47–48
  Troster, Singer & Co., 81
Merkin & Co., 44, 116
Merrill Lynch, 75–76, 139, 193–195
Meyers, John J., Jr., 9
M.H. Meyersohn & Co., 73
Mintz, Robert A., 134
Mooney, Wilma, 177
"Morality in Business" sermon, 44
Moran, Dorothy, 136
Morano, Jerry, 150
Morgan Stanley, 124
Morgenstern, Stanley, 104
Morris, Robert, 163
Moudis, Ted, 103, 148, 160
Mount, Alan, 111
Mount & Nadler, 111, 147, 157
M.S. Wien & Co., 81, 104
Mulligan, Jerry, 48
Museum of American Finance, 31, 130–131, 154, 157–158
mutual funds, 17–18
Mutual Shares Corp., 94, 109, 116

Nadler, Hedda, 111
NASCA (Numismatic Antiquarian Service Company of America), 50
NASD (National Association of Securities Dealers)
  comprehensive audit of Herzog & Co., 64, 83
  founding of, 20
  "Investor Attitudes in the spring of 1988" survey, 135

monitoring quotations
entered into Nasdaq,
122–123
regulatory criticism against
Herzog, 122–123
requiring individuals to
register, 23
as self-regulatory
association, 20
Nasdaq
Buzzy objecting to new
rules, 176
class action, 178
establishment of, 20
Fixed Income Pricing
System (FIPS), 160
gaining respect, 76
national market system
concept, 117
price fixing, 161, 176
publishing quotations in
1/64th increments, 159
reticence in joining, 70–71
National Association of
Securities Dealers
Automated Quotation
system. *See* Nasdaq
national market system
concept, 117
National Over-the-Counter
Clearing Corporation, 55
National Securities Clearing
Corporation (NSCC), 96
National Security Traders
Association (NSTA),
19, 104
National Stock Exchange, 62
"Nature and Timescale of
an Electronic Trading
System" talk, 118
negotiated markets, 164–165
Nelson, Steve, 173
net settlement process, 96
Neulander, Harold, 9, 11
New York Curb Market, 4
*The New York Daily Investment
News*, 10–11
The New York Post, 174–175
New York Security Dealers
Association, 19
New York Society of Security
Analysts, 23–24

New York State Abandoned
Property account, 49
New York State Employment
Agency, 52
New York Stock Exchange
200th anniversary, 149–150
international companies
trading on, 172
private wires and, 3
rule changes, 123–124
SuperDot system, 158–159
The New York Times
"Let's Reform the O-T-C
Market," 134
"The Narcotic of Crime on
Wall Street," 148
"O-T-C Issues: New
Wariness," 134
Newburger, Loeb & Co., 29
North Carolina Society,
172–173
Northern Pacific, 141
NSCC (National Securities
Clearing Corporation),
96
numismatic auction business,
49–50

obsolete securities. *See*
inactive securities
offering price, definition of, 9
Olliff, Barry, 113, 117, 128
Oni, 78
on-line order flow, 187
open mindedness, 54
Operations Department, 81,
83, 91, 131
Opinion Research
Corporation, 135
Options Industry Council, 179
options investment area, 179
order-handling rules, 184
over-the-counter market
in bank and insurance
stocks, 4, 9
fairness in, 117
Forbes article on, 127
length of time for trade, 70
speculative, 17

Padala, Charles, 100, 138
par value of stock, 11–12

Parmer, Devore, 3–4
Parmer, Herzog & Chadwick,
3
Pasternak, Kenneth, 189
Paul II (pope), 168
Pearl Harbor attack, 23
Pelorex, 102
penny stocks, 177
Peterson's International Code,
17
Phelan, John, 112
Philadelphia office, 181
Philadelphia Stock Exchange,
100
Philbro, 124
"Planning for Uncertainty"
(Drucker), 150
portfolio insurance, 129
position limit, 13, 72
Premtaj, Tom, 157
Price, Michael, 94, 109, 122,
134, 135–136, 140
The Price of Liberty
(Anderson), 49
private wires
adding additional turrets
and wires, 67
description of, 3
to Ernst & Co., 36
with Merrill Lynch, 76
to Newburger, Loeb &
Co., 29
research for, 31
profit-sharing plan, 94–95
program trading, 125
Project Lightyear, 193
put and call business, 78

Questioned Trades problem,
131
Quick & Reilly, 150
Quigley, Hugh, 132

R. M. Smythe & Co., 47, 49, 50
railroad bankruptcy securities,
85, 140
Raquet, Walter, 108–109, 110,
136–137, 145, 189
Reagan, Ronald, 124, 133
real-time trading system,
110–111
reconstruction in Europe, 3

Index

regulations
 banking, 142
 Federal Reserve, 19
 as helpful, 18–19
 to protect customers, 118
 SEC, 36
 systemic abuse of, 148
 technology keeping up with, 185
ReliaStar, 180
Republic Pictures Corp., 118
rescission checks, 37
Retail Division, 138–139, 186
retirement plans, 181
"Revenue Enhancement and Cost Cutting Survey," 145
Rockefeller, John D., 142
Roditi, Nick, 116
Rona, Geza, 7
Rona, Laci, 7
Rosenberg, Kurt, 139
Rukeyser, Louis, 109
Russian Exchange Center, 154

Sahar, Gmul, 195
Sarnoff, Paul, 78, 84
Sawyer, Miles, 138
Schneider, Bernet & Hickman, Inc., 100
Schroder Securities, 116
Schwab & Co., 182
Schwartz, Robert A., 187
Scotch week, 15–16
Scott & Stringfellow & Co., 8, 72
scripophily, 49
secondary reserves, 14
securities
 bankruptcy, 109, 136, 140–141
 delivery and receipt of, 10, 43
 inactive, 43, 49
 investment grade, 11
 lack of transparency, 17–18
 laws, impact of, 18
 railroad bankruptcy, 85, 140
 regulations, 18–19
Securities Act of 1933, 18
Securities and Exchange Commission (SEC)
 compliance requirements of, 20
 on continuing education, 155
 creation of, 12
 Levitt as president of, 155
 underwriting regulations, 36
Securities Exchange Act of 1934, 19
Securities Industry Association, 78, 108
Securities Industry Institute, 187
Securities Investor Protection Act of 1970, 65
Securities Investor Protection Corporation (SIPC), 49
"Security Analysis" (Graham), 18
Security Dealers of North America (SDNA) directory, 8, 15, 56
Security Traders Association of Chicago, 66
Security Traders Association of New York. See STANY
Security Traders Handbook, 131–132
"A Selected List of Growth Companies in the Over-the-Counter Market" publication, 138–139
self-underwriting, 36
Senior Subordinated Debt, 180
Service Bureau, 54–55, 56–57, 83
short positions, 21, 35, 53
short seller, 13
short term self-liquidating loans, 14
SIA conference, 192
SIA Webmaster Roundtable, 180
Siebert, Muriel F., 134
Siegel, Jeremy, 192
signature guarantees, 43
Simmons & Co., 3
Singer & Mackie, 73
SIPC (Securities Investor Protection Corporation), 49
Sloane, Leonard, 134
Small Order Execution System (SOES), 110, 154

Smith New Court, 122, 125, 193
Smythe. *See* R. M Smythe & Co.
Snyder, Harry, 78, 84, 102, 119, 131
SOES bandits, 154
Sofiyskiy, Vasiliy, 154
Soros, George, 146
specialist book, 73
Spink, 50
Standard Oil Building, 103
STANY (Security Traders Association of New York), 19, 57, 125–126, 134
"Staying Committee," 168
Steichen, Edward, 7
Stern, Henry, 140
Stevenson, Malcolm, 175
STIF (Stock Transfer Incentive Fund) law, 93
Stix Friedman & Co., 72
stock delivery, 24–25
stock loan exposure, 119
subordinated loans, 77, 102, 111, 119, 149, 180
Summers, Lawrence, 129
SuperDot system, 158–159
Svenson, Arthur, 44
"Swing into Spring" party, 79
Sylla, Richard, 158
synthetic fiber stocks, 17

technology
 Auto-Ex, 126, 127
 British telecom, 177
 COLT (Continuous On Line Trading) terminal, 110–111
 computerized batch system, 57
 data processing, 62, 83–84
 electronic trading network, 186–187
 Fixed Income Pricing System (FIPS), 160
 Instinet, 186–187
 Internet, 177, 180
 Maxi-Quote, 154
 real-time trading system, 110–111
 Small Order Execution System, 110
 SuperDot system, 158–159

telecom systems, 107, 177
Technology in Trading
    conference, 136–137
telecom systems, 107, 177
teletype service, 15
tiger (logo)
    announcing opening of
        Philadelphia office, 100
    introducing, 95
    to tell firm's story, 103
    in trade ads, 99–100
    See also advertising activity
Tiger Online News, 177
Tobin, Jim, 129, 180
Toczek, Peter, 44, 80
Tognino, John, 75–76
Traders Magazine, "Herzog
    Heine Geduld at 65," 147
traders/trading
    after hours, 188, 189
    personality types of, 164
    position limit, 13, 21–22
    taking risks, 42
    uncompared, 131
"Trading with a Passion"
    article, 131–132
Travelers Corp., 124
Trust Company of North
    America (TCNA), 9–10

uncompared trades, 131
Unlisted Security Dealers
    Association, 19
U.S. Manufacturing, 44
U.S. Treasury bonds, 14

Vilas & Hickey, 159, 160, 171
Vista Industries, 44
V.S. Wickett & Co., 52

Wacht, Harvey, 137, 142, 186, 189
Wall, John, 117
Wall Street Letter, "Herzog
    Leaves Jersey City for
    NYC," 105
Wall Street Race, 150
The Wall Street Transcript,
    "Money Manager
    Interviews," 154–155
Wasserstein Perella, 193
Watergate hearings, 80
Waters, Jim, 29
Weeden, Don, 97
Weeden & Co., 97
Weingarten, Claire, 28
Weingarten, Louis, 15, 21–22,
    24, 28, 43, 121
Westchester Country Club, 7

When Issued contracts, 12, 16
"Who Are the Best Traders"
    survey, 147
Widenski, Theodore J., Jr., 62
Williams, Ethel, 175
Williams, Len, 38–39, 42, 43
wires. *See* private wires
Woolard & Co., 72
World Trade Center, 152
Wriston, Walter, 142

Xetra, 189

Y2K, 191
Y2K plan, 186
Yager, "Luv" Elaine, 156–157, 167, 171, 178
year-end bonuses, 59, 65, 183
yen-dollar relationship, 129–130
Yom Kippur, 54

Zaglin, Eileen, 122
Zarb, Frank, 184
Zicklin School of Business, 187
Zoline, Orrin, 4, 13